TREES AND WOODLAND IN THE BRITISH LANDSCAPE

The Complete History of Britain's Trees, Woods & Hedgerows

REVISED EDITION

Oliver Rackham

PHOENIX
PRESS

5 UPPER SAINT MARTIN'S LANE
LONDON
WC2H 9EA

A PHOENIX PRESS PAPERBACK

First published in Great Britain
by J.M. Dent in 1976
Revised 1990
This paperback edition published in 2001
by Phoenix Press,
a division of The Orion Publishing Group Ltd,
Orion House, 5 Upper St Martin's Lane,
London WC2H 9EA

A CIP catalogue record for this book is available from the
British Library.

Printed and bound in Great Britain by
Butler & Tanner Ltd,
Frome and London

ISBN 1 84212 469 2

In memory of
COLIN EDWARD RANSON
who studied the woods
of Suffolk and Essex
with me

Contents

Plates

Text-figures

Preface to the First Edition

[which was part of the *Archaeology in the Field* Series]

Archaeology is nowadays taken to mean the study of objects which provide evidence of the activities and environments of the men of past centuries. Woodland and trees sometimes come within the archaeologist's province, because of their longevity and continuity and the many ways in which they interact with human affairs. In the case of some woodland the continuity of the plant community extends beyond the life-span of the individual trees.

As a rough rule I propose to exclude any tree or group of trees that has obviously been planted for some designed life-span that has not yet expired. A commercial orchard or forestry plantation acquires archaeological interest only if, for some reason, it is allowed to remain in existence beyond its commercial life-span and so to tell us about past, rather than current, practices. On similar grounds I shall seldom refer to the trees of gardens or town streets. Such exclusions leave us with woods that, in their present form, have not (or not obviously) been planted; with hedgerows; and with the trees of parks, meadows, commons, farmyards, and places like Epping Forest. These form the subject-matter of this book.

Except for gardens and forestry plantations, which have been charted by a number of competent historians but have relatively little archaeological interest, the literature on the history of trees and woods is very unsatisfactory. Some scholarly works have been written by foresters, whose interests are in plantations rather than in alternative and older methods of handling trees. Others have been written by historians who have worked among archives and are reluctant to put on their boots and discover what the land itself, and the things that grow on it, have to say. At a more popular level, the subject has suffered from a long tradition of plagiarization and an unusually extensive corpus of folk-mythology; when they use contemporary evidence at all, many writers pay more attention to the exhortatory side of works like Evelyn's *Sylva* than to accounts of what actually happened in particular places.

The making of the [Norfolk] Broads by J.M. Lambert and others (1960) was a pioneer work in historical ecology, taking into account vegetation as a third dimension in a historical and archaeological synthesis. It is only in the case of hedges that this dimension has yet been constructed on anything like a national scale, but there are some half-dozen regional and local studies involving woodland and trees. Usually these are done by botanists, for they require a basic knowledge of the properties of indigenous trees and other plants which is seldom possessed by historians and not always by foresters. Such a historical outlook is to be found, for instance, in Mr Colin Tubbs's book on the New Forest, Dr Ruth Tittensor's study of the Loch Lomond oak woods, and Dr G.F. Peterken's work in Lincolnshire and Northamptonshire.[1]

In the present state of knowledge it would be impossible to cover the British Isles uniformly without resorting to facile generalization. As long ago as 1897 F.W. Maitland warned us in *Domesday Book and Beyond* that we ignore at our peril the intricate regional variation, so characteristic of Britain, of which much still remains despite all the levelling-out influences of the last 250 years. This book says more about the English lowlands than about highland regions, because of the nature of the subject; as far as we know it is chiefly in the lowlands that a stable relationship has developed between men and trees. The bias towards 'Eastern England' – Norfolk, Suffolk, Essex, and Cambridgeshire – results from my own research interests, which make it possible to tell a reasonably comprehensive story for this region and to point out how far other people's study areas differ. Eastern England is a particularly well-documented region which throughout historical times has had relatively little woodland though plenty of trees. It abounds in delicate variation and intricate detail. It has been less thoroughly swept by changes in silvicultural fashion than have many better-wooded areas, and is still rich in the fabric and traditions of medieval woodland.

In writing at this stage in the development of the subject I hope I may encourage readers to work on the many districts and counties that are still unexplored. Time is running out. The historical flow of change in the countryside – an erratic trickle with spates now and then – has turned since 1950 into a devouring flood from which little, at least in the eastern half of Britain, is safe. To plan rationally for the future we need to know about the origins and past maintenance of the details that we now prize. I hope that conservation-minded readers may be helped to identify features which are worth preserving or restoring, and to avoid wasting effort on sites where preservation is impossible, unreasonable, or not worth while. Even if they fail in their objects, if they do their work properly they will have the satisfaction of ensuring that the achievements of our past civilization have not been allowed to perish unrecorded.

Preface to the Second Edition

In thirteen years much has happened in historical ecology. Although little needs to be unsaid, new knowledge has caused much of the book to be rewritten. This is especially true of prehistory. The first edition was written when the making of the landscape was being back-dated to much earlier than we used to think; it has since been back-dated further still.

Roughly half the books and articles mentioned in the Bibliography and References have appeared since I wrote the first edition. These include two major books: G.F. Peterken's *Woodland conservation and management*, and W. Linnard's *Welsh woods and forests*. As I expected, many regional and local studies have been done by myself and others. I can name only a few at random: J.G. Kingsbury's account of woods near Worcester, J.A. Best's mighty work on King's Wood, Corby (Northants), the survey of Herefordshire woods, and Mary Edwards's study in Merionethshire.[2] Ireland and southern England are no longer neglected: for example the work of W.A. Watts and D. L. Kelly on Killarney, M. Jones's study of the Wicklow woods, the Hampshire woodland survey,[3] and A. Wheaten's investigation (unpublished) of the Blean near Canterbury. In general it turns out that although the woods may be very different from one region to another, the cultural aspects are often similar, despite huge variations in the amounts of woodland. The practical and many of the technical terms of East Anglia are repeated in the woods of West Yorkshire, studied by G. Redmonds.[3a] The Cambridge woodland historian in Sussex, Cornwall, Wales, the Lake District – or even in Ireland, S.W. Scotland, Normandy or eastern America – is not in an unfamiliar world: he will find some, if not all, of the woodbanks, giant stools, boundary pollards, special plants and other familiar features of ancient woodland. Eastern England is unusual chiefly in that its woods are better preserved than most, and easier to understand: they maintain still in use, or only recently disused, cultural features that in other places declined long ago.

The conservation chapter has been entirely rewritten after a dramatic change in the fortunes of ancient woodland in the late 1970s. The anthropology of woodland has come to be a fascinating subject in itself. Why does the public believe a complete pseudo-history that is at variance with the real history? Why is there what David Dymond calls a 'hunger for false information'? Why does pseudo-history grow to accommodate new events that ought to explode it?

Acknowledgements

In the first edition I thanked – for help, comments, or the use of unpublished information – the late Dr D. Chapman, Mrs J. Deacon, Mr D.P. Dymond, Mrs A. Hart, Dr W. Liddell, Mr J. Hunter, Mr P. Nicholson, Dr C. Owen, the late Mr W.H. Palmer, Dr G.F. Peterken, Dr C.D. Pigott, the late Mr J. Saltmarsh and Mrs R. Tittensor. I must now add Dr Margaret Atherden, Dr K. Kirby, Professor W. Linnard, Mr D. Morfitt, Mr L. Sisitka and Dr P. F. Williams; together with a host of others – memory would fail in the naming of them all – who have drawn my attention to, or asked my opinion on, matters of interest over the years. The work has been made possible by the kind help of many archivists and keepers of records, and the cooperation of the owners of hundreds of woods.

I have drawn on work financed by the Natural Environment Research Council, the Nature Conservancy Council, and Kerrier District Council. I acknowledge the help of Corpus Christi College, Cambridge.

My special thanks are due to Colin and Susan Ranson for many years of encouragement, hospitality and help in the field and in the archives. David Coombe, James and Ann Hart, Hildegard and George Heygate, and (in America) Susan Bratton and Jennifer Moody have been faithful colleagues and friends. Mrs J. Evans kindly read and commented on the text.

English Measures

1 inch		= 25 mm
1 foot	= 12 in.	= 0.30 m
1 yard	= 3 ft	= 0.91 m
1 mile	= 1760 yards	= 1.6 km
1 modern acre	= 4840 square yards	= 0.40 ha
1000 modern acres		= 4.0 km^2
£1	= 20 s. (shillings)	= 240d. (pence)

The medieval penny must be thought of as something like sixpence in the money of the seventeenth century, a shilling in the mid-nineteenth, and about £3 today.

1

The constant spring: how woods and trees work

Robert de Corneville was summoned [to explain] why he had committed waste contrary to the orders of our lord the king in a wood in Parva Tolleslund [Tolleshunt Knights, Essex] ... he felled the great oaks in the war and afterwards allowed his own cattle and oxen to eat the stool-shoots, so that he did waste and damage to the value of 60 shillings.

Curia Regis Rolls, A.D. 1220

Regions

For hundreds of years Britain has been one of the least wooded countries in Europe, and Ireland has been less wooded still; but not all parts are equally poor in woodland, nor are they poorly wooded for the same reasons. Suffolk, at one extreme, has long been one of the less wooded counties, yet locally grown timber and wood have been very important to its inhabitants. More than a thousand years ago, men learned to live with their woods, to run them as a self-renewing resource, to get woodland products from small wooded areas intensively managed, and to devote the rest of Suffolk to other uses. At the other extreme, most of Scotland was a comparatively thinly populated land, where trees were less important because there were plenty of alternative resources of coal, peat and building stone. Some ancient woodland survives, often by accident rather than design, in remote places; but the populous parts of Scotland owe more to later planting than to the medieval traditions of conservation and symbiosis which have shaped the Suffolk landscape.

The Scottish Highlands and Suffolk are the two extremes of woodland history in Great Britain. Intermediate are the rest of Scotland,

Wales, and the Highland Zone of England (Fig. 1) – lands of moors, dales, and a mountain way of life. The ancient woods tend to be of oak, and have often not been as intensively managed as those of Lowland England. This last, however, often turns out to be an illusory distinction: the management traditions existed in highland areas, but declined earlier than in the lowlands.

A further distinction must be made. It was once thought that the typical lowland countryside of hedged fields and small woods was derived from the Enclosure Acts of the eighteenth and nineteenth centuries, before which England had been farmed in great open prairie-farming fields. This is indeed true of much of the middle of England, from York and King's Lynn to Weymouth. I call this the *Planned Countryside* of post-1700 enclosure. Here the landscape was usually laid out hurriedly in a drawing-office at the enclosure of each parish, and has a mass-produced quality of regular fields and straight roads. The other half of England, the *Ancient Countryside*, has a hedged and walled landscape dating from any of forty centuries between the Bronze Age and the age of the Stuarts. The fields here are of very varied origin, but they all have a characteristic irregularity resulting from centuries of 'do-it-yourself' enclosure and piecemeal alteration (Frontispiece).

This is one facet of a distinction that cuts deep in European social history from France to Crete. Ancient Countryside, the *bocage*, is the land of hamlets, of medieval farms in hollows of the hills, of lonely moats in the claylands, of immense mileages of quiet minor roads, holloways, and intricate footpaths; of irregularly-shaped groves and thick hedges colourful with maple, dogwood and spindle; and of pollards and other ancient trees. Planned Countryside, the *champagne*, is the land of brick farmhouses in exposed positions, of flimsy haw-thorn hedges, of ivied clumps of trees in corners of fields, of big villages and few roads, and above all of straight lines; it does, however, often contain medieval woods, Anglo-Saxon hedges, and ancient trees that the enclosure commissioners failed to destroy. I shall return to this distinction in Chapter 10; for a full account I refer the reader to my *The History of the Countryside*.

Forestry, woodmanship, wood-pasture and farmland trees

Throughout history, trees have been part of our cultural landscape and have been managed and used. There are six traditional ways in which trees interact with human activities. Orchards, and trees of streets and gardens, are outside the scope of this book. The other

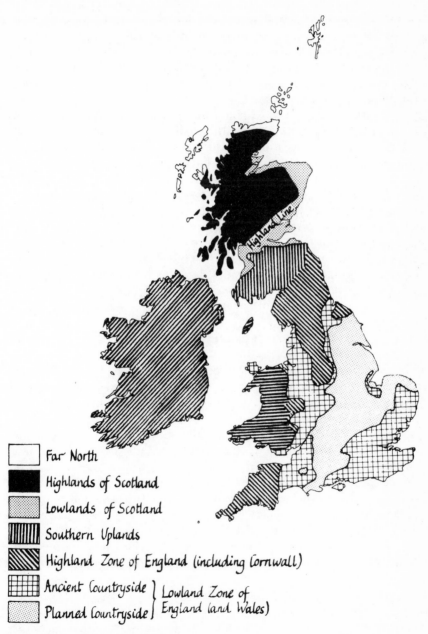

Far North

Highlands of Scotland

Lowlands of Scotland

Southern Uplands

Highland Zone of England (including Cornwall)

Ancient Countryside } Lowland Zone of

Planned Countryside } England (and Wales)

Fig. 1. Regions of the British Isles.

traditions are:

1. ***Woodland.*** Woods are land on which trees have arisen naturally. They are managed by the art of ***woodmanship*** to yield successive crops of produce in a perpetual succession, making use of the facility that most British trees have of growing again after felling.

2. ***Wood-pasture.*** This involves grazing animals as well as trees. There is a conflict, in that the shade of the trees spoils the pasture and the livestock eat the regrowth of the trees. Methods have been devised for reconciling the two uses.

3. ***Plantation.*** Here the trees are not natural vegetation: somebody has planted them. Plantations are usually of just one or two species, often conifers, and do not maintain themselves. The ground is cleared and the trees planted, grown, and harvested just like an arable crop; the stumps are then intended to die, and the ground is either replanted or put to some other use. This is ***forestry*** as generally practised in Britain and Ireland. It is much the most recent of the traditions.

4. ***Non-woodland*** trees in hedgerow and field.

Some kinds of tree, such as the ordinary 'pedunculate' oak, occur equally on all kinds of tree-land, while others are more restricted. One seldom sees Sitka spruce outside plantations or service except in a wood; black poplar is a non-woodland tree.

Native, naturalized and exotic trees

The British tree and shrub* flora comprises between fifty and seventy ***native*** species, such as ash, hazel and holly, which arrived here by natural means in prehistoric times. (Some elms may have been imported by prehistoric men.)

A few trees are *naturalized*. Originally imported from overseas, they now behave like natives in that they maintain themselves without further human intervention and have invaded native vegetation. Sweet-chestnut was introduced in Roman times, and has become part of our wildlife to such an extent that it is only through pollen analysis that it has been proved not to be native. Sycamore was introduced probably in the sixteenth century, and became wildlife in the eighteenth.[4] *Rhododendron ponticum* became abundant in the nineteenth century.[5] Foreign trees have not overrun the landscape at large to the

---

* The botanists' distinction between trees (with one main stem) and shrubs (which branch below or near ground level into several main stems) is not very useful to us because many trees, such as oak and ash, have often been grown in a multi-stemmed form. To save vain repetition the word 'tree' throughout this book will be taken to include big shrubs such as hazel.

extent that they have in some other countries.

Several hundred kinds of tree are *exotic*, imported from overseas at different times and not, or rarely, maintaining themselves. Connoisseurs of historical films will remember the anachronisms of Sir Thomas More being executed against a background of horsechestnuts, and King Charles I riding among Corsican pine plantations. This is not a matter of the passage of time. Walnut was introduced at the same time as chestnut, but shows no sign of becoming wildlife. Exotic trees, such as Sitka spruce, Norway spruce (which does not come from Norway) and Lawson cypress, predominate in plantations and gardens. London plane and some poplars are among the many trees which were invented by gardeners and nowhere grow wild.

Scots pine survives as a native tree only in the Scottish Highlands, while beech (with rare exceptions) is native only south-east of the line Weymouth–Swansea–Cromer. Both trees are widely planted and naturalized far outside their native ranges.

Tree-planting runs in fashions, like architecture or costume. The Wheatley Elm is typical of the 1930s, and the Huntingdon Elm of the 1890s; the Victorians were fond of Atlantic cedar, and the Georgians of the cedar of Lebanon. This book is mainly about wild, not planted, trees, but the occasional fashion tree can be a valuable clue to the history of a wood or park.

How trees are replaced

Poets have accustomed us to the notion that trees, like the rest of us, reproduce their kind by sexual methods, in this case by acorns and other seeds. This is partly true, but the matter is not simple. For instance, it is extremely easy to grow an oak tree from an acorn in one's garden, but it may be extremely difficult to do so in an existing wood. (What would become of the world if as many as ten out of every million acorns actually grew into full-sized oaks?) Some native trees such as small-leaved lime are very seldom observed to establish themselves successfully from seed. The checks and balances of natural population control among trees are still poorly understood. One important factor is that most British trees do not like shade. They do not grow up underneath bigger trees of the same species, but only in natural or artificial clearings, or sometimes under the lighter shade of other tree species. Beech is shade-resistant, and sometimes grows up through an oakwood and takes it over. Oak grows up under birch (though less often now than it used to). Birch demands light and will grow up only in the open.

Table 1. Summary of the properties of the principal trees in this book

	Older vernacular name	Botanical Latin Name	Methods of Regeneration				Preference for woodland	Ability to form secondary woodland	Tolerance of poor soils
			Seed	Suckers	Coppicing	Pollarding			
NATIVE									
Alder	—	Alnus glutinosa	++++	O	++++	?	−	+++	++
Apple (crab)	Wilding	Malus sylvestris	+++	O	+++	?	+	O	?
Ash	—	Fraxinus excelsior	++++	O	++++	++++	O	+++	+
Beech	—	Fagus sylvatica	+++	O	+++	++++	+	+	+++
Birch (black)	—	Betula pubescens	++++	O	+++	?	O	+++	++++
(silver)	—	B. vertrucosa	++++	O	+++	?	O	+++	++++
Blackthorn	—	Prunus spinosa	++	++++	O	O	−⏐	++	+
Cherry (wild)	Gean	P. avium	++	++++	O	O	+	+	++
Elder	—	Sambucus nigra	++++	O	(+++)	?	O	+	O
Elm (wych)	—	Ulmus glabra	+++	O	+++++	++++	O	O	O
(smooth-leaved)	—	U. carpinifolia (minor)	+	++++	(+)	++++	O	+++	+++
(English)	—	U. procera	O?	++++	(+)	(+++)	−	++	++
Hawthorn (hedgerow)	Whitethorn, Quickthorn	Crataegus monogyna	++++	O	+++	O?	O	+++	++
(woodland)	—	C. laevigata (oxy-acanthoides)	++	O	++++	+	+++	O	+
Hazel	Nuttery	Corylus avellana	++	O	++++	+++	+	O	++
Holly	Hulver	Ilex aquifolium	+++	O	+++	+++	O	+	+++
Hornbeam	Hardbeam	Carpinus betulus	+++	O	++++	+++	++	+	++++
Lime (small-leaved)	Linden	Tilia cordata	+	+	++++	(+++++)	+++	O	+++

Maple	—	Acer campestre	+++	O	+++	+++	O	+++	+	+
Oak (pedunculate)	—	Quercus robur	+++	O	+++++	++++	O	+++++	++++	+++++
(sessile)	—	Q. petraea	++	O	+++++	+++++	++	(+++++)	+++	+++++
Pine (Scots)	—	Pinus sylvestris	++++	O	O	O	++	O	+++	+++++
Poplar (aspen)	Asp	Populus tremula	+	+++	O	O	++	O	+	+
(black)	Popeler	P. nigra	O	+	O?	O	--	O	O	O?
(white)	Abele	P. alba	O?	+++	O	O	--	O	++	+++
Rowan	Quicken	Sorbus aucuparia	+++	O	+++	+++	O	?	+++	+++
Sallow	—	Salix caprea	+++++	O	+++	+++++	O	(+++++)	++	+++
Sallow		S. cinerea (atrocinerea)	+++++	O	+++++	+++++	O	(+++++)	++	+++
Service	—	Sorbus torminalis	+	+++	+++	(+++++)	+++	(+++)	+	+++
Whitebeam	—	S. aria	+++	O	+++	+++	O	(+++)	+	+++
Willow (crack)	—	Salix fragilis	+++++	O	(+++++)	+++++	--	+++	O	++
(white)	—	S. alba	+++++	O	(+++++)	+++++	--	+++	O	++
NATURALIZED										
Chestnut (sweet)	—	Castanea sativa	+++	O	+++++	(+++++)	++	(+++++)	O?	+++
Rhododendron		Rhododendron ponticum	+++++	O	(+++++)	O?	O	O?	+++	+++
Sycamore	—	Acer pseudo-platanus	+++++	O	(+++++)	+++++	-	(+++++)	+++	++

Traditional woodmanship, however, normally bypasses the seed process. As every gardener knows, some trees such as pines can be got rid of by cutting them down, but many species grow again from either the stump or the root system. Maple, oak, lime, hazel, ash, wych-elm, alder, hornbeam and many others *coppice*. The stump sends up shoots, called *spring*, and becomes a stool from which an indefinite succession of crops of rods, poles or logs can be cut at intervals of years (Fig. 2). Aspen, most elms and cherry *sucker*: the stump dies but the root system remains alive indefinitely, sending up successive crops of poles and growing into a circular patch of genetically identical trees called a *clone*.

Coppicing and suckering are very efficient and reliable methods of establishing a new crop. The new spring can grow at more than 2 inches *a day*; sallow sometimes reaches 11 feet high in the first summer after felling, while even oak can stand 7 feet high and an inch thick after one season's growth. Such shoots are too big for voles, rabbits, hares and other destroyers of seedlings. But, as we see from the quotation at the head of the chapter, the spring is greedily eaten by cattle, and also by sheep and deer. For this reason, boundaries and security have always been important in woodland history. Different methods were needed in wood-pasture and non-woodland places where these animals could not be fenced out.

Pollarding or *lopping* is the practice of cutting a tree at between 6 and 15 feet above the ground, leaving a permanent trunk called a *bolling* (to rhyme with 'rolling'). This sprouts in the same way as a coppice stool, but at a height where animals cannot reach the spring, and yields an indefinite succession of crops of poles. Pollarded trees survive mainly in eastern England and the Lake District, but once were nearly universal. Before the modern bow-saw, pollarding was disagreeable work – axes and ladders don't go well together! – and coppicing was preferred where possible. Trees that coppice can also be pollarded, and so can some others, such as suckering kinds of elm. A variant of pollarding is *shredding*, in which the side-branches are repeatedly cut off, leaving a tuft at the top ot the tree. This yields (at the cost of hard work and risk to one's neck) crops of poles, or leafy boughs on which to feed animals, and a trunk that one hopes may be of use as timber. I know of no surviving shredded trees in Britain, but the practice seems frequently to be referred to in medieval documents, and such trees can still be seen in France, Italy and Norway. Pollard trees also serve to mark land boundaries, and for this purpose may be cut only 4–6 feet high, when they are known as *stubs* or *cant-marks*.

It might be thought that coppicing and pollarding are very artificial practices, whereas seedlings and suckers are natural. However, some

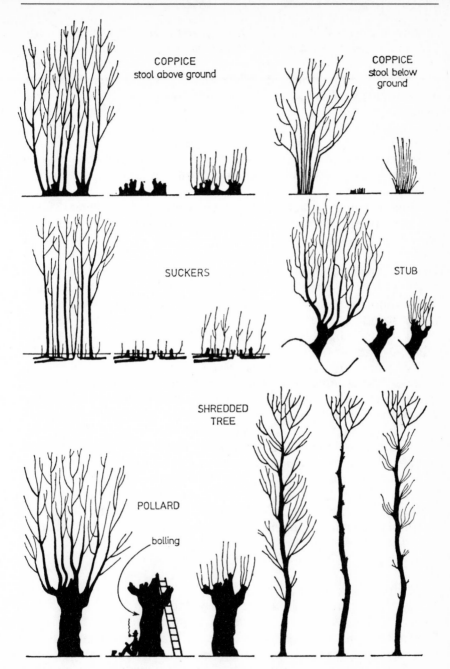

COPPICE
stool above ground

COPPICE
stool below
ground

SUCKERS

STUB

SHREDDED
TREE

POLLARD

bolling

Fig. 2. Ways of managing wood-producing trees. For each method the tree, or group of trees, is shown just before cutting, just after cutting, and one year after cutting. All drawn to the same scale.

American trees have a tendency to self-coppice and self-pollard (p. 32). Our hazel is self-coppicing; if frustrated in this tendency (as by cattle eating the young shoots) it grows a massive trunk. Lombardy poplar illustrates self-pollarding by its habit, when about 80 years old, of snapping in a gale to leave a tall stump from which new stems arise to continue the cycle.

Timber and wood

Woodmanship, like other crafts, has left its mark on languages. *Timber* and *wood* traditionally mean different things. Timber (Medieval Latin *meremium*, modern French *bois d'œuvre*) is big stuff suitable for making planks, beams and gateposts; wood (Latin *boscus*, French *bois d'industrie*) is poles, rods etc. suitable for light construction or firewood (faggots, logs or charcoal).* The distinction has been important in law and practice – for instance, tithes were payable on wood but not timber – and exact definitions, such as that wood is anything less than 2 feet in girth, have been laid down. Even now we talk of 'timber' buildings and 'wood' fires.

Wood consists either of *underwood* (Latin *subboscus*), the poles produced by cutting coppice stools, pollards or small suckers, or of the branches of trees felled for timber. Timber trees, sometimes called *standards*, may be *maidens*, grown from seed, but have often themselves originated from coppicing or suckering.

It has been the normal practice for a wood to consist of coppice stools with a scatter of timber trees. A typical park contains timber and pollards; an ancient hedge contains coppice stools, suckers, pollards and timber. Underwood is felled at more frequent intervals than timber trees; underwood and timber in the same wood often belonged to different people. In the past, wood was generally the more highly valued crop.

The longevity of trees

Trees are long-lived creatures which are easily and permanently altered by their environment and by human activities. An ancient tree (Plate

---

* **Brushwood** is the very smallest twigs, especially of birch, used for making brushes.

XX) stores up information about what has gone on around it. Its very existence may tell us something of land use at the time when it originated. Its shape and branching and the scars of old injuries record the vicissitudes of centuries. When it is cut down, its annual rings tell us how old it was and form a record of the good and bad seasons in its lifetime.

Middle-aged and old trees are poorly understood. Foresters are concerned with trees in the first quarter, at most, of their life-span. Middle-aged trees are more difficult to understand – human life isn't long enough – and have no commercial interest. The grower of an oak for timber will think about felling it as 'mature' at 100 years; after 150 years it becomes a store of capital increasingly at risk from decay; if still standing at 200 years it may be cut down on the plea that it is 'dangerous'; but if left alone it may live to the age of 400 or much more.

Timber trees of more than 250 years' growth are not normally to be found in woods. Occasionally a wood happens to pass through the hands of a succession of owners each of whom forgets to fell the oaks or values them for their beauty; Londoners will know the magnificent old oaks of Ken Wood in Highgate. Ancient timber trees are to be found mainly in parks and hedges, where they are valued for beauty or shade. Trees whose function is not timber – pollards and coppice stools – may live much longer than timber trees. The cutting process prolongs their lives, and they go on doing their job of producing useful crops of poles despite old age or decay.

A tree does not have a predetermined life-span as we do. Every year it is obliged to lay down a new annual ring of wood over its trunk and all its living boughs, twigs and roots. The new wood comes from material made by the leaves, the amount of which is determined by the size and spread of the tree's crown of branches and foliage. The vigour of a tree depends largely on the ratio between the size of its crown, which determines its annual 'income' of new wood, and the surface area of trunk, branches etc., which forms the 'commitments' over which the new wood has to be spread. In its youth, the tree grows in height and its crown gets bigger each year. Eventually it reaches its maximum height and crown size, and enters middle age. Its commitments inexorably rise as its trunk, etc. thicken; but its income remains fixed, apart from the effects of the weather of good and bad years, and of room for expansion which may come from the felling of neighbouring trees. All this is recorded in the form of wide or narrow annual rings. Old age begins when the tree can no longer meet its commitments and branches die.

Dieback of branches is a normal process in a tree's life from youth onwards. It usually leads to infection by wood-rotting fungi. Trees have no healing process as we know it, but are not passively at the mercy of decay. They have definite damage-limiting programmes which wall off the rot and confine it to parts of the wood where it will not matter.[6] These processes have been properly studied in America, but they occur in European trees too. Many a tree that would have been pronounced 'dangerous' through having been 'weakened' by decay withstood the great storm of October 1987, while its young, sound neighbours collapsed all around.

The life-span of a tree is determined partly by the length of time which it takes to reach old age, and partly by the length of time which old age lasts. The onset of old age is determined more by the size of the tree than by the number of its years; a tree that grows fast when young is likely to reach an early middle and old age. When growth is slowed by an adverse environment or by pruning or cutting, life is likely to be prolonged, as we see to an extreme degree in the long lives of the bristle-cone pines of the Arizona mountains and the bonsai of Japanese gardeners. With pollards and coppice stools, the increase in the tree's commitments is interupted each time it is cut; ageing begins from the date of the last cutting.

The power of a tree to prolong its old age depends on its capacity for retrenchment and for damage-limitation. Retrenchment is illustrated by the 'stag-headed' oaks of hedges and parks (Fig. 3), whose dead upper boughs show that they once had a larger crown. Stag-head has been misunderstood as a symptom of a 'dying' tree, and various more or less implausible causes have been proposed. In reality, many such trees have been stag-headed for fifty years or more: the bark and sapwood of the dead boughs have rotted away, and the remaining crown is healthy. Stag-head is a normal process of retrenchment by which a tree reduces its commitments and grows a new, smaller, crown. This works best in oak, sweet-chestnut, ash and lime, which have efficient damage-limiting devices.

The recipe for longevity in an oak is that it should grow in a non-woodland site with plenty of room, on a poor soil; it should form a small crown; it should be a pollard or otherwise useless as timber; and it should have burrs and ridges on its trunk (genetically determined) which will enable it to form new boughs late in life. Parkland oaks can be astonishingly tenacious of life. All major branches may have been abandoned so long ago that even their heartwood has vanished; the tree may be reduced to the shell of a gigantic bolling; areas of bark may have died and rotted away; yet well-defined strips of living tissue still cover burry ridges and maintain a small but healthy crown and a moss-like growth of short living twigs.

Fig. 3. Stag-headed tree.

How old is a tree?

Working out the age of a living tree comes from practice rather than from books. The student should never pass a stump without counting its annual rings, which are the ultimate authority for the ages of trees. Even better is to cut a slice to examine at home: ring-counts done hurriedly or in poor light are usually underestimated.

Even if a tree is hollow, as most old trees are, one can often find a place where rotten but readable wood reaches nearly to the centre. In estimating how many rings have disappeared from a hollow tree, one must remember that trees usually grow faster when young. Sometimes one can find a section in a living tree, for example in a sawn-off branch, or exposed sideways in a fissure in a bolling. Hollow borers for taking cores seldom work with big, and especially rotten, hardwood trees.

A useful rule, due to Alan Mitchell, is that a free-standing tree has one inch of girth (measured at 'breast height', 5 feet from the ground) for every year of its age; a tree in a wood has $\frac{1}{2}$ inch of girth per year. These figures correspond to mean annual ring widths of 4.0 mm and 2.0 mm per year. This works quite well for *maiden* trees of a variety

13

of species in *middle age*. A few famous big oaks have been measured repeatedly for many years; on this basis Mitchell estimated that the Major Oak in Sherwood Forest, 402 inches in girth ($10\frac{1}{2}$ feet in diameter) in 1965, was then between 400 and 650 years old.[7]

Very large trees, however, are usually on good soil and are not necessarily the oldest. A moderately large tree with a small crown on a waterlogged or infertile site may be older than a well-favoured giant with a big span of branches. Pollards tend to be older than maidens of the same size: a pollard has a very small crown, especially in the first few years after each cutting, and hence the bolling expands very slowly. After pollarding has ceased it may form a full-sized crown and grow at much the same rate as a maiden. I have found oak pollards in Epping Forest of only 50 inches girth which are at least 350 years old, having maintained an average ringwidth of 0.4 mm since 1720; this must be close to the slowest rate at which an oak can grow and yet remain alive. Oaks which are much retrenched in old age probably grow at about this rate.

An age of at least 400 years is not uncommon among oaks, especially pollards, in parks and Royal Forests. A few giants on poor sites go back much further, like the oak whose shattered bolling stands before the Dower House in Ickworth Park, Suffolk, and whose visible annual rings suggest an age of about 700. The Doodle Oak in Hatfield Forest (Essex), which died in 1858, was estimated from a ring-count in 1949 to have dated from *c*.950. Also about a thousand years old are the Queen's Oak at Huntingfield (Suffolk), and the wonderful pollards of Windsor Great Park, some of which were photographed in 1864 and have changed little since.[8]

Other species rarely live beyond 500 years, except yew, which is long-lived by tradition but is difficult to date objectively. The pollard beeches of Burnham Beeches (Bucks), Epping Forest and Felbrigg (Norfolk) are known or suspected to be about 400 years old – even though beech is not good at damage-limitation. Ancient slow-grown beeches and hollies can sometimes be recognized by nineteenth-century graffiti (Fig. 4). Other pollarded trees – elm, ash, hornbeam, hawthorn, small-leaved lime – live at least as long. Pollard willows appear to be relatively fast-growing and short-lived.

Longer-lived still are coppice stools. These are completely self-renewing and capable of living indefinitely as long as they are not overshadowed by timber trees. An old stool spreads, without loss of vigour, into a ring of living tissue with a hollow centre and often an interrupted circumference. Some species are cut on a high stool, which can be sectioned to observe annual rings from which the rate of spread can be estimated. On a waterlogged site an ash stool 2 feet across can

Fig. 4. Graffito on a slowly-growing beech-tree. The bark of beech and holly stretches as the trunk expands; the degree to which an inscription has been distorted gives a rough estimate of how much the tree has grown since it was cut. Genuine nineteenth-century graffiti have carefully executed lettering, often (as here) in two different styles.

be 300 years old,[9] while on a good site a 300-year-old ash stool may be 5 feet across. Ancient stools can reach three times this diameter (Plate VI). Stools in the Bradfield Woods, Suffolk, are up to $18\frac{1}{2}$ feet across, and on this rather wet site may be among the oldest living things in Britain (at least a thousand years); they still yield good crops of poles.

Small-leaved lime, elm, sweet-chestnut, beech, alder and oak also form such *giant stools*. Elm and sweet-chestnut grow faster than ash; but even so the imposing chestnut stools in Holbrook Park (S.E. Suffolk), up to 16 feet across, can hardly be later than Plantagenet times. Big single stools should not be confused with the groups of stools formed by *layering* – bending down coppice poles and pegging them to the ground to take root – a method formerly used in some districts to propagate underwood.

Europe in general is a continent of young or youngish trees, like a human population with compulsory euthanasia at age thirty. One can go from Boulogne to Athens without seeing a tree more than 200 years old. But at least since Shakespeare, the English have loved the beauty and mystery of ancient trees: of Herne's Oak, the Gospel Oaks, the Oaks of Reformation, the Major Oak, the Tortworth Chestnut (Plate XXI), and many such. We have painted their portraits, sung verses and danced dances in their honour, and have preserved them to give dignity to new parks. It is right that we should: such trees are part of our history and a record of our civilization. But lately it has been appreciated that *ancient* trees are the home of special animals and plants: hole-nesting birds, wild bees, and the bats that roost in hollow pollards; the peculiar lichens of old dry bark and overhangs; and a host of specialized beetles, spiders and other invertebrates. Ancient trees are full of meanings which young and middle-aged trees do not have at all, and it has become the duty of the English to cherish them.*

What annual rings tell us

The annual rings of a middle-aged or old tree show seemingly random fluctuations which express the effects of weather or caterpillars year by year. These do not concern us directly, although they enable archaeologists to date oaken artefacts by recognizing particular sequences of good and bad years. These yearly changes are super-imposed on longer-term variations which reflect the general vigour of the tree. We can get a *release cycle* of wider rings (Fig. 5a) when a

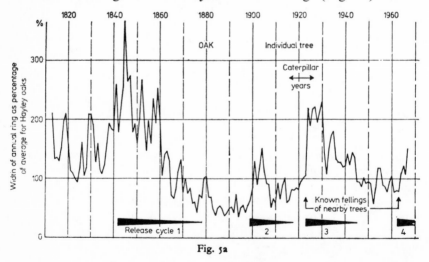

Fig. 5a

* The Greeks also venerate ancient trees. Greece (and especially Crete) are full of sacred planes and cypresses, mighty oaks in different styles of pollarding (yes, there is still one at Dodona), olives of Byzantine or Roman age, medieval chestnut pollards, etc.

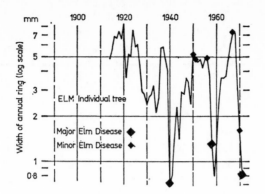

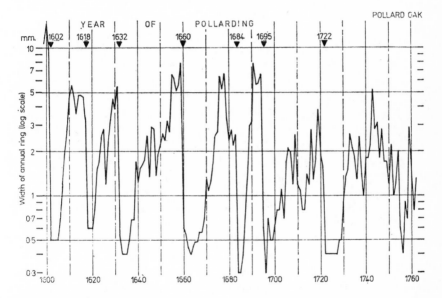

Fig. 5. Tree-ring sequences.

(a) A woodland oak, showing four periods of faster growth attributable to the felling of neighbouring trees. These ringwidths are expressed as percentages of the average ringwidth in each year, in order to separate the release cycles of this particular tree from the effects of weather, etc., which are common to all trees. Hayley Wood, Cambridgeshire.

(b) A woodland elm, showing two cycles of slow growth following severe Dutch Elm Disease. A third major attack killed the tree. Hayley Wood.

(c) Bolling of a park pollard, showing seven cycles of sudden decline on pollarding followed by gradual recovery. Intervals between pollardings varied. Year-to-year fluctuations are superimposed on this pattern. Ipswich.

17

neighbouring tree dies and our tree expands to fill the gap. Conversely we can get a *damage cycle* of narrower rings (Fig. 5b) when our tree suffers some accidental loss of branches which are gradually replaced. A useful kind of damage cycle is seen in sections of bollings and of the bases of stools (Fig. 5c); it enables us to work out when, and at what intervals, the tree was pollarded or coppiced.

Woods of different kinds

Botanists used to think of nearly every wood as an oakwood, except on chalk soils where nearly every wood is a beechwood. It was supposed that if Britain had never been civilized the 'natural' vegetation would everywhere be dominated by either oak or beech, except in those few places where neither tree could grow.

The truth is much more complex. Oak is not prominent just from natural causes, but because men have encouraged it by design or default. By long tradition a woodman, meeting an oak, does not cut it with the underwood but lets it grow on to become timber – unless the wood is so full of oaks that there is no choice. Oak also does well out of grazing, or allowing fields to revert to woodland, both of which give it a start over its competitors. A truer notion of the character of a wood is given by the underwood. The connexion of beech with chalk soils is even more artificial. In the eighteenth century the notion got around that beech was pre-eminently the tree of chalklands, and people planted it in fulfilment of that misapprehension.*

In reality, as well as oakwoods, we have a rich variety of maple-woods, alder-woods, hazel-woods, limewoods, elmwoods, hornbeam-woods, etc. These variations, which make every ancient wood unique, are described in Chapter 6. Wood-pastures, on the whole, are less variable and have fewer kinds of tree.

Primary and secondary woodland: succession

Woodland and wood-pasture may have been formed from fragments of wildwood – the original prehistoric forest – that were brought under management without ever having been anything but woodland. These will be termed *primary*. In contrast, *secondary* woods and wood-pastures have been formed on areas that at some time in the historical

---

* Note that many areas of chalk *rock* do not have chalk *soils*, but acid soils (from clay-with-flints or loess) on which beech more often grows naturally.

period have been farmland, moorland, etc.

We must not suppose that because a wood has arisen on former open land it was necessarily planted. The natural tendency of almost any land in Britain is to turn into secondary woodland. Let a field be abandoned – as has happened to many fields down the centuries – and in ten years it will be overgrown with scrub (which is young woodland) and difficult to reclaim; in thirty years it will have 'tumbled down to woodland'. The same would happen, and often is happening, to most chalk downs and heaths, and to some moors and mountains. In eastern North America, where agriculture collapsed in the last century, secondary woods, full of field-walls, are to be found from Florida to Nova Scotia; their total area is much larger than the *entire* British Isles.

The forester, no less than the farmer, is concerned to prevent his land from turning into natural woodland and to prevent native 'weed' trees from competing with the planted trees. He does not always succeed, and many plantations have turned into secondary woodland through neglect; a few conifers may live to tell the tale.

An abandoned field or plantation can be invaded by many species of tree, depending above all on what trees are growing near which can seed or sucker into it. In the classic example – Broadbalk Wilderness at Rothamsted, Herts – an area of arable land was abandoned as an experiment in 1882 and within thirty-two years had become an oak-sycamore grove.[10] Birch, elm, oak, ash and hawthorn are the commonest early colonizers.

This is an example of *succession* – the spontaneous replacement of one kind of vegetation by another. This can go on for centuries: for instance, a new oakwood may be invaded by hornbeam after a hundred years. As we shall see later, succession can also happen in ancient, even primary, woods and wood-pastures: sometimes after a change of management, but also spontaneously for no apparent reason.

Elms, limes and poplars

Elms, especially in woods, are the most complex genus of British trees. They are extremely variable, and their variations are indefinitely perpetuated by suckering. Some variation is natural, and some has been induced by elms' long symbiosis with civilized mankind. This is a summary of my treatments in *Ancient Woodland* and *The History of the Countryside* (and of the book that might easily be written). Despite Dutch Elm Disease, it is not difficult to find examples of most elms left alive; one should look in woods and away from roads.

Wych-elm, Ulmus glabra, the common elm of the north and west, does not sucker, but coppices and reproduces its kind by seed like a 'normal' tree. It is not gregarious. It has a spreading, forking habit with big, broad, very rough leaves with hardly any stalk (Fig. 6).

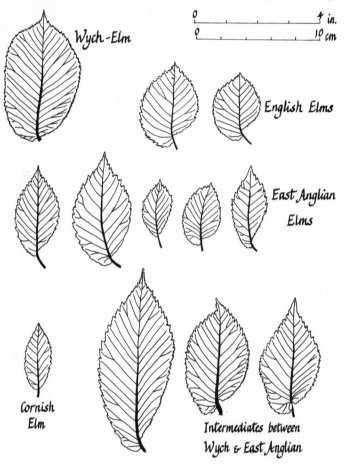

Fig. 6. Typical leaves from different groups of elm. Sometimes leaves are shown from different clones within the same group, to show the range of variation.

Most other elms sucker and are gregarious, growing in clonal patches. They are very variable, and are divided into three groups:
1. **English Elm**, *'Ulmus procera'*, the traditional elm of most of middle and south England, and its relatives in the north and in Dublin. A very big, upright elm with heavy masses of dark foliage; leaves small-ish, broad, usually all rough. Very susceptible to the present Dutch Elm Disease: no big elm left alive, except in the Brighton area, can be

a typical English Elm. (There are plenty of suckers, which have reached about 25 ft high in 1989.)

2. *East Anglian elms*, known collectively as *'U. minor'* or *'carpinifolia'*, the common wild elms of East Anglia, north Essex, the NE Midlands and east Kent (and through Europe as far as Crete). Very variable, with many local varieties. Graceful or rugged in habit; rounded, upright, pentagonal or one-sided in outline. Leaves narrow, often pale, smooth, often with long stalks and very asymmetric bases.

3. The *Cornish Elm*, *'U. stricta'*, and its relatives wild in Cornwall, Devon and the Channel Islands, together with tree-planters' elms such as the Wheatley Elm. Stiffly upright, often with short stubby boughs. Leaves very small, tough, dark green, smooth, nearly symmetrical.

There are many intermediate elms, possibly the result of hybridization. The Huntingdon Elm, which lacks suckers, has a formal habit with a short trunk forking about 12 feet up into an inverted cone of big boughs; it is another planters' elm, and (being resistant to the present Dutch Elm Disease) is the chief elm surviving in cities. The Dutch Elm, forking in habit like a wych-elm but suckering, is common in Cornwall and Ireland, and said to be a relic of a planting fashion associated with William of Orange. The Lineage group of elms, intermediate between wych and East Anglian, coppice like wych but are gregarious; they are a distinctive and ancient feature of some eastern woods.

Among limes, the 'common' lime, *Tilia vulgaris*, planted in millions in towns, villages and wherever men plant limes, is a hybrid between two native species, 'large-leaved' lime, *T. platyphyllos*, and pry or 'small-leaved' lime, *T. cordata*. It became fashionable in the seventeenth century. It was valued by nurserymen because easily propagated from suckers, but is not naturalized. Pry is a magnificent tree with graceful, bluish, heart-shaped, long-stalked, not sticky leaves. It is one of the most important historic trees, but, alas, has attracted the caprice of fashion in recent years. Large-leaved lime is much rarer and largely confined to limestone rocks. Although a common lime in a wood is almost certainly planted, natural hybrids are to be found, sometimes in woods with no pure *platyphyllos*.

Among poplars, the more familiar kinds, such as Lombardy and balsam poplar, are all exotic or artificial. The commonest native poplar is aspen, a clonal woodland tree often referred to in medieval documents and then used as timber.

The black poplar is one of the rarest and most distinctive native trees. No other native tree can compete with it in rugged grandeur. It is recognizable a mile off by its outline (Fig. 7), with a vast, straight, usually leaning trunk and heavy branches with arch and sweep down.

21

Fig. 7. Black poplar.

The trunk and boughs are covered with great bosses; the bark is very deeply ridged and appears black from a distance. It grows in hedges and especially meadows and is never known in woods (except where the wood is young and has grown up round the poplar). All poplars have two sexes. The female black poplar is very rare indeed (unlike aspen, where I find it to be the commoner sex). Denied the opportunity to set seed, black poplar reproduces by falling over and taking root from the fallen trunk – appropriate behaviour for a tree which (like cottonwood, its American equivalent) would originally have grown on the unstable flood-plains of rivers. It is often mentioned in documents, and in the middle ages was one of the common non-woodland trees of Suffolk and Essex; its timber occasionally survives. It has become rare with the rise of planting and the introduction of cultivar poplars.[11]

And what is the abele? The word is commonly supposed to mean white poplar and to have been introduced, along with that tree, from Holland in the seventeenth century. However, in medieval Suffolk and

Essex the word *abel* is used for a common non-woodland tree connected with, but distinct from, [black] poplar.[12] Is white poplar, therefore, either native or an earlier introduction? If so, why does it not survive? White poplar is strongly clonal and, once introduced, should persist for ever, but is rare in Suffolk today, apart from recent plantings. I am tempted to equate *abel* with grey poplar, a much better-established clonal tree for which we lack a medieval word. But grey poplar is found (by experiment) to be a hybrid between white poplar and aspen.[13] How could it have spread, as early as the thirteenth century, in the absence of one of its parents? There must be a mistake somewhere, but I cannot yet find it.

History, pseudo-history, anthropology and the Triumph of Unreason

The sort of 'History' that was taught in Narnia under Miraz's rule was duller than the truest history you ever read and less true than the most exciting adventure story.
C.S. Lewis, *Prince Caspian*

A fascinating aspect of anything to do with trees and woods is that there is a rival version. I do not refer to conflicts of evidence and differences of scholarly opinion. The reader will doubtless be aware that woods were destroyed by people felling trees to build houses and ships, that medieval England was still very wooded, that forests were preserved for hunting by severe laws and barbarous penalties, that there was a 'timber famine' in the Tudor period, that iron was smelted with coke because there was no wood left, that there was no conservation, that replanting was taken in hand after Evelyn wrote *Sylva* (1664), and that the last remnants of the old woodland perished when cut down in the First (or was it the Second?) World War. All this (and much more) forms a consistent, logical, and widely accepted story – which, however, cannot be sustained from the records of actual woods or Forests. It is a *pseudo-history* which has no connexion with the real world, and is made up of *factoids*. A factoid looks like a fact, is respected as a fact, and has all the properties of a fact except that it is not true.

Pseudo-history is not killed by publishing real history. In a rational world, this might lead to a controversy in which either the new version was accepted or the old version was shown to be right after all. In our world, the matter is not controversial: either the old version is re-told as if nothing had happened, or authors try to combine the two versions as if both could be true at once. Pseudo-history is not static but alive and growing: as we shall see in Chapter 11, new factoids are even now being devised and added to the temple of Unreason. It wins ground at the expense of real history. Seventy years ago, the natural succession of farmland into woodland was a hot theme of ecology: research was done, and books written, and students examined on how this happens. Succession is as true as ever, but is now all but forgotten. How many recent books on conservation and the countryside devote so much as a chapter to it?

What is there about trees and woodland (and the landscape generally) that makes them specially, perhaps uniquely, productive of canards? Authors confuse the history of woodland with the history of woodland *folk* or the history of what people have *said* about woodland. These are very different things. Landscape changes through natural causes and human default as well as human action. People notice the sudden felling of trees but not their gradual growth; they may put on record the grubbing-out of a wood as an investment, but not the making of a new wood by neglect, which costs nothing; they take far more notice of oak than of hornbeam.

Historians forget that trees and woodland are living things, and have lives of their own independently of what men do to them. They are not mere artefacts, and are not wholly predictable. As living things, trees are very unlike us and unlike each other. They are much less anthropoid than dogs or codfish; an ash is less like a pine than a dog is like a fish. Each species has its own behaviour, and we do not understand them fully. A huge inverted pyramid of argument has been built on the belief that trees die when cut down – a factoid which flatly denies the whole basis of woodmanship as practised over the last 5000 years.

In this field, authors copy one another; each repeats his predecessors' errors and adds a few of his own. Plagiarism often goes back to a first statement by Evelyn. One example (the notion that ivy kills the tree it grows on) can be traced all the way back to Theophrastus in the fourth century BC, without anyone stopping to think whether it can be true!

Scholars do not always resist the temptation to argue *a priori*, often to avoid admitting ignorance. Time and again, one meets the statement that tree X grows in place Y because its wood was used to make Z. It is easy to make such an assertion; much easier than to study the behaviour of X and to find out why it chooses to grow in Y. People are surprisingly ready to accept that a would-be maker of Z planted trees, did something else for 50 years, and came back and made Z when the trees had grown. They rarely ask whether Z is really made of X, and whether another wood would not do instead. (In practice, timbers are surprisingly interchangeable: there are very few uses for which a particular species is really necessary.)

Pseudo-history is a fascinating subject, part of the anthropology of human motives and attitudes to woodland. But it does matter. It is all the history that most of the public – and some Cabinet Ministers – ever read; much of what passes for conservation is based upon it. We must try to get the story right. Is Hatfield Forest the last reasonably intact wooded royal Forest of medieval England, or is it a fourth-rate nineteenth-century landscape park? On the answer depend both our estimate of the importance of the Forest, and the practical choice of what to do about its future.

How to investigate the history of trees and woodland is illustrated in the following chapters. Certain principles must be emphasized.

1. The woodland history of the British Isles is the sum of thousands of histories of individual woods, every one different from every other. We must work from the particular to the general. Only then can we go back to general writers such as Evelyn, and decide whether they were right.

2. Documents, though valuable, are not the whole story. I seldom enter a wood, however well documented, where there is not something more to be learnt from the wood itself. If we rely on documents, we never find out anything about periods when nobody was writing, and we overemphasize the achievements of people who had much to say for themselves. The more independent kinds of evidence there are to corroborate an argument, the stronger will be the conclusions.

3. Beware of bias in the documents. Most records were made for some purpose other than telling posterity objectively what the landscape was like. They were often written by accountants or lawyers; it is wrong to infer that woodland management was necessarily dominated by economics or law. Many things and activities are not put on record; this usually means that they were commonplace and taken for granted.

4. Do not be afraid to say you don't know. Canards are started by scholars clutching at straws.

Let no-one suppose that by sifting out the factoids we shall be left with a grey, banal, workaday residue. Quite the contrary. Trees and woodland have been poorly served by grey-minded pseudo-historians; but even had this not been so, no writer could have imagined the colourful tale of human achievement and folly, the independent lives of trees and plants, the doings of deer and the nemesis of Nature, which is the actual story of a place like Hatfield Forest. The real history of trees and woodland is more romantic than the romance.

2

Wildwood and prehistoric beginnings

The dominance of lime in the Post-Glacial warm period has only lately been realized. Examinations of peat-bogs can easily give an exaggerated impression of the significance of oak ... Lime flowers are pollinated by insects and thus do not disperse the pollen so effectively as the other common forest trees, which have flowers specialized for wind-pollination ... Lime was much more frequent and oak was much more scarce than the pollen diagrams would appear to suggest.

J. Iversen, *Danmarks Natur* (1967)[14]

The history of woodland and trees in Britain begins about 11,000 BC. There have, of course, been trees of various sorts in the land for hundreds of millions of years, but these are not directly relevant to our purpose because the ecological continuity of the vegetation has been broken by the ice ages. For the last million years the normal climate of Britain has been arctic, interrupted from time to time by relatively brief warm periods, of a few tens of thousands of years, during which the trees and other plants and animals that had retreated to southerly latitudes have been able to return to the British Isles. We live in one of these *interglacial* periods, which we think of as the *post-glacial*.

The events described in this book have all happened in the twinkling of a geologist's eye. The history of British woodland is not so very much longer than that of civilization: the gulf of time which separates us from the end of the last glaciation is only about six times as great as that between us and Julius Cæsar. I shall therefore discuss the development of plant communities, in relation to the changing environment and the impact of human affairs, rather than the evolution of species. With a few special exceptions (e.g. elms), our trees have not had time to adapt themselves to their present environment to any great degree. They sink or swim with the genes that they inherited from their earlier history.

Before written records, all the evidence for the history of trees has to come from actual remains. These can range from whole tree-trunks embedded in peat to fragments of nutshell from an archaeological excavation. Many plants, especially trees, produce large quantities of pollen grains, which can be extremely resistant to decay.[15] Pollen accumulates in stratified deposits such as peats and lake muds and also, though in a manner more difficult to interpret,[16] in acid soils on dry land. Individual grains can be recognized to some extent under the microscope as coming from particular plants. For instance, it is easy to tell lime pollen from oak; the two species of lime can be separated with difficulty; some progress has been made towards distinguishing different elms;[17] but as far as we know it is impossible to tell apart the pollens of the two native oaks, of different poplars, or willow from sallow.

For most of the post-glacial period the predominant vegetation of the British Isles has been continuous forest of various kinds. To avoid adding further to the meanings of the overworked word 'forest', I shall call these prehistoric forests, before the coming of civilization, by the general name of *wildwood*.*

Development of wildwood

At the beginning of the post-glacial Britain and Ireland were tundra and moorland. A series of waves of colonization by different trees spread across the country from the south. The earliest wildwoods were formed by birch, aspen and sallow, whose pollen, in the deposits, replaces those of the previous grasses, heather etc. About 8500 BC pine and hazel spread to replace birch, which became generally uncommon (though it never disappeared) until its very recent resurgence. Pine was followed by oak and alder; next by lime and elm; then by holly, ash, beech, hornbeam and maple.[18]

This process was rather like the making of secondary woodland now. Distances were greater, but there was no farmland to stand in the way of the advance, nor at first was there an English Channel or Irish Sea. Birch, aspen and sallow are relatively arctic trees. The later species were either trees of warmer climates (hornbeam, maple) or bad colonizers (lime). The earlier trees spread throughout Britain and Ireland, except the far north of Scotland; alder reached Ireland shortly before it was cut off by rising sea-level. Beech and lime scarcely

---

* Incautious reviewers should note that The Wild Wood is to be found in the works of Kenneth Grahame, not A. A. Milne, and has nothing whatever to do with wildwood.

penetrated beyond the Lowland Zone of England. Latecoming trees were slow to become abundant, for there was no vacant ground to occupy; they had to wait for existing trees to die.

The arrival of lime began a long period of relative stability – roughly 7300 to 4500 BC – during which the various tree species fought each other by the natural processes of succession to form a series of 'climax' wildwood types. At the end of this *Atlantic Period*, readily recognized in pollen profiles by a sudden fall in the abundance of elm, almost the whole of Britain was covered with forest which had not yet been affected by civilized human activities.

The fully developed wildwood

A picture of the wildwood just before the Elm Decline was compiled in 1975 by Dr John Birks and his colleagues from 140-odd pollen profiles from all over the British Isles.[19] There were then a number of gaps which have been filled in by later work.

Pollen analysts used to regard the climax wildwood of 4500 BC as a rather monotonous 'mixed oak forest' of oak, alder, elm, hazel as a shrub, and a little lime and pine. We now know the reality to have been much more complex. Lime and ash have been greatly underestimated in the past because they shed less pollen than oak or birch. Hazel has been under-valued because it was thought to be an understorey shrub; it is in fact a canopy tree, and produces little or no pollen if shaded by taller neighbours. Alder has been overestimated because it is a wet-land tree, specially common around the edges of those wet places in which pollen is preserved.

Discounting alder, including hazel, and allowing for the different pollen production of the various trees, we find that wildwoods fall into five regional types or provinces (Fig. 8). Within each province there were many types of woodland, to some extent reflecting the different soils; these included, in special places, outliers of woodland more typical of other provinces.

The Pine Province covered the eastern Scottish Highlands, with outliers on mountains in England and Ireland. The Birch Province occupied the western Scottish Highlands. In it there were outliers of pine and oak: Dr Hilary Birks has shown that the patchwork of pinewoods and oakwoods, still existing around Loch Maree, dates from 7800 BC.[21]

The Oak–Hazel Province stretched from middle Scotland to Land's End. Since hazel does not flower under the shade of oak, we must suppose a mosaic of hazel-woods and oakwoods. There were patches

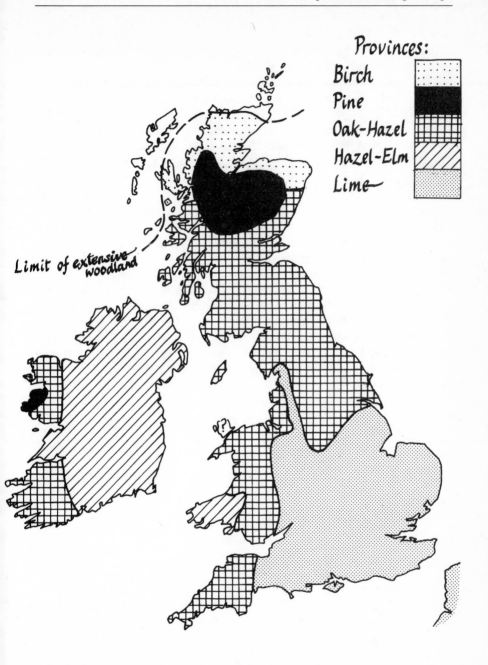

Provinces:
Birch
Pine
Oak-Hazel
Hazel-Elm
Lime

Limit of extensive woodland

Fig. 8. Wildwood provinces in 4500 BC. Derived from the work of H. J. B. Birks and others.[19,20]

and outliers of other types of woodland: for instance, of elmwood and pinewood in County Durham[22] and of limewood in the Lake District. Hazel and elm dominated most of Ireland.

The Lime Province covered Lowland England. Although in most pollen profiles lime comes out as the commonest tree, the second and third commonest vary widely from place to place. In Norfolk, for example, four sub-regions can be distinguished (Fig. 9): the Broads with an extreme predominance of lime, south Norfolk with abundant ash, the Breckland edge with predominant hazel and some birch, and the Fens with pine. There were evidently at least seven local types of wildwood – limewood, hazel-wood, ashwood, elmwood, alder-wood, pinewood, and probably oakwood – and maybe others based on mixtures of trees.

Even in 4500 BC we see some features which persist in ancient woods to this day. The pinewoods, birchwoods and oakwoods of the Scottish Highlands are still with us and still have much the same distribution. In the Highland Zone of England and Wales, oakwood – in which oak is so overwhelmingly abundant that it has been treated as underwood and not just as timber – is still by far the commonest. Hazel-woods, which would have grown on the more fertile soils, have been grubbed out and now survive chiefly as patches within the oakwoods. In Ireland, this process has gone further: the very little

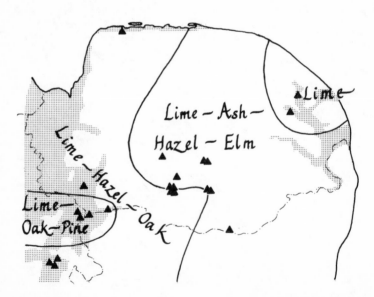

Fig. 9. The sub-provinces of wildwood in Norfolk. Triangles show the actual sites of pollen deposits.[23]

ancient woodland that survives is oakwood, representing the special wildwood of the least fertile soils. Nearly all the hazel-woods have gone, and elm-wood, being the woodland of ordinarily fertile soils, has been reduced to a few acres in the whole of Ireland.

In Lowland England woods, now as then, are still a patchwork of tree communities. Different woods, and different parts of the same wood, are composed of different mixtures of trees. Oak, though reserved and encouraged as a timber tree down the centuries, is not the natural dominant: oakwoods are either recent, or artificial, or are the special woodland of very infertile soils. Native lime is now much less common than in 4500 BC, but is unobtrusive and is not so rare as is often thought. Limewoods are still to be found, if one looks for them, over the exact prehistoric range of the tree from Cornwall and Kent to the Lake District and County Durham. Lime (pry) is still the commonest tree of ancient woodland within a definite area centred on Sudbury, Suffolk (Fig. 10). Other groups of limewoods exist in Norfolk, Lincolnshire, Derbyshire, Herefordshire, etc. and are mysteriously separated by wide tracts of country in which even ancient woods contain no lime at all. Of the two species of lime, *Tilia platyphyllos* was much rarer in wildwood than *T. cordata*, and still is today.

Pollen analysts have to take their deposits where they find them.

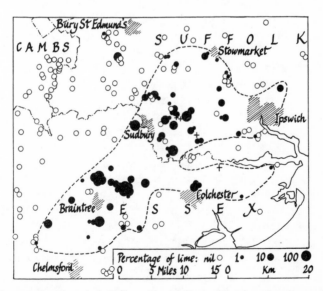

Fig. 10. Limewoods of south Suffolk and north Essex. The size of each spot is related to the proportion of pry in the wood. Crosses: sites of former pry-woods. Circles: woods without pry.

We can still only speculate on how far the ash and maple woods of the Midlands, beechwoods of the Chilterns, and hornbeam-woods of Essex and Suffolk reflect vegetation differences already established in the Atlantic Period. Ashwoods certainly then existed, but have increased down the centuries and still increase today, partly as secondary woodland on former farmland, and partly through ancient woodland turning into ashwood for reasons yet unknown. Beech has greatly expanded following human activities; most of what are often mistaken for natural beechwoods, especially on chalk, are very recent plantations.

What did wildwood look like? What was its structure? How did it reproduce? What lived in it? For possible answers, we look at the (surprisingly small) areas of surviving wildwood in eastern North America. The trees here are of different species from ours, but of much the same genera. American wildwoods show the same pattern of regional, sub-regional and local variation that I have described for ours. There is a huge variety of structures. The mighty hemlocks and tulip-trees of damp fertile valleys in Tennessee grow to 180 feet high and 7 feet thick. Some of the 'bog oaks' and pines dug up in the peat of our Fens reached almost this size, but may have been peculiar to this habitat. At the other extreme are the Lilliput-like oak and pine wildwoods of New England mountain-tops; these are approached by the small oaks and pines which Dr Margaret Atherden has shown me in the bogs of the North York Moors. The prevalence of hazel in our pollen record means that wide areas of wildwood were of low enough stature to allow hazel to reach the canopy.

American wildwoods reproduce in various ways. In general they are full of saplings, which our present woods are not: partly this is because of our recent management (or neglect), which has given few opportunities for new saplings to arise; partly because we happen to have few native trees (chiefly beech and yew) that can grow up in the shade of other trees. In America, sometimes a giant tree crashes down and makes a gap in which successors (often of different species) can grow. Sometimes a whole area of trees is destroyed by storm or fire, and is replaced by an area of trees all of the same age. Most American trees reproduce by seed, but some, such as American beech, sucker. Several species are self-coppicing; an American lime, for example, rots at the base, crashes down, and is succeeded by shoots previously sent up from the base. Even pollarding occurs naturally, for example in tulip.

The structure of British wildwoods will have depended on how particular trees fell down. A big beech may be uprooted when still alive and crash down on its neighbours, making a wide gap in which other species can grow. A big lime rots at the base and crashes down, leaving a stump which sprouts and continues to occupy the spot. An oak usually dies standing and takes about thirty years for the roots to rot through, by which time the gap may have been filled by the expansion of neighbouring trees. An elm falls to pieces branch by branch, doing little damage and leaving a gap to be filled by its own suckers. Catastrophes, rather than such single events, probably played a lesser part with us than they do in America. Except for pine, no British wood can be destroyed by fire. After the 1987 storm, it can no longer be claimed that our woods are immune from hurricanes on the American model. However, that storm uprooted chiefly planted trees and had less effect on ancient woodland; where it felled areas of woodland, most of the uprooted trees remained alive and will recover.

Most woodland herbs and undershrubs are poorly recorded because they produce very little pollen. We know that brambles, dog's-mercury, bluebell, wood anemone, etc. go back to prehistoric times, and suspect that some of them increased when men began to fell and manage woodland. Wildwood was not quite continuous: this is shown by the constant presence of grass pollen as well as by occasional grains from plants such as buttercup, cuckoo-flower, ragged robin, bugle and devil's-bit, which do not flower in shade. These are now part of the 'woodland grassland' flora of rides and wood edges. In wildwood there were presumably glades where deer and wild oxen congregated and ate any tree saplings which appeared among the herbage. Such glades appear to have been more abundant in the wildwood of earlier interglacials, being maintained by the great beasts that then lived or by Palaeolithic men.

Destruction of wildwood

It has been assumed that until men began to till the soil they had no more effect on vegetation than the beasts on which they preyed. Mesolithic and even Palaeolithic men had axes, and made temporary clearings around their homes;[24] but their numbers were so small that they could have made little impact even if they had nothing else to do but cut down trees.

Hunting and gathering were probably not simple amateurish activities, but may have involved the definite management of land and vegetation. Some North American Indians, whom we would call 'Mesolithic', produced a kind of wood-pasture by periodic burning,[25] but this would seldom have been possible in British wildwood. Whether plants will burn or not depends on whether they make resins

33

or other combustible chemicals. It happens that Nature has given us rather few inflammable plants, and most of these, such as heather, are not trees. Pine is our only tree that can be killed by setting fire to it, and its early disappearance from most of England has been ascribed to Mesolithic burning, but this may not have been so. Pines are not inflammable by misfortune: many foreign species *need* to be burnt (by lightning) from time to time, otherwise they are infiltrated and replaced by competitors. Scots Pine is not necessarily one of these, but it springs up abundantly after a fire, and the occasional burning may not eliminate it.

Mesolithic men certainly began in a small way the creation of heathland.[26] Once formed, a heath would have provided pasture for edible wild beasts, and could be kept in being by periodic burning of the heather. More surprising is the recent discovery that small areas of chalk downland, in the Yorkshire Wolds, go back to this period.[27] It has been claimed that Mesolithic men are somehow responsible for the great abundance of hazel in the post-glacial; they are known to have eaten largely of the nuts.

The earliest evidence of interference on a large scale comes with the Elm Decline. Within a century or two of 4000 BC, half the elm vanished from Europe. This decline is everywhere associated with a sudden increase in agricultural weeds such as plantains and stinging-nettle, and often – both in Britain and Ireland – with archaeological evidence of Neolithic settlement. Explanations that have been pro-posed include climatic change; deterioration of soils; pollarding of elms for leaves on which to feed cattle and sheep; selective grubbing-out of elms because they grew on the most promising agricultural soils; and Dutch Elm Disease. The first two possibilities can be ruled out because the decline was so sudden, so universal, and affected only elm. The third and fourth cannot be the main causes, because the Elm Decline occurred everywhere regardless of whether elms were common or rare: with elms covering about one-eighth of the entire British Isles, there would not have been enough Early Neolithic men to have pollarded or grubbed them, even if they spent all their time on this one task. This leaves Elm Disease as the only sufficiently powerful and specific cause. Elsewhere I have shown that this disease has a long history, and could well have been present in the Neolithic; it is plausible that early pollarding and agriculture could have favoured the spread of the disease.[28] Two recent discoveries support this theory. First, one of the bark-beetles that transmit the disease was already present.[29] Second, the Elm Decline does not mark quite the beginning of the Neolithic, but was preceded by several decades of small-scale agri-culture;[30] this removes the happenstance that a virulent form of the

34

disease should have appeared at the exact moment when agriculture arrived.

Destruction of wildwood for cultivation began just before the Elm Decline, and continued throughout the Neolithic and Bronze Age. On the light soils of the East Anglian Breckland, where there was a dense, and even an industrial, Neolithic population, wildwood vanished never to return. The same happened on much of the chalklands, the Somerset Levels and the coastal Lake District. Elsewhere, many Neolithic clearances were temporary; the pollen record suggests a scene rather like what can still be seen in South Tirol or Macedonia, where grazing, cultivation, shredding, coppicing and scrub coexist uneasily with no definite boundaries.

During the Bronze Age (2400–750 BC) clearance of wildwood continued and extended into high altitudes. The period of greatest activity was probably the early Iron Age, when axes and ploughshares became cheap and heavy ploughs made it easier to till clay soils. I hazard the guess that half of England had ceased to be wildwood by 500 BC; some archaeologists would put it earlier. The lands now being won included the bulk of the present farmland and also moorland.

At various times in the late Neolithic and Bronze Ages lime decreased in many places. This change is attributable to the deliberate grubbing-out of limewoods,[31] presumably because they were on the more rewarding soils, leaving other wildwoods to be dealt with later.

Even at high altitudes most of the new land was put to the plough for a time, as for example around the Bronze Age village of Grimspound on top of Dartmoor; but in that environment farming could not be sustained, and the land went to pasture and then moorland. Some moorland is probably of natural origin. The far north of Scotland has always been open tundra, and the boundary between tundra and woodland has crept southward as the marginal woodland soils have become leached and overgrown by peat. A change to a wetter climate may have helped this process.[32]

To convert tens of millions of acres of wildwood into farmland is the greatest achievement of our ancestors: even in these bulldozing days it is no light investment to dig up a few hundred acres of English coppice. It belongs to an age far beyond record or memory, and we know little of how they did it, of what men were involved, how they were organized, how much of their time they spent on it, how many man-hours it took to clear an acre, or what they lived on while doing it.

Speculation is guided by analogy with the methods used by settlers in America, by old-fashioned farmers in the wilder parts of the world, and by the modern destroyers of rain-forest. Archaeologists in

Denmark and England have simulated ancient methods of winning land and growing crops.[33] But let us not extrapolate these observations too hastily to the prehistoric British Isles. The destroyer of an Amazon jungle meets with less resistance than in an English wood. Our woods (except for pine) burn like wet asbestos; they are not readily killed by felling because they coppice or sucker. Stone axes are said to compare favourably with metal ones (and even with chain-saws!) for cutting down smallish trees, but this only begins the task. Felled trees will not burn where they lie, but have to be cut up and stacked. A log of more than 10 inches in diameter is almost fireproof and is a most uncooperative object. There is the bigger problem still of digging up or ploughing round the stumps and preventing regrowth. The regrowth problem might be reduced by burning up the felled trees on top of as many of the stumps as possible. Trees too big to fell might be killed by lighting fires round them or, less reliably, by ring-barking. Stumps and big logs would have to be ploughed round, as in Dickensian North America, for many years.

Cattle, sheep and goats probably helped the axe-clearance by browsing the young regrowth shoots and eventually killing the stumps. Farm animals too were probably allowed to roam the remaining wildwood and to scratch a living from such herbage as it contained. They would naturally eat tree seedlings as well; this could, in theory, change wildwood into grassland with trees, as old trees died without being succeeded by young ones, and eventually into treeless grassland. This process tended to happen in medieval wood-pasture (p. 144); but we should not exaggerate it. It takes a lot of browsing to stop regeneration altogether. Places like the unenclosed New Forest and Hatfield Forest have been heavily grazed for centuries and still have plenty of trees. At Hatfield the present stocking of one bullock to $1\frac{1}{2}$ acres of plain, which has often been exceeded in the past, is only just enough to prevent trees from increasing.[34] In prehistoric times there can hardly have been so many cattle except very close to settlements.

Prehistoric woodworking and woodmanship

Archaeologists are conditioned by the preservation of their material to think in terms of stone, bronze, iron and pottery. Most prehistoric artefacts were wooden, and if more of them survived we would think instead in terms of inventions and fashions in woodworking. In recent years something has been done to remedy this imbalance: a variety of woodwork has been excavated from waterlogged deposits, illustrating many of the crafts, but not yet all.[35]

Woodworking goes back far into the Palaeolithic, as is shown by the Clacton bowstave, the world's oldest wooden artefact, from two ice-ages ago. From the Neolithic we have the many 'trackways' of the Somerset Levels: wooden structures built as walkways across soft peat, and entombed and preserved by the growth of the peat. Some of them are made of logs or mere branches, but others are of hurdles, exactly like a modern wattle hurdle except for such differences as come from using stone tools. The earliest of all, the Sweet Track, at 3900 BC, is the most elaborate and sophisticated, with poles of oak, ash, lime, hazel, alder and holly, of different sizes and selected for particular functions in the structure.[36]

The late Bronze Age built the biggest wooden structure there has ever been in this country, at Flag Fen near Peterborough: a gigantic crannog or artificial island in the then submerged Fenland, four acres in extent, with many buildings on it.[37] This one artefact consumed at least five times as much timber as the largest of Nelson's warships.

Also from the Bronze Age comes the biggest single timber known to carpentry in these islands, the Brigg Logboat, a dugout boat made from an oak trunk 48 ft long and $5\frac{1}{2}$ ft in diameter at the small end. Such an oak in this country today would be a named and famous tree. This boat is, alas, destroyed, but her younger and slightly smaller sister, the Hasholme Logboat, is the pride of Hull Museums, and demonstrates that by the Iron Age the design of carpenters' joints was as masterly as it has ever been.[38] In the Iron Age a house was an elaborate round structure, often as big in span as a cathedral; reconstructed examples can be seen at Butser Hill Ancient Farm, Hampshire. The Iron Age also brought wheelwrighting to a perfection not regained until the nineteenth century and never surpassed.

These examples show that early woodworking could equal, both in scale and elaboration, anything in historic times. There was nothing primitive about it: each separate craft attained, and sometimes surpassed, the sophistication which it has today. For example, the joining of planks edge-to-edge reached its zenith in Roman ship-building and has gradually declined ever since.

What does this imply for woodmanship? Rods, poles and most timber did not come from wildwood. Occasional giant trees were used for making dugout boats or woodhenges, but for ordinary purposes such trees would have been impracticable to cut up or transport: as on the modern Amazon, most of the trees that came from destroying wildwood were wasted. Instead we find, from the earliest times, a distinction between underwood and timber, most of the latter coming from smallish trees. The oaks in the Flag Fen crannog were typically less than a foot in diameter.

Early Neolithic people had already made the discovery which is the key to woodland management: that the regrowth shoots from a stump are more useful than the original tree. The various sizes of poles in the Sweet Track appear to come from a mixed coppice like the Bradfield Woods, managed on a rather complex coppicing system.[39] Later Neolithic hurdle-tracks are more obviously the product of coppicing, but are not so simple as they look. The rods are accurately matched for size (since there was no metal tool to split the thicker ones) and are therefore of different ages, for some grew faster than others. Neolithic woodmanship turns out to be an elaborate practice, involving not the felling of whole areas of underwood but the 'drawing' of rods here and there from the stool. Some rods had had their tops cut off a few years previously and allowed to grow on: the main purpose of the wood may have been to grow leaves on which to feed livestock.

From Neolithic times onwards, parts of the wildwood, instead of being grubbed out, were evidently turned into managed woodland. The twentieth century, conditioned to think in terms of timber, finds it difficult to grasp the immense importance of *underwood* in almost everyone's life in prehistory. Whole buildings were made of it: an Iron Age round-house comprises rods and poles grown to various sizes for different parts of the structure. It was the normal material for roads, fences, vehicles and equipment, and the normal fuel for cooking, heating, metalworking and pottery. Coppice-woods, cut on various rotations, were evidently a usual part of the landscape, but beyond this I cannot yet go. I have found some evidence for Roman or earlier woodbanks, but cannot say whether timber trees were scattered among underwood or grown separately; nor do I know how many surviving coppice-woods were already coppiced in antiquity.

3

From Claudius to
Hugo de Northwold

Start from Twyford along the road to Bracken Ridge, from there along the road to Carrion Barrow; then in a straight line to the pear tree; then along the road to Ceardic's Barrow; then to Withy Grove; then to the road that shoots over the ditch; then along the road to the pollard oak; from there along the road from where it adjoins the wood ... by the little hedge along the spinney ... along the hedge to the old maple tree ... from there to the hoar [i.e. lichen-covered] apple tree; then along the ditch out to the river Test; to its southern bank; then along the bank; then below the timber weir to the northern bank; along the bank back to Twyford.
Boundary of Hurstbourne Priors (Hants), dated A.D. 901[40]

The first twelve centuries after the birth of Christ are a significant period in the making of the British countryside, but what they signify is a matter of debate. By AD 1200 much of the modern landscape was already recognizable. Nearly all our villages and most hamlets existed then; the proportions of farmland, moorland and woodland were not enormously different from what they are now; what are now Ancient and Planned Countryside were distinct; and many actual woods and hedges still extant had come into being. The things that distinguish woodland from wildwood – the separation of woods from each other, the naming of woods, their private ownership and defined boundaries, and above all *management* by rotational felling to provide a succession of crops and by fencing to protect the young growth from grazing animals – had become widespread and systematic. When I first wrote this book I supposed that all these had come into being in what was then the dark age of the late Anglo-Saxon and early medieval periods, and that the Roman age had been a time of comparative wilderness. Archaeology and systematic study of the documents have since illuminated much of the darkness. The landscape is earlier than we used to think; much of it is inherited from the Roman period; and a good deal was already there when the Romans came.

By this time pollen analysis, though useful, is no longer our chief source. Where the deposits have not lost their upper layers through peat-digging or erosion, they become progressively more uncertain of interpretation as the area from which they collect pollen develops into a pattern of land uses. As woodland plays a decreasing part, it becomes difficult to sort out what is happening to the remaining woodland.

The first four centuries

The Romans, invading England in AD 43, came to a land with a fully-developed agriculture. Wildwood had vanished for ever from river gravels, flood-plains and chalkland. With the coming of the furrow-turning plough, claylands too had long been widely cultivated, although in some regions grassland predominated. For example, the pollen diagram from Diss shows that south Norfolk ceased to be wooded about 1000 BC, but for centuries was mainly pastured.[41] Land belonged to somebody, and was sometimes divided up by grids of parallel (but sinuous) field boundaries going on for mile after mile. This prehistoric rural planning – we have no idea what it was for – can be seen today: about a quarter of Essex still bears traces of it. There has been nothing like it in England for two thousand years. (For a modern example we go to the American Mid-West, with its grids of fields and roads sometimes covering an entire state.) Archaeology has begun to show that hedges existed.

England and Wales was a rich and densely populated province of the Roman Empire. Farming had long since ceased to be confined to easy terrain: it extended into the heavy soils of Suffolk and Essex, deep into what were later to be great woods, and even into the Fens. There can be little doubt that England was almost as agricultural as it is now. Much of what was not farmland was moorland; England can hardly have been very wooded by the standards of today.

Roman Britain was also an industrial land on a scale not to be repeated for well over a thousand years. The Romans dwelt in cities and had great timber-framed buildings, bridges and ships; they indulged in things like baths, bricks, hypocausts, corn-driers, and articles of iron, lead and glass. This implies organized woodmanship to secure permanent supplies of both timber and wood. Not only, as in earlier times, had poles and rods to be grown to sizes which were difficult to get from wildwood; it would now have been necessary to conserve a limited resource and to organize supplies to woodless places. For example, among their many activities in the Weald the

40

Romans had military ironworks, whose output has been estimated by Dr Henry Cleere at 550 tons a year.[42] From this figure I calculate that these ironworks could have been sustained permanently by 23,000 acres of coppice-wood. There were many other ironworks in the Weald, whose total influence on the landscape could hardly have been surpassed even in the seventeenth-century heyday of the iron industry.

The Romans were familiar with woodmanship in Italy; they even planted coppices and worked out the yields and the labour required. Columella, the first-century author, recommended cutting chestnut underwood at five years' growth and oak at seven. Although this is only a textbook recommendation, derived from Italian practice, the Romans did introduce chestnut to England. Some ancient chestnut coppices still extant (e.g. Stour Wood near Harwich) may possibly be derived from Roman plantations. More often, acording to charcoal identifications, woods in Roman Britain seem to have been mixed coppices not unlike those of East Anglia in the middle ages and today.[43]

We know little about the details of Roman woodmanship, nor of where the woods were. There were probably two kinds of region: those with a patchwork of woodland and farmland (e.g. Herts, Essex), and those with little or no woodland (the great river-valleys and most of the chalklands). Many of the *big* wooded areas of later centuries – which the medievals thought uncultivable – have Roman or earlier settlements in them. Wychwood Forest (Oxon), Rockingham Forest (Northants), Grovely Forest (Wilts), and Micheldever Wood (Hants) cannot then have been so continuously wooded as they were later to become.

Roman woods may exist today, but have we any hope of recognizing them? It is quite possible that the Romans normally surrounded woods with woodbanks, but only where the wood has grown bigger have we any hope of separating these from later banks which overlie them. In S.E. Essex the Rayleigh Hills have been for 2000 years an island of woodland and heath in the midst of an organized grid of fields. In the surviving woods I have mapped successive layers of woodbanks, and find, underneath the Anglo-Saxon, medieval and later boundaries, faint earthworks which probably mark a different set of wood edges in Roman or earlier times.[44]

The coming of the Anglo-Saxons

The end of the Roman Empire is still a dark age, and research has not dispelled the mystery. Roman Britain, in the fourth century, can hardly have numbered less than five million people, speaking Welsh and Latin. These folk, plus maybe tens of thousands of immigrants from Germanic lands, somehow turned in 250 years into at most $1\frac{1}{2}$ million English-speakers in a landscape with hardly a word of Welsh except river-names. Something very drastic had happened. Wars rarely shed blood on so vast a scale, but writers of the time mention epidemics as well. The most plausible theory is plague, which becomes possible through the recent discovery that Roman Britain had rats.

The archaeological and ecological record indicates recession rather than genocide. Had the rural population vanished, secondary woodland would have covered even the good farmland within thirty years, and we would have some record of its subsequent destruction. In fact, we find all over the country bits of Roman road, fragments of field systems, and sometimes large areas of organized Roman and pre-Roman landscape – features which could survive only through continuous use. Doubtless there were many more which did not survive the vicissitudes of later centuries, or which are still there but not recognizable as ancient. On Hertfordshire or Suffolk claylands and in many other places, the map shows disconnected straight lanes, the remains of what were once Roman through roads. The towns at either end have long vanished, but all through the Dark Ages there was somebody in the intervening hamlets who had a use for a mile or two of the road and was prepared to take a billhook to the encroaching oak and blackthorn.

The site of Stansted Airport appears in Domesday Book as the third largest wooded area in Essex. Surveys and excavations have shown that this clayland began to be settled in the Bronze Age and was largely farmland in Roman times. At the end of the Roman period habitation abruptly stopped and was not resumed until Norman times.[45] Here the archaeology neatly fits the historical expectation, but this is rather exceptional and is not repeated in other 'backwoods' areas. At Shakenoak, in the Wychwood area of Oxfordshire, a Roman villa remained in use for three centuries into the Anglo-Saxon period and only then was abandoned and given over to woodland.[46] At Rivenhall in Essex the villa was never abandoned, but was gradually transmuted into the Anglo-Saxon church and medieval manor-house which are still in use today.[47]

The post-Roman recession hit towns hard: even London was semi-derelict for a time. In the countryside, circumstances were reduced but life went on. Surprisingly little, even of the worse soils, was abandoned to woodland, and where this did happen it was from local rather than general causes. Pollen diagrams point to an *expansion* of farmland in the last remaining wildwood of the Lake District and southern

Scotland. At Bloak Moss, Ayrshire, Dr Judith Turner has found extensive clearance of the fifth or sixth century, which involved not a general thinning of the woods but the making of defined clearings within them.[48]

Anglo-Saxon woodmanship

Although industrial uses of woodland declined, we must not suppose that management lapsed altogether. Men could no longer afford bricks and glass, and worked less in iron and copper, but they still cooked and warmed themselves, made pots and built houses. Anglo-Saxons were carpenters rather than masons. Despite their long experience with stone for churches they always built houses, even royal palaces, of timber. We know how they did this from tantalizing excavated remains and obscure literary references; from the church door at Hadstock, Essex, still in daily use after a thousand years; and from the mysterious church at Greensted, Essex, with its clever design and skilled workmanship.

The Anglo-Saxons did not go in for the 'log-cabin' buildings of the Continent, a building system that demands straight trunks, especially of conifers, and would not work with the crooked trees of Britain. Our traditions, beginning in prehistoric times and continuing right into the twentieth century, are of timber-framed buildings with upright posts separated by panels filled with wattle-and-daub. This does not call for big trees, but for a supply of small timber and of poles, which need be only moderately straight. These would normally have to be grown in coppice-woods. Without power-driven tools, one soon learns not to cut down trees that are bigger than strictly necessary for the job in hand.

At Colwick on the River Trent, the hurdlework of an Anglo-Saxon weir (for catching fish) has been excavated and analyzed. The staves and rods were grown in a way which reproduced exactly the complexities of Neolithic woodmanship, nearly 4000 years earlier, rather than the simpler practice of medieval and modern times.[48a]

Anglo-Saxon buildings had posts set in the ground; these would have rotted, and their frequent replacement would have increased the demand for timber. The *groundsill*, a horizontal sleeper-beam into which the feet of the posts are morticed and which acts as a damp-course, came in very gradually towards the latter part of the period. (This is why Anglo-Saxon timber buildings are so very rarely still standing.)

Surviving scraps of early literary evidence include tariffs of compensation for criminal damage which show that trees could be valuable private property. King Ine of sixth-century Kent, for instance, decreed that a smallish tree, under which thirty swine could stand, was to be valued at sixty shillings: in Anglo-Saxon England one could get away with murder for 200 shillings. In South Wales a mere hazel stool was equivalent to $3\frac{3}{4}$ sheep.

Anglo-Saxon charters

These documents give us the chance to escape from treacherous generalities on to the firmer ground of describing some identifiable piece of country. It was customary, in the days before maps, for a deed of gift or sale of a piece of land to contain a **perambulation**, or description of the boundaries. The example at the head of the chapter shows how this was done. By careful fieldwork it is often possible to identify exactly the sites. There are about 840 such documents, attached to charters bearing dates from about AD 600 to 1080; on the whole the later ones are more informative.[40]

Reading the perambulations one is struck by how little England has changed in the thousand or so years since they were written. They conduct us through a familiar world of rivers, mill-streams, ditches, hedges and hedgerow trees, roads, lanes, paths, bridges, heaths, thorns, stumps, pits and old posts – and of barrows, hillforts, 'heathen burials', 'ancient cities', and Roman roads. The landscape of the charters is unmistakably England. As we shall see in Chapter 11, it was already divided into Ancient and Planned Countryside, though not exactly in their medieval forms.

England in even the earliest charters was definitely not a very wooded land. Many features such as downs are explicitly non-woodland; others, such as trees, would have been of no value as landmarks in a wood. Woods in the charters had individual names and were permanent: at least one in four of the woods was still there in the twentieth century. A very early perambulation, that of Shottery by Stratford-on-Avon in *c*. 704, mentions a *Westgrāf*; the map still shows a Westgrove Wood in Hazelor. Also in Warwickshire, the bounds of Long Itchington, dated 1001, pass through 'a high oak in the middle of Wulluht grove'; at this point there is still a 200-acre wood bisected by the Ufton–Itchington parish boundary.*

Woodland was not always situated in the place to which it belonged. The charter for Benson (Oxfordshire) in 996, having traced the

* Mr D. R. Morfitt assures me that no modern evil has befallen it.

44

boundary, then says 'These are the bounds of the wood that belongs to the land', and goes on to perambulate a separate territory some miles away in the Chilterns. About twenty such detached woods are described in detail, and many more are named.

Charters do not set out the uses of woodland, but they let slip incidental details which make it clear that woods were managed and used. There are many references to coppicing and the supply and transport of rods, fuel and other wood; less often to timber. Wood-pasture is differentiated from other woodland, and common woods from private woods:

Pasture for 70 pigs in that wooded common ... which the country-folk call Wulfferd-inleh [Wolverley, Worcs] and 5 wagons full of good rods and every year one oak for building ... and wood ... for the fire as necessary.

Grant by Burgred, king of Mercia, 866

60 fothers of wood ... in the wood at Horn. And 12 fothers of grove and six fothers of poles.

Annual supply to Sempringham, Lincs, 852

[Horn is in Rutland, 16 miles off, and was by no means the nearest wood. A fother was a kind of cartload. I do not know what 'grove' was as a woodland product.]

A place in which salt can be got and with [right of] access for 3 carts into the wood which is called Blean.

Grant at Lenham, Kent, 850

[The Blean, still the second-largest wooded area in Kent, is 15 miles away.]

The old coal-pit where the three boundaries go together.

Apsley Guise, 969

[A coal-pit in Bedfordshire has to be a pit for making charcoal.]

The Anglo-Saxon language had many words for woodland: *wudu* 'wood', *grāf* 'grove', *scaga* 'shaw', *hangr* 'hanger', and now-forgotten terms such as *bearu*, *holt*, and *fyrhþ*. These may be technical terms for different kinds of woodland, but there is no real evidence as to what they meant.

Woods were valuable private property: a wood at Powick (Worcs) was the subject of a complicated lawsuit in 825. We might expect their boundaries to have been demarcated, and as we shall see there is evidence that some woodbanks are as old as this. There are 93 instances in the charters of a mysterious word *wyrtruma* or *wyrtwala*, literally 'plant-strength' or 'plant-wall'. This was a linear feature like a hedge and was usually associated with woodland: for instance at Rimpton (Somerset) one passed along the *wyrtruma* of a wood called Eatan bearu. Although it is not quite certain that the *wyrtruma* was always at the edge of a wood, it is hard to resist the conclusion that this is the Old English technical term for a woodbank.

45

Evidence of place-names

Place-names are a sharp two-edged sword. Many of them date from the Anglo-Saxon period, often from even earlier than the charters. But the interpretation is full of pitfalls. Scholars traditionally over-interpret place-names and read into them more than they say. Brent-wood does not mean 'wood destroyed by burning'; it means just 'burnt wood', and there is nothing to suggest the nature of the burning or that the wood was destroyed (which would be physically almost impossible). Place-names are difficult to date, and may be much older than the earliest written record. England is fortunate in that the language has changed over time and gives some clue to dating; even so, a chance mention by the Venerable Bede or in an early charter may back-date to the seventh century a place-name which would otherwise be guessed to be at least 400 years later.

Place-names referring to kinds of tree might seem straightforward provided we avoid the trap of assuming that trees imply woodland. The most frequent trees in English place-names are thorn and ash, followed closely by willow (including sallow and withy) and oak, then by alder, hazel and elm. But are places named after common trees, or after trees which were sufficiently uncommon to be notable? How many Actons (*ac* = oak) and Oakleys are so named because they had the only oak for miles around? Was a wood called 'Birch Wood' really a hornbeam wood distinguished from other hornbeam woods by one conspicuous birch tree at the edge?

Another ambiguity is illustrated by the *ley–wood–grove–tree* series of place-name elements (Fig. 11). The Anglo-Saxon *lēah* appears to have had a reasonably definite meaning, a permanent glade or clearing in woodland. Names of villages and hamlets ending in *-ley* or *-leigh* (or the Viking equivalent *-thwaite*) therefore imply that much woodland remained at the time they were formed. 'Grove', Anglo-Saxon *grāf*, has the opposite meaning, a small, defined, probably managed wood, normally surrounded by non-woodland; it therefore carries a presumption that there was **not** much woodland where the name was formed. The implications of 'wood' (*wudu*) are somewhere in between. 'Wood' and 'grove' place-names, unlike 'ley' names, have of course been formed continuously from Anglo-Saxon times until now. 'Tree' (*trēow*) place-names tell us next to nothing about the landscape: many areas with no woodland have plenty of trees.

Despite these limitations, place-names if used with care can tell us much about woodland or trees. Names that refer to rare trees are usually more informative than those naming common species. *Ac*ton or *Ash*croft – whatever their exact meaning – are unlikely to tell us

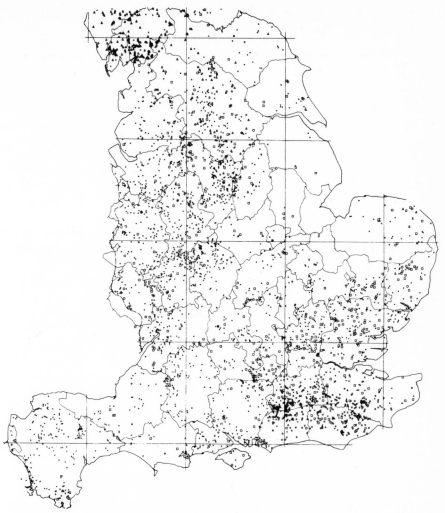

Fig. 11. Names of towns, villages and hamlets involving 'ley' (dots), 'hurst' (circles), or 'thwaite' (triangles), and of towns and villages involving 'field' (squares). 'Hurst' seems to have the same significance as 'ley'. 'Field', Old English *feld*, in this context appears to mean not so much a field as an open space within sight of woodland with which to contrast it.

much about oak or ash that we did not know already; but an early *Chesteyns* in Essex adds to our medieval evidence for sweet-chestnut (p. 98), while *Hulver* Street in Suffolk refers to holly. The Domesday Book village name *Lin*wood, Lincs, reminds us of the wood of small-leaved lime which existed nearby until coniferized thirty years ago.*

Names referring to the destruction of woodland may include Roding, Stocking, Stubbing, and Assart. *Roding*, with its variants Ridding, Redon, Reed, Royd, etc., is cognate with German *roden*, to grub out woodland, and probably with the English word *riding*, now shortened to *ride*, a gladeway or track through a wood. *Stocking* is a place which, perhaps hundreds of years earlier, contained 'stocks', that is tree-stumps. *Assart* does not always imply grubbing out woodland: it is a legal term for an encroachment which could equally involve heath or moorland. (For the names of woods themselves see Chapter 6.)

Domesday Book

The great survey of 1086 makes it perfectly clear that England was not very wooded. Out of 12,580 settlements for which adequate particulars are given, only 6208 possessed woodland. This is not due to random under-recording, for wooded and woodless areas form a definite pattern (Fig. 12). For 35 miles around London nearly everywhere had a wood; there were well-wooded areas in the west Midlands, Derbyshire, east Somerset, etc. There was almost no woodland in the Breckland, the Fens, or a belt extending from east Yorkshire across the central Midlands to Wiltshire. This distribution is entirely supported by documents from later centuries.

For more than half England, the sizes of woods are given, either in terms of length and breadth or as so many acres. They can be converted to modern areas on the basis that a Domesday woodland acre was 1.2 modern acres, and the area of an irregular wood is, on average, 0.7 times its length times breadth. We cannot expect great accuracy, but then all official statistics of woodland are bedevilled by problems of definition as well as measurement.

In the eastern counties woods are usually given as 'wood for so many swine'. Such entries refer to the ancient practice of driving tame pigs into woods in autumn to fatten on the acorns (or beechmast if any) before being slaughtered and salted down. Unfortunately this is not the down-to-earth method of estimating the area of a wood that it seems to be. Acorns and beechmast are notoriously variable crops, which often fail. Medieval records, and a few Anglo-Saxon wills, make it clear that they were equally unreliable then. It is unrealistic to expect an objective equation between pigs and acres. By 1086 the wood-swine had become swine of the imagination; real pigs were counted

* Maybe it has now come back to life – see Chapter 11.

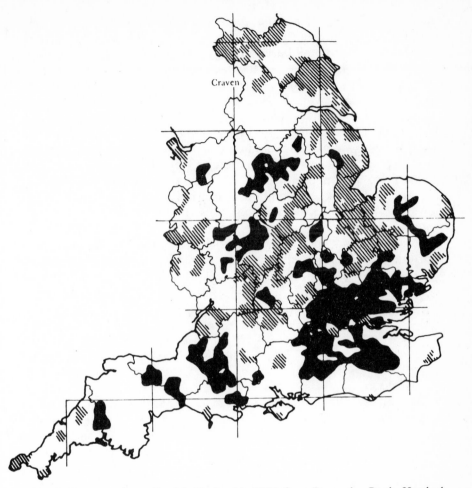

Fig. 12. Presence of woodland in England in 1086, from Domesday Book. Hatched areas: no woodland recorded. White areas: some settlements had woodland but not others. Black areas: every settlement had woodland. No account is taken of the amount of woodland. There are no usable returns for five northern counties nor for Craven.

separately and fed in other ways. We cannot objectively tell whether a wood for only a few swine was a small wood, a hornbeam wood (not yielding acorns), a coppice wood (lacking big oaks), or a wood owned by a pessimist. Nevertheless it is possible, by comparing Domesday with thirteenth-century records of the same woods, to form a rough impression of how much woodland there was.

In S.E. England the entries are in the form of 'wood rendering so many swine for pannage'. To interpret these involves even more guesswork, since rents in general tend to reflect obsolete land-uses. In very big wooded areas, especially the Weald, swine-rents represent a branch of the economy based on pigs fed at *denns*, secondary settlements often far from the place to which the entry applies. For example, Tonbridge, though a quite important place, is hidden in the entry for Otford, ten miles away. The denns have been investigated in detail in books by K. P. Witney and Alan Everitt.[50] Although the Weald was a stronghold of pannage, even here it was becoming obsolete by 1086 and the denns were changing into conventional hamlets.

The results of the calculation are given by counties in Table 2 and in the form of a map in Fig. 13. Domesday Book covers 27 million acres of land; of these 4.1 million, that is 15%, were woodland (including wood-pasture). Rough though these figures necessarily are, they show that England was not well wooded even by the standards of twentieth-century, let alone eleventh-century, Europe. It had a proportion of woodland between those of modern France (20% of the

Table 2 Woodland as a percentage of land area in Domesday England

	% woodland: in 1086	in 1895	Ratio 1086/1895	Form of record
The Weald	70?	18.1	3.9	●
Gloucestershire (W. of R. Severn)	50?	31.2	1.7	●
Worcestershire	40	4.2	9.4	●●●●
Staffordshire	32	5.3	6.1	●●●●
Hertfordshire	c30	6.1	4.9	●●●
Middlesex	c30	3.8	2.1	●●●
Cheshire	27	3.8	7.0	●●●●
Buckinghamshire	c26	6.7	3.9	●●●
Derbyshire	26	4.0	6.6	●●●●
Surrey (except Weald)	20?	c9.6[a]	2.1?	●●
Berkshire	20?	7.7	2.6	●●
Essex	c20	3.2	6.5	●●●
Warwickshire	19	3.5	5.5	●●●●
Oxfordshire	16	5.5	2.9	●●●●
Flintshire (N.E. Wales)	16	5.0	3.2	●●●●
Yorkshire (W. Riding)[b]	16	4.8	3.3	●●●●
Hampshire (except Isle of Wight)	15?	12.6	1.2?	●●
Bedfordshire	c15	4.1	3.6	●●●
Kent (except Weald)	13?	c8.5	1.5?	●●
Dorset	13	6.0	2.2	●●●●

Table 2 Woodland as a percentage of land area in Domesday England

	% woodland: in 1086	% woodland: in 1895	Ratio 1086/1895	Form of record
Wiltshire	13	6.0	2.2	••••
Nottinghamshire	12	5.3	2.4	••••
Norfolk	c12	4.1	2.9	•••
Yorkshire (North Riding)	c12	3.9	3.1	••••
Somerset	11	4.4	2.4	••••
Gloucestershire (east of R. Severn)	9.6	4.7	2.0	••••
Rutland	9.6	4.0	2.4	••••
Suffolk	c9	3.7	2.4	•••
Northamptonshire	8.8	4.4	2.0	••••
Herefordshire	8?	7.8	1.0?	•
Shropshire	c8	5.9	1.1	••••
Huntingdonshire	7.4	2.0	3.7	••••
Isle of Wight	6?	5.1	1.2?	••
Sussex (except Weald)	6?	c5.1	1.2?	••
Yorkshire (E. Riding)	4.4	2.3	2.0	••••
Lincolnshire (Lindsey + Kesteven)	4.0	3.0	1.3	••••
Devon	3.8	5.2	0.74	••••
Cambridgeshire (except Isle of Ely)	c3.5	1.9	1.7	•••
Leicestershire	3.3	2.7	1.2	••••
Cornwall	3.2	3.6	0.91	••••
Isle of Ely	c0.8	0.0	0	•••
Lincolnshire (Holland)	2 woods	0.0	–	••••
Total, Ancient Countryside	18.7			
Total, Planned Countryside	8.2			
All England	**14.9**	**5.4**	**2.8**	

The counties are the traditional ones (Fig. 11), which are not exactly the same as those in Domesday itself. The modern woodland area comes from Board of Agriculture returns for 1895 (a date chosen in order to exclude most modern plantations).

Northumberland, Durham, Cumberland and Westmorland are omitted, and the records from Lancashire are too vague to include.

••••	Woods recorded by area or by length and breadth.
•••	Woods recorded mainly in terms of swine.
••	Woods recorded in terms of swine-rents.
•	Record is little more than an informed guess.
a	Much of the 1895 woodland was then recent.
b	Excluding Craven, for which there is no record.

52

land) and modern Denmark (9%).

Woodland was more unevenly distributed than its remains are today. What is now Ancient Countryside was more than twice as wooded in 1086 as the present Planned Countryside. No Planned Countryside district was more than averagely wooded, but most Ancient Countryside (Devon and Cornwall being conspicuous exceptions) was around average or above.

In the 800 years following Domesday, woodland was to decline by nearly two-thirds, but more in well-wooded areas. Worcestershire, for example, 40% woodland in 1086, lost nine-tenths of its woodland and became no more wooded than most counties. Staffordshire was to lose four-fifths of its woodland. On the other hand, among the least-wooded counties, all the losses in Leicestershire can be accounted for by the single biggest wood, while in Cornwall and Devon there seems to have been a net *gain* of woodland between the eleventh and the nineteenth century.

We noted in the charters that many woods were detached from the places to which they belonged. Research into medieval documents has revealed many examples which are hidden in Domesday Book. In 1086, S.E. Warwickshire and north Oxfordshire appear to have had a little woodland, but this was really located many miles away in the more wooded parts of these counties.[51] Similar anomalies of recording appear in south Somerset, S.E. Wiltshire and S.E. Essex. Detached woodland – like a smaller version of the Weald – seems to have existed in most places where a big wooded area was surrounded by a wide tract of woodless terrain. The woodless areas were thus even more devoid of woodland, and the wooded areas were slightly more wooded, than Fig. 13 makes them.

England in the eleventh century would not have looked like modern Borneo, but rather like modern France. In both we find a sharp distinction between wooded and unwooded areas. The Norman Weald, like the modern Vosges, was well over half tree-covered, but penetrated by roads and full of villages and hamlets in clearings. In the Fens, Breckland and Yorkshire Wolds – as around Chartres

Fig. 13. Area of woodland in England in 1086. In counties for which Domesday gives the sizes of woods, areas are mapped by 10-km National Grid squares: each black spot represents, at the scale of the map, the total woodland area possessed by places in the square. (Except for Amesbury (A) in Wiltshire, no attempt has been made to redistribute woodland belonging to places located in a different square.) In the eastern and south-eastern counties, for which returns are in the form of swine or swine-rents, each black spot is an estimate of the woodland area of a whole county (or of the Weald or Chilterns separately). Stippled circles in Oxfordshire represent Forests, of which an unknown proportion was woodland.

today – one could go many miles without seeing a wood. Between these extremes, the general landscape consisted of farmland with islands of wood.

In some counties a distinction is made between *silua minuta*, an early expression for coppice-wood, and *silua pastilis*, 'pasture wood'. Lincolnshire, for example, covered 1.43 million acres (excluding the fenland subcounty of Holland), of which 4.0% was woodland. Of this, 1.54% was *minuta* wood, in 270 separate woods; 1.56% was *pastilis* wood, in 93 separate woods; and 69 woods, totalling 0.92% of the area, were recorded as *pastilis per loca*, 'pasture in places' – evidently woods that were partly coppice-woods and partly wood-pasture – or otherwise. As we would expect, *minuta* woods were, on average, smaller than *pastilis* woods. In Nottinghamshire and the North Riding, each with 12% total woodland, and in Derbyshire with 26%, underwood (with a contribution from the *per loca* woods) comes to about 2% of the total area. Coppice was evidently the more important kind of woodland, but each community needed, and could maintain, only a limited area of it; any surplus went to the less intensive *pastilis* use. *Minuta* woods are recorded occasionally, but not systematically, in many other counties.

Domesday rarely names individual woods, and never mentions trees. It is, however, sometimes possible to show indirectly that a wood is 'mentioned in Domesday Book'. For example, Wayland Wood in S.W. Norfolk has a Viking wood-name (p. 107). Domesday refers, not directly to the wood, but to Wayland *Hundred*, or division of the county, named after the wood, where the hundred court would have been held. This was therefore a grove of assembly, perhaps even of heathen worship, long before the Conquest. This wonderful wood – it is also the Babes-in-the-Wood wood, and much of its underwood consists, almost uniquely outside northern England, of bird-cherry (*Prunus padus*) – still survives and belongs to Norfolk Naturalists' Trust.

Domesday occasionally gives industrial uses of woodland, such as the continuous supply of cartloads of wood to the Droitwich saltworks. There are rare references to secondary woodland: for instance that grim little note about what had been eleven settlements on the Hereford-Radnor border, the scene of a frontier incident some thirty years before. 'On these waste lands woods have grown up, in which the said Robert has the hunting and takes away what he can get. Nothing else.'

Changes after Domesday

It is unlikely any wildwood still remained in England in 1086. The best case that can be made out is for the Forest of Dean. By 1250 Dean was extensively coppiced and pastured, but this state of affairs was probably not long established.[52] On the Domesday map there is a blank, which appears to result from a real lack of activity rather than an anomaly of recording. Between 1241 and 1265 Henry III gave 71 oaks out of Dean to make timbers for the Dominican friary at Gloucester, where they remain to this day.[53] They have been sawn from huge oaks, about 2 ft 3 in. in diameter at the middle and 50 ft in usable length. These are very unlike the oaks typical of later medieval buildings (though there are some similar timbers in the earliest (twelfth-century) roofs of Lincoln Cathedral). Oaks in wildwood may well have looked like this, though it has to be said that Dean had been inhabited and industrialized in the Roman period.

With this possible exception, woods in England in 1086 were part of the cultural landscape: every wood belonged to some person or community, and was used. But the use seems not to have been so intensive as in later centuries. In better-wooded areas many woods were still used chiefly as wood-pasture. Domesday records very few changes in woodland, doubtless because it came at a time of recession, after twenty evil years in which men had won lands by the sword and not the mattock. However, in Norfolk, Suffolk and Essex, in one wood in 17, it is stated that the swine-assessment had decreased between 1066 and 1086. This change was not systematically accompanied by an increase in farmland,[54] and was therefore due to some alteration in the quality rather than the area of woodland. The most likely cause is an extension of coppicing. Among the places affected were Dereham, Shipdham and Pulham in Norfolk, all of which had important woods in the thirteenth century.

The evil years after the Conquest mark a pause in an expansion of population which was shortly to be resumed. Between 1086 and 1250 the population at least doubled,[55] and pressure on land was becoming extreme. Already before the Conquest the Fens had begun to be re-drained, and the Weald to be made into farmland. Together with a re-advance of cultivation into moorland, these had added substantially to the farmed area of England by 1250.

Over the next 160 years, woodland in Domesday Book was destroyed at an average rate of at least 20 acres a day. The uses of the remainder finally crystallized into either coppice-wood or wood-pasture. At least half the Domesday woodland is never heard of again, but these years are poorly documented. There are many records of assart, but those of an acre or two are vastly commoner than of hundreds of acres, and all the known assarts together can add up to only a fraction of the two million or so acres involved. As well as being deliberately grubbed out, woodland was grazed away into heath. More disappeared from the better-wooded areas, which often became no more wooded than the rest of the country. For an example, let us return to the Stansted Airport site. In the archives of Colchester Abbey there survive some records of assarts and new arable land within these 5000 acres or more of woodland.[56] By the late thirteenth century the whole area had again become farmland with only scattered wood-lots.

Wildwood into woodland

We used to think of the Angles and Saxons as colonizing peoples, rather like the seventeenth-century English in America. They came to a land of boundless wildwoods, and spent much of their time making fields; but despite all their efforts, civilization (we were taught) remained local and precarious throughout the Anglo-Saxon period.

This view seems to be supported by place-names, especially the thousands of clearing-names. However, these place-names, and the great woods which they imply, were by no means ubiquitous. If wildwood had really been everywhere in Anglo-Saxon times, then leys, hursts and thwaites ought to be as common in Lincolnshire and east Gloucestershire as they are in Hertfordshire or west Gloucestershire.

All the other kinds of evidence run against the traditional view. Domesday says that at least five-sixths of the original woods had gone by 1086. If this was the work of the Anglo-Saxons, then the average Old Englishman would have spent as much time digging up trees as his descendant now spends before the television; but there is no hint in Anglo-Saxon literature that this was an everyday occupation. The charters have remarkably little to say about change. They occasionally mention new hedges or the sites of former trees, but they give a strong impression of stability. Never once does a charter expressly mention the site of a former wood.

Let us not make too much of the 'clearing' place-names. A clearing can arise as easily by the retreat of agriculture – by the surrounding fields becoming woodland – as by new fields being made. Place-names tell us nothing of when the clearings were made, or how, or by whom. Only archaeology can tell us how many leys and hursts were made by the Anglo-Saxons themselves.

The distribution of woodland in Domesday Book agrees remarkably closely with the earlier distribution in the charters, and the earlier distribution still from place-names. There are some points of discrepancy: the charters, for example, evidently caught almost the last of the vanishing woods of the Fens. But on the whole the areas lacking woodland in 1086 also lack evidence for woodland in the charters and place-names.

Much of the English landscape existed in the time of the Anglo-Saxons, but was not necessarily created by them. Sometimes they were indeed colonizers, making and enlarging leys and hursts. Alan Everitt has made a good case for Jutish colonization in Kent – but Kent, then as now, was much more wooded than average. Elsewhere there were areas of stability, of reorganization, and even of retreat. Woodland was already, as it has been ever since, something inherited from an earlier era. Why were many woods awkwardly detached from the places they belonged to? Is this not the Anglo-Saxons' attempt to parcel out and use a distribution of woodland which they had inherited from a more highly organized past?

The distinction between Ancient and Planned Countryside began not later than the Roman period. In the former, woodland was extensive, though there had also been heaths, farms, villas, and cities like St Alban's. The Anglo-Saxons re-named, extended, and sometimes abandoned the Roman clearings; the landscape retained, and still has, a piecemeal and individualistic character. In the latter, nearly all the woodland was already gone and did not return; what woodland remained was precious and was conserved. Here the Anglo-Saxons and their successors had little room for expansion; instead they collectivized the landscape, reorganizing farmland into open-fields and grouping the farmsteads into villages. They thus set the scene for Enclosure Acts nearly a thousand years later.

Wales and Ireland

Outside England the records are much sparser. Only place-name evidence is copious, but it is even more difficult to date, because Celtic languages are very conservative.

For S.E. Wales there is a group of early charters in Welsh. They are rather laconic, but give the impression of a land as wooded as the more wooded counties of England. (This area was still relatively wooded in the nineteenth century.)

In Ireland the Iron Age went on well into the Christian era, and was a time of high civilization and dense population. The earthworks of at least 30,000 *raths* – Iron Age farmsteads – are found throughout the island and leave no room for continuous woodland: they sometimes occur in what were later big woods. Archaeology reveals a coppicing tradition (p. 89).

Irish place-names often allude to trees and woods. Elm is occasionally mentioned, which suggests that something was still remembered of the prehistoric elmwoods. For example, the Gaelic *Leamhchoill*, 'wood of the elm', has been transmuted into Loughill or even, it is claimed, Longfield.[57] By far the commonest such name is *derry*, an 'oket' (p. 108) or wood composed of oaks. Oakwood, a relatively minor type in the wildwood, had evidently become the commonest, doubtless because it grew on poor soils and in inaccessible places. Hundreds of derries are islands in bogs; even these inhospitable places had usually been made into farms by the time they are first recorded in writing.

4

Classical woodland management: the Middle Ages and after

A certain Wood called Heylewode which contains 80 acres by estimate. Of the underwood of which there can be sold every year, without causing waste or destruction, 11 acres of underwood which are worth 55s. at 5s. an acre.... A certain other Wood called Litlelond which contains 26 acres by estimate. Whose underwood can be sold as a whole every seventh year. And it is then worth in all £6 10s. at 5s. an acre.

Earliest surviving management plan of
Hayley Wood, West Cambridgeshire, dated 1356 [58]

The first detailed woodland records

In the year 1251 Hugo de Northwold, Bishop of Ely, caused a great survey to be made of the estates belonging to his bishopric. This work, the *Old Coucher Book of Ely*,[59] is a field-by-field account of lands and tenants in dozens of parishes scattered over eastern England. It names scores of woods, with estimates of acreages and various particulars of their uses. The Coucher Book begins a new era in detailed land recording. It is followed by a number of other estate surveys, particularly on the lands of the abbeys of Ramsey (Huntingdonshire) and Bury St Edmund's; and by the Hundred Rolls of 1279, the second, and even now the most detailed, national survey of land tenure, although the rats have eaten most of it.

Part of the Coucher Book entry for Barking, Suffolk, reads:

The woods
Item, there is one small park which contains nine acres, including a laund, measured by the aforesaid perch.[a] Which would be worth every year, including the laund, four shillings if it were not for the beasts.

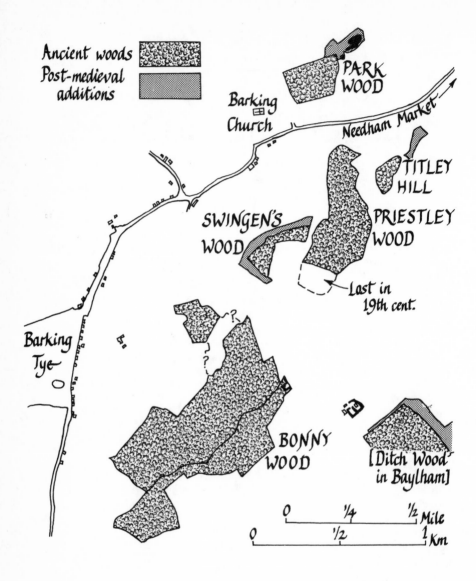

Fig. 14. Ancient woods of Barking, Suffolk, as they are now. (Early large-scale maps confirm that Bonny and Priestley Woods have had exactly the same outlines for over 350 years.)

Item, there is one grove which is called Tykele which contains five acres by the aforesaid perch. And a certain other grove which is called Prestele which contains thirty acres by the aforesaid perch. And a certain other grove which is called Wetheresheg which contains seven acres by the aforesaid perch. And these groves are worth sixteen shillings every year.

Item, there is one big wood which is called Boynhey which is estimated to contain ninescore acres. It is worth £4 10*s*. per annum.

ᵃ The size of the local acre depended on the length of the perch, which did not always have its modern value of 16½ feet. In Barking we are told that the perch, and therefore the acre, were of the modern size.

It is obvious that this is an essentially modern countryside, with islands of wood surrounded by farmland. The park and laund will be explained in Chapter 8. A glance at the map raises the suspicion that at least four of the woods are still there; for in Barking there are woods called Park Wood, Titley Hill, Priestley Wood and Bonny Wood, which correspond roughly with those of the 1251 survey (Fig.14). As it happens there are many documents and maps from the intervening centuries which confirm that this is so; indeed the missing wood, Wetheresheg, is still in existence under another name. We see in Table 3 that the acreages agree to a surprising extent over 740 years. The wood areas appear to have been underestimated in the thirteenth century, as they often were.[61]

This is by no means an isolated case. The same continuity can be shown for many other woods in the Ely Coucher Book, such as Hayley Wood, Cambridgeshire, and in other thirteenth-century surveys.

Table 3 The Barking, Suffolk, woods

1251		c.1639[60]		1988	
	acres		acres		acres
Parvus Parcus	9	Parke woode	14	Park Wood	13.9
Grava de tykele	5	Tickley woode	4	Titley Hill	4.7
Grava de prestele	30	Presley wood	43.5	Priestley Wood	43.5
Grava de wetheresheg	7	Swynsey woode	13	Swingen's Wood	14.2
Magnus boscus de boynhey	180	Boyney wood at least	100	Bonny Wood	126.0

Nearly half the Coucher Book woods, including small ones like Titley, still existed in 1945; so did, for example, at least eight of the twelve woods in Whepstead (Suffolk) listed in the Cellarer's Cartulary of Bury St Edmund's Abbey, and nearly all the West Cambridgeshire woods mentioned in the Hundred Rolls. In 1945, medieval woods were roughly as numerous as medieval churches.

There is no reason to suppose that the start of continuous records corresponds to any sudden change in the woods themselves. For all we know, they may have been unchanged for centuries before. We have seen some pre-Conquest examples in the last chapter. Even the tiny Knapwell Wood, Cambridgeshire (Fig. 22c) can be taken back almost to the Norman Conquest.

Woodland in the medieval landscape

In the time of the Ely Coucher Book, rural society, land tenure and land use were much more complex than today: bewilderingly complex, it seems to us, where open-field was involved. There were systems of multiple land use in which a number of people had different rights in the same piece of land. Hardly any land was unused: the large areas of 'waste' do not mean derelict or unoccupied land, but land whose uses were communal rather than private.

The place of woodland in the English countryside was well established. Woods producing underwood and timber were differentiated, as in earlier centuries, from the various categories of wood-pasture. They were pieces of property with definite boundaries; usually they were privately owned, though some woods had small common-rights. Unlike modern plantations, here today and gone next decade, woods were permanent. Although woods could be converted to other uses such as arable or wood-pasture, or vice versa, these were rare events in the life of any one wood, and many woods (like those of Barking) were hardly altered by them.

Woods were managed intensively and conservatively. In the Middle Ages, men expected to have to live off renewable resources, and managed woods on the basis that whenever a tree was felled it would grow again or another would grow in its place. Usually this is taken for granted: surveys either state a coppicing rotation for woods or give a figure for the expected annual return. Occasionally, we find the self-renewal principle stated explicitly, as in the quotation at the head of this chapter. Felling at short intervals of years ensured vigorous and trouble-free regrowth. In 1269–70 the monks of Beaulieu Abbey (Hants) drew up a schedule of the various products to be expected from an acre of wood of twenty years' growth: firewood of various kinds, faggots, vine-stakes and charcoal, with the methods of measuring and transporting each, and the prices expected either in the wood or delivered.[62]

Great attention was paid to boundaries and security. Usually a wood boundary consisted of a bank and ditch combined with either a fence or a hedge. We hear occasionally of new earthworks being made: for example there is the contractor's account for making some four miles of new woodbank round Norwich Cathedral Priory's two woods at Hindolveston (Norfolk) in 1297–8; a hedge was planted on it, with eight gates secured with 'feterloks' and a bridge at each gate.[63] But many woodbanks appear to be much older than this. For Knapwell Wood the Ramsey Cartulary refers in the early twelfth century to 'the grove of Cnapwelle and the arable land which is inside the ditch [*foveam*] which surrounds the grove'.[64] Even at that early date the wood had been reduced in size within an earthwork that had marked its old boundary.

Manorial court records are full of trespasses against woodland, which incurred fines like other petty offences against property. Letting one's sheep get into the lord's wood was prosecuted in much the same way as letting them into his cornfield. Stealing acorns or underwood was a common peccadillo: often the 'fine' appears not to be deterrent at all, but merely a means of collecting the money from a casual sale. Occasionally there were graver proceedings, a very early example of which is quoted on p. 1.

The records are curiously silent about woodland rides, most of which seem to have been cut after the middle ages. Previously there had been irregular tracks winding among the stools, as can still be seen (hardened into permanence) in Chalkney Wood, Earl's Colne (Essex).

Management of underwood

Most medieval woods were of the type that books now call coppice-with-standards. The site was shared by standard trees and underwood; the latter produced an annual return of wood, while the former yielded timber at longer and less regular intervals. More often than not, wood was the more important product and the one we hear more about.

Coppicing, well established in 1086, by 1251 had spread to nearly all woods. This is not true just of Eastern, or even of Lowland, England: coppicing records of the Helford River oakwoods in Cornwall go back to this period. Woods were cut at irregular intervals;

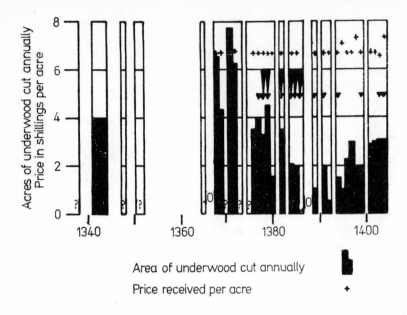

Fig. 15. Acres of underwood felled each year in Hardwick Wood, Cambridgeshire, from 1341 to 1495, together with the price per acre and the years in which oaks and other timber trees are known to have been felled.[65] 0 indicates a year in which it is said that no wood was cut; ? is a year in which the records do not mention wood, and probably also indicates nil output. Gaps in the time-scale indicate missing records.

the average cycle was an abstraction, and surveyors did not always see fit to estimate it. Medieval felling rotations were usually short: eight years, seven as at Hayley, six, five or even four years (as at Pulham, Norfolk). The twenty-year cycle envisaged at Beaulieu would then have been unusually long.

Hardwick Wood, which still exists in Cambridgeshire, was supposed in 1356 to be cut on a five-year cycle;[58] there also survive annual accounts (Fig. 15) which show that, while this was a good estimate of the average, the actual acreage cut fluctuated widely from year to year. In later centuries some woods, particularly those with specialized functions, were cut with strict regularity every so many years. As anyone who manages a wood knows, such an inflexible programme is impractical. There are many reasons for felling different acreages in different years: a dry summer, a long winter depleting people's woodpiles, a part of the wood growing more slowly, or a man falling sick. One of the woodward's skills is knowing when to fell underwood.

We have not only accounts of underwood, but the stuff itself preserved in wattle-and-daub – the wooden reinforcement in the clay used

Hardwick Wood

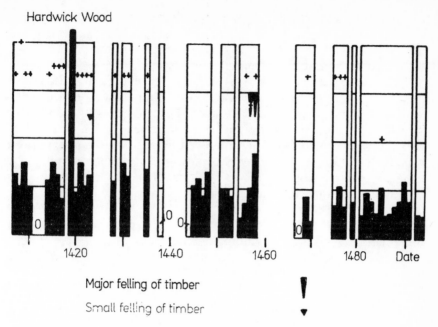

1420   1440   1460   1480   Date

Major felling of timber

Small felling of timber

in the various wattling systems that fill the panels of timber-framed buildings. The rods are usually of sallow, hazel or elm, less often of maple or ash, and I have seen birch and lime (Plate IX); they are tied together with withies (one-year-old sallow shoots) or string. Some-times laths, rent from oak timber, are used instead. Wattle is very durable, and often after 500 years as good as the day it was made. (Restorers should on no account throw it away.) The annual rings in the rods confirm that woods were felled usually at seven or eight years' growth, and grew again at least as fast as they do now.

Medieval woodmen took little interest in the composition of under-wood, and did not try to influence or even to record it. Only in some surveys of Tudor times are we told the species systematically. From casual references in court rolls and accounts we learn that woods were mixtures of much the same underwood species as they are still: ash, hazel, maple, thorn, sallow, elm, lime, birch, crab, oak.

The commonest uses of wood were fuel and fencing. The usual firewood was underwood (or the boughs of felled timber trees) bound into faggots. Fencing was an important item in an age when wire was a jewellers' speciality. One of the commonest kinds of fence was a row of stakes interwoven with *ethers* – long flexible rods – either standing on its own or reinforcing a hedge. For portable fencing, the two modern types of hurdle both existed: the kind that is woven from small hazel rods, and the kind carpentered from bigger underwood to look like a small seven-barred gate. Wattlework had many other uses, notably for sea-defences and revetting river-banks (it has been found in many waterfront excavations). Broaches and ethers, then as now, were used in holding down thatch.

These varied uses explain why the species of underwood did not matter much. Some trees had special uses, but the more specialized underwood crafts used relatively little. The bulk uses of wood were for purposes such as fencing and especially fuel, for which any tree would do at a pinch. Nothing, not even twigs and hedge-trimmings, was wasted. Except in wood-pastures, where young spring might be exposed to browsing, there was nothing to be gained by allowing underwood to stand for a long rotation.

Fig. 15 shows how the coppice cycle in Hardwick Wood during the fifteenth century became longer (fewer acres were cut each year) and more regular. This is the beginning of a tendency which I have noticed in woods in general.

Management of timber

Timbers preserved in buildings are a more valuable supplement to written records than is underwood. Building was a major use of timber: written records suggest that it used over half the timber produced by woods. Structures that are grand and well-known, such as hammerbeam roofs and great barns, may not be representative; but recent research has shown that examples of workaday buildings – the homes of humble 'peasants', and even workshops – occasionally survive from as early as the thirteenth century.

Our age treats timber as if it were plastic. Sawmills and other machines are designed to reduce trees, regardless of their natural shapes, to exact rectangular sections. Our predecessors were more cunning: they selected trees for size rather than cutting them to size, and made much more efficient use of the tree. Although they could saw trees lengthwise to make two rafters or a pair of crucks, they avoided lengthwise sawing unless they had a special reason. Building practice adapted to using a certain size of tree implies a woodland practice that regularly supplied it.

All buildings have timber roofs and sometimes floors. Why some buildings should be timber-framed, while others have walls of stone, brick or earth, is still a mystery of local fashion and architectural etiquette. It is not related to whether or not there was woodland. Medieval Cambridge had abundant easily-worked stone and no local woodland; but apart from colleges and churches it was a timber-framed town. Well-wooded north Norfolk had less timber-framing than poorly-wooded Suffolk or even the woodless Breckland. The only generality is that, where a region has not much timber-framing, it will be urban: for example, the timber (or timber-fronted) buildings of Edinburgh, York, Dorchester (Dorset), Exeter, Fowey and formerly Dublin. Timber was an architectural medium: even in the smallest cottage 'a wealth of exposed beams' did more than merely hold up the structure.

Over 90% of building timbers are oak; the second commonest species is elm, followed by ash and (surprisingly) aspen. (The great curved crucks of cruck buildings are occasionally made of black poplar, which grows in the appropriate shape.[66]) Humbler houses contain more of other trees, but usually have *some* oak. Oak is used no less in the Chilterns beechwood area and in oakless Cambridge than in regions where it was a common tree.

Ordinary medieval buildings contain large numbers of small oaks, felled usually at 25 to 100 years of age. The carpenter chose the smallest tree that would do the job, and squared it with a broad-axe or adze, usually leaving the corners *waney* or rounded where they met the outside of the log. Often the sapwood and even bark were left on. Wild oaks, then as now, were crooked, and carpenters made ingenious use of their irregular shapes and curves. In the cruck buildings of Wales and west and north England, naturally-curved trees were chosen for a special purpose. Sometimes, especially in the later Middle Ages, a log was sawn lengthwise into two timbers. (It is often said that trees were split, but most British oaks are too knotty to split well; most halved timbers in fact bear saw-marks.) Carpenters cannot now be persuaded to follow this practice, and Victorian 'copies' of medieval timber frames, or modern replacements of original timbers, are instantly detectable by their rigid straightness. The modern carpenter often claims that oaks can no longer be found to match those used by his predecessors: this is untrue, and results from his insistence on eliminating sapwood and waney edges, which calls for a bigger tree than would have been used in medieval times.

Medieval timbers are thus impressed with the shape in which God made the tree. It is possible to decide how many trees went into a building, and also their ages, shapes and sizes. Grundle House, Stanton, a timber-framed farmhouse a little bigger than the average of hundreds built in Suffolk in the fifteenth century, contains some 350 trees, one-fifth of them elm. Half the trees were less than 9 inches in diameter at the base; 32 trees were as small as 6 inches; but only three exceeded 18 inches, a usual size for a 'mature' oak nowadays. A similar but smaller and probably older house at Rochford, Essex was made of 173 trees of a similar mix of sizes, also including some elm. A very small thirteenth-century house – the oldest survivor of the boundary-houses where the commoners of Hatfield Forest dwelt (Fig. 37) – is made of smaller trees still, mostly oak poles less than 4 inches thick, but including some aspen.

The roof, floors and internal walls of the mid-fourteenth-century Old Court of Corpus Christi College, Cambridge, contained about 1,400 oaks, mainly less than 9 inches diameter. Turning to upper-class buildings, the great hall of the Prior of Prittlewell, Essex, involved at least 273 oaks, mostly of a little less than a foot in diameter. The fifteenth-century main roofs of Norwich Cathedral contained some 680 oaks, mostly around 15 inches in basal diameter. (These examples happen to be from eastern England, but the principles applied wherever there were timber-framed buildings.)[67]

Timbers of ordinary buildings are usually up to 20 feet long; those that are longer are often crooked, knotty and tapering where they reach into the crown of a tree that was not really long enough. Many timbers were shorter than this, and we then find the top-length – the upper, more crooked and knotty part of the trunk – used in some less conspicuous place in the building. However, some medieval buildings contain an excess of top-lengths, evidently left over from some more important structure on which the butt-ends had been used. I am surprised to find these leftovers composing quite grand buildings such as Southchurch Hall, Essex and the barn of New College at Widdington, Essex.

The high roofs of cathedrals and abbeys can include large numbers of timbers with a reasonably straight length of as much as 30 feet. Particularly costly structures, such as the great Perpendicular roof now hidden by the vault of King's College Chapel, Cambridge, may contain *outsize* oaks 30 inches or more in diameter. The grandest timber frame of all, the Octagon of Ely Cathedral, built after 1328, has an inner timber tower with eleven posts at least 60 feet long. This is sustained by sixteen struts which are meant to be 40 to 45 feet long by $13\frac{1}{2}$ inches square, but – with all England to draw on – the carpenter evidently had to make do with getting the utmost length out of trees that were not quite long enough. Such oaks can still be admired in the twelfth- and thirteenth-century timber church towers of Essex and Herefordshire. By the 1320s they were harder to find than ever before or since.

The records agree with this evidence from buildings. We are seldom given dimensions of trees, but the prices and charges for felling and transport tell us something about the range of sizes. Accounts for Hardwick and Gamlingay, Cambridgeshire, document, year by year, the part played by timber trees in intensively managed woodland. Oak was the most valuable as well as the commonest timber tree: for instance in 1334 the Gamlingay bailiff claimed that he had been overcharged by 2*s*. 7*d*. 'for maples which they made out as oaks in the previous account'. Oaks were very variable in size. In 1333–4, for instance, 91 oaks were sold at Gamlingay at from 5*d*. to 20*d*. each. At Hardwick, between 1377 and 1403, about 1800 'wrangelons' (probably big, crooked poles, usually oak but sometimes ash or maple) fetched from 0.31*d*. to 2.0*d*., and there were sales of oak stakes at 0.23*d*. to 0.30*d*. each.[65,68] In the money of 1989, oaks felled in woodland could be worth anything from less than £1 to over £40.

There existed oaks very much larger than these. The post on which a windmill stood had to be *bought* at a cost varying from 18*s*. to 25*s*., more than ten times as much the largest oak sold from Gamlingay Wood. This post would have been about 2 feet square by at least 40 feet long, weighing about 4 tons. There is an item for 'mending a cart which broke under the great post of the mill'.

A few oaks were felled each year for maintaining local buildings, ploughs and carts, besides bridges, weirs, the pound and the machinery of justice (e.g. stocks). But numbers of standard trees varied enormously in consequence of big fellings for new buildings (Fig. 15). The 40 acres of Gamlingay Mertonage Wood supplied at least 561 trees of various sizes in 1333–7, and about 180 trees, mainly oaks, in 1358–9.[67] Various Norfolk woods in the following century had from 5 to 40 timber trees to the acre.[69]

Timber was felled as occasion demanded. The carpenter would go into the wood, choose and fell trees for the job in hand, and work them at once. For example, Gamlingay never had a stockpile of seasoned timber, except in the years after 1333, when 269 oaks had been felled for a building which was cancelled. Much of the warping and sagging of ancient buildings can be shown (from early alterations) to have arisen in the first few years, owing to the movement of unseasoned oak as it dried.

This method secured a continuous yield of timber. Replacement of felled trees cannot have been a problem, else we should not find so many very small oaks used. Medieval oak timbers often have a curved butt end with a very wide first annual ring, which suggests that much use was made of regrowth from stumps. The stakes and other very small oaks sold may be superfluous poles cut away in the operation of 'promoting' coppice-grown oaks to form the next generation of standards. Felling oaks young encouraged such regrowth, gave the flexibility needed to cope with unpredicted new building or the emergencies of fire and sack, and avoided the heart-rot which often develops if oak stands beyond a hundred years. To use timber immediately made it easier to work and reduce the problems of organization.

As with underwood, nothing was wasted. Account rolls mention monies received for the branches, bark, 'loppium et chippium', twigs and even leaves of felled trees.

Minor uses of woodland

Although woodland grasses are of little food value, there was some demand for them. *Agistment*, grazing of farm animals, was seldom permitted in woods, except sometimes during the latter part of the coppice cycle, when little damage was likely to be done. *Herbage* seems to have been akin to the practice in Hatfield Forest, Essex, recorded in 1612, of

reaping the Grass & carrying it away in Baggs wch would be a great hindrance to the commoners in neglect of Business of greater Weight.... Except it be a poor Body that hath nothing else to do ... and he perhaps may lye in a Copice reaping grass a whole day together....[70]

Pannage sometimes lingered on in woods into the Middle Ages, but like agistment is more a wood-pasture practice. Other woodland products included acorns and hazel-nuts (gathered by the tenants at Barking as part of their labour services), bracken, and bast (the inner bark of lime-trees used as fibre). The bizarre German practice of burning a wood after felling and growing a crop of rye among the stools[71] seems not to be recorded in Britain.

Sporting uses were less prominent before the days of firearms. Pheasants, introduced by the Normans, occasionally figure in poaching cases. The art of cock-shooting was to catch woodcock in a net strung across a re-entrant angle in a wood. A specially shaped cockshoot-wood will be seen in Fig. 18.

What a medieval wood looked like

A normal wood consisted of underwood of a mixture of species cut on a short rotation. There was a variable scatter of timber trees of a continuous range of sizes from about 18 inches basal diameter downwards; these were mainly oak, up to 70 years old, and chiefly of the smaller sizes. The 20-foot length of building timbers results from the growth of the underwood, suppressing the lower branches of the standard trees but allowing them to form a crown above this height. The division between timber trees and underwood was not always sharp; there was sometimes an intermediate class of large coppice poles allowed to stand for two or three underwood cycles. Fig. 16 is a reconstruction of such a wood.

This can still be seen in working order in Felshamhall Wood and Monks' Park at Bradfield, Suffolk (Fig. 17). Bury St Edmund's Abbey was one of the mightiest houses of the monkish world, and several of the abbey woods remain as witnesses to its pre-Reformation wealth. Felshamhall Wood (for the wood's name see p. 107) is still within a great meandering boundary bank set with pollard trees; the earthworks of Monks' Park are more complex because it was once a deer-park. Underwood is still cut at irregular and rather frequent intervals; there are now two coppice cycles of 8–10 and about 25 years. Coppicing records go back to 1252. The underwood consists of various mixtures of ash, hazel, alder, maple, both birches, lime, sallow, elms, occasional oak and other trees. After cutting, new growth sometimes reaches ten feet in the first year. Oaks tend to stand in groups. As in the middle ages, they are very variable in size, age and appearance; they are mostly less than a century old, and often of stool origin. In contrast to nearly all woods nowadays, the oaks replace themselves without difficulty. There were major fellings of timber in the 1650s and 1920s. Permanent bracken glades are another medieval feature.

The Bradfield Woods are remarkable in other respects. They are among the richest of all British woods in plant life, with some 350 flowering plants recorded, including 42 native trees and shrubs. This results from their probable origin in wildwood, long and continued history of management, freedom from planting, their long-established rides and glades, their wet site, and their remarkably complex soils. The woods are noted also for mammals and birds, including coppice-loving species such as the dormouse and nightingale, and for insects and a wealth of strange fungi. Much of Monks' Park fell victim to the craze for arable land in the 1960s. In 1970 the woods were acquired, by the energy and generosity mainly of Suffolk people, by the present Royal Society for Nature Conservation; they are now managed by Suffolk Wildlife Trust.

How does pollen analysis link wildwood with managed woodland? The silt of an ancient pond in Monks' Park begins to give the answer. The woods had even more plant species in recent centuries than they have now.[72] The tree pollen is dominated by oak and hazel to a much greater extent than we would expect from the actual vegetation, but these trees are over-represented. Oak produces a full pollen output because it is treated as a standard tree. Hazel does so because it flowers from the second year onwards after felling. Most other underwood trees, especially lime, take several years to reach flowering size and

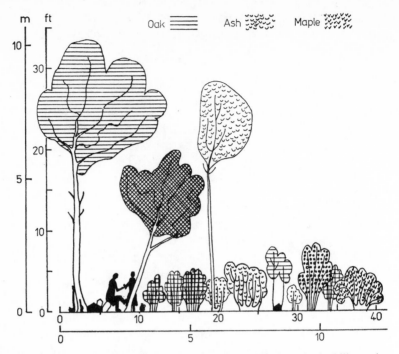

Fig. 16. Reconstruction of what a wood such as Hayley might have looked like under normal coppice management. The underwood of the left-hand half was felled last winter; that of the right-hand half has had five seasons' growth and could (if needed) be felled again. Five small timber trees are shown.

therefore produce only a little pollen, if any, before they are cut again.

Working coppice-woods enable the historian to learn from experience about the biological, social and economic practicalities of woodmanship. Records, for example, do not reveal that much of the woodman's labour consists of the hard and unpopular task of 'humping' wood from the stump to the nearest point that a cart can reach. Nor do they tell us that, while the trees in mixed underwood live happily together on a short coppice cycle, once the cycle exceeds fifteen years the lower-growing species, especially hazel, start to be overshadowed and eliminated by their taller sisters. At Bradfield the social links still continue: the woods supply some poles to a local factory making rakes, scythe-sticks etc. and to other woodworking businesses, while the remaining underwood supplies the neighbourhood with stakes and fuel.

The Bradfield Woods are a place of wonder and delight, with the varied colours of the leaves and bark of the different underwood trees; the strangely gnarled ancient stools; the brilliant colours of oxlip,

Crabapple 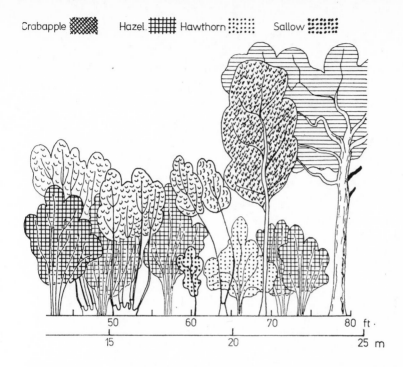 Hazel Hawthorn Sallow

wood-spurge, wood-anemone and water-avens, flourishing on different soils in the second and third springs after felling; bush-crickets chirping on hot nights; robust ferns, stately sedges and delicately coloured toadstools; and the aquatic vegetation of the mysterious so-called 'Fishpond' that separates the two woods. Beauty and colour went with traditional woodmanship.

Although most coppice woods resembled Bradfield, we occasionally hear of small groves 'of no annual value because of the abundance of big trees';[73] these evidently consisted of timber only. From early times it was recognized that the more timber trees you grow in a wood the less wood you will get. At Bradfield every oak has a patch of poor underwood beneath it; the claim was made in 1669 that as a result of felling 'a great part of the Timber trees' the underwood 'is become of a greater value by a third part than it was when the timber was standing'.[74] It would seem logical to try to gather the timber trees together into a part of the wood reserved for them, but only in west Cornwall have I seen this done: in that very windy climate, timber trees are congregated into sheltered ravines within the woods. Against the benefits to both timber and underwood of growing them separately, the coppice-with-standards practice had the advantage that it would have been relatively easy to keep up a succession of different sizes of

73

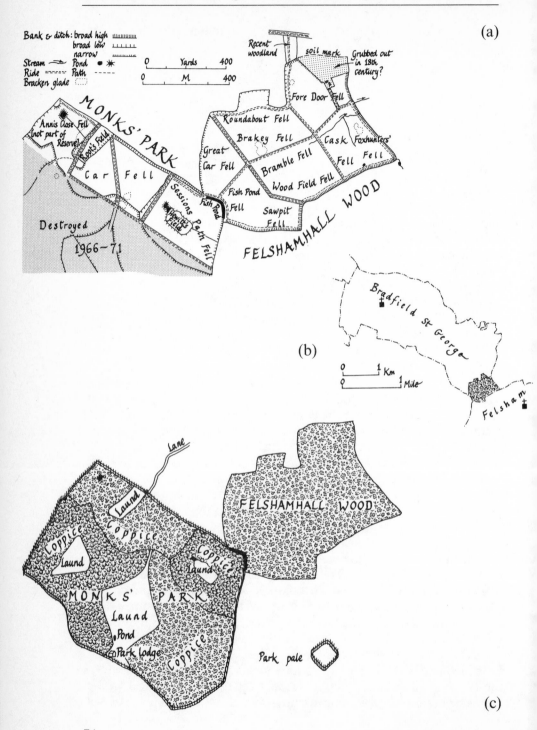

oaks. With timber trees scattered among underwood there would always have been room for the next generation.

Woods in society

A wood usually formed part of a farming estate, rather than being an estate on its own. Some produce was used by the lord of the manor on his own demesne farm. Some was allotted to tenants as a customary right. In Hayley Wood in 1251, for instance, each of 43 local inhabitants could demand a specified quantity of wood each year. Rights to timber or wood for specific purposes are often described as *hedgebote*, *firebote*, *housebote*, *cartbote*, *gatebote*, *stilebote*, and 'other customary botes'. These terms could define a common right to be exercised in the lord's wood. Elsewhere they refer to **hedgerow** trees, which ordinarily belonged to the landlord but which a tenant might cut for specific purposes.

Even where there was a wood, not everybody had rights in it, and many places and whole districts had no woodland. Woodland could not always be relied upon to yield all the right kinds of produce when wanted. Hence from at least the thirteenth century there was a well-established trade in both timber and wood. Some was sold locally to people who could not claim it by right. Some was sent from one estate to another in the same ownership: in 1412 the men of Hardwick cut wood in 'the lord's wood of Heylee',[65] apparently because Hardwick Wood had temporarily run out. Woodless places might get timber from local non-woodland trees, or from woods twenty miles and more away. For example, the woodless Breckland parish of Brandon, belonging to the Bishop of Ely, used local black and white poplar trees, and drew timber from the Bishop's woods at Shipdham and Hitcham, 18 and 29 road miles away. Some of the Hitcham timber was sent on to the Bishop's manor at Somersham near Huntingdon, 50 miles away by water, even though Somersham had big woods of its own.[75]

Outsize trees, especially, were transported long distances, often from Forests and other wood-pastures. For example, in 1251 Henry III gave thirty oaks to the monks of Bury St Edmund's, to come from Inglewood Forest near Carlisle, over 250 miles away;[76] the transport

Fig. 17. The Bradfield Woods. (a) Woods as they are today; the 'fell' names are given as in the 1850s. (b) Position of Felshamhall Wood, as its name implies, in 'the Felsham corner' of Bradfield St George parish. (c) Reconstruction of woods as in the middle ages; for the compartments in Monks' Park see p. 157.

cost, 18*s*. each, would itself have bought a big oak.

There was also a large import trade from Norway, the Baltic and Central Europe. Pine did not grow in England; so when, as in a building in Ely, we find a thirteenth-century roof largely made of small pine trees,[77] we are reminded of the purchases of pine scaffolding-poles from Norway in the fabric rolls of Ely Cathedral. Documents speak of a large trade in boards of both oak and pine. These could be used in grand structures – there are pine boards in the thirteenth-century doors of the Chapter-house at York Minster – but were often put to humble uses, such as a shed, even in places that had woodland. Making boards was a specialized job, and the local carpenter did not always have the skill or equipment, or the right trees for it. Imported oak 'wainscot' boards can be seen in church furniture and doors. They do not carry the stamp NOT MADE IN ENGLAND as obviously as pine does; yet with practice one can distinguish the giant, straight-grained, slow-grown oaks of Central Europe, accurately sawn in a board factory, from the small, crooked, fast-grown local oaks used for the structural frames of the same buildings.[78]

Woods down the centuries

In 1250 woodland, although valuable, was rapidly being grubbed out, especially in what remained of the more wooded areas. This age of expansion and over-population came to an abrupt end with the Black Death in 1349. Thereafter woodland became stable, or in some areas, such as the east Midlands, increased.

Changes came in the sixteenth and seventeenth centuries. The population began once again to catch up with the land available. Although the standard of living in general declined, there was widespread new building, amounting in some areas to a 'Great Rebuilding' of most of the medieval houses (sometimes occasioned by a big fire, as in Wymondham, Norfolk). The dissolution of the monasteries in the 1530s caused woods to change hands (often with a period of neglect) and released second-hand timber from demolished monastic buildings. Capital needed to pay for monkish lands, or to meet fines for religious or political offences, was often raised by selling timber.

The demand for underwood should have risen through winters getting colder (the Little Ice Age), increasing population, changing standards of domestic heating (wood was burnt in chimneys instead of on a hearth in the middle of the floor), the growth of fuel-using industries, rising sea-level (leading to more underwood needed for sea-defences), and the increase of hop-growing (a large user of big poles).

Against these must be set competition from coal. In the middle ages coal had been a special, expensive fuel; by 1600 it had captured much of the market for heating in cities, and in London was causing serious trouble with acid rain.[79] Coal was cheap to produce, though expensive to transport, and without it there would have been a crisis in wood supplies.

Timber for house-building was found with little difficulty. At first, massive timbers were displayed in what seems to us vulgar taste. In many medieval buildings, my own college among them, I find that the biggest timber is not original but a Tudor insertion. But new houses, though larger, tended to be less solid. Trees grew bigger and were sawn lengthwise, or medieval timbers were reused. Timbers were now covered up and merely needed to hold up the structure. This, like all fashions, began at the top of the social scale; the use of massive exposed beams as part of the architecture lingered into the seventeenth century in new homes of the relatively poor. Without these changes there would have been a crisis in timber supplies.

Outsize trees were now more easily come by. The biggest of all were fifteen oaks, each apparently 80 ft long, in the towers of Nonsuch Palace; Henry VIII brought them from four different places on a specially-built 'Great Wain'.[80] When the nave roof of St Paul's Cathedral was burnt in 1561 a new roof was promptly framed from huge timbers in Yorkshire.[79] Still extant is the wonderful roof, with timbers nearly 40 ft long, framed in 1632 on the ruined Abbey Dore (Herefordshire), which had become a humble parish church.[81]

Other countries have forestry policies and laws, to which students of forest history devote inordinate attention, but in England these are few and unimportant. In 1416 there was a statute forbidding clogs to be made of aspen in order to prevent competition with the makers of arrow-shafts. Everyone remembers the statute of 1543, which required woods to have a minimum of twelve timber trees per acre, to be fenced after felling to prevent them from turning into wood-pasture, and not to be grubbed out. All these had, of course, been normal practice for centuries. The statute purported to prevent changes, but had so many loopholes as to be almost unenforceable; much as with modern tree preservation orders, an offender could escape by claiming that the trees felled had been 'seere and dead in the toppes'.[82] I know of only two prosecutions. This Act, and others like it, probably had some effect by influencing the terms of leases, which it did for over 200 years.

Woods were among the most enduring and successful of all medieval institutions, and were remarkably resistant to the vicissitudes of the centuries (Fig. 18). They were not in a constant state of flux. Changes,

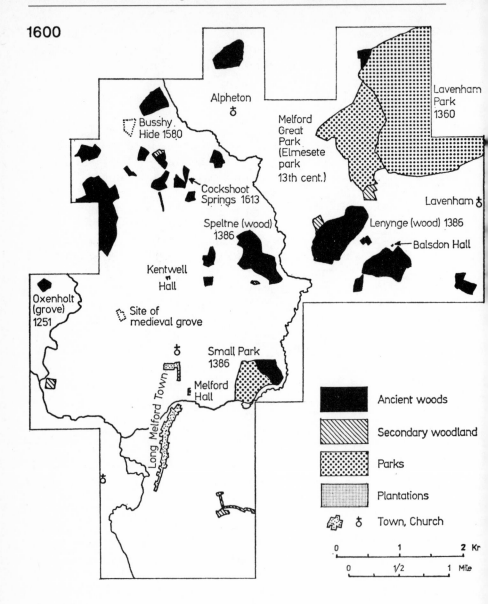

1600

Alpheton ♂

Lavenham
Park
1360

⌐⌐⌐ Busshy
└┘ Hide 1580

Melford
Great
Park
(Elmesete
park
13th cent.)

Lavenham ♂

Cockshoot
Springs 1613

Lenynge (wood) 1386

Speltne (wood)
1386

Balsdon Hall

Kentwell
Hall

Oxenholt
(grove)
1251

Site of
medieval grove

Small Park
1386

Long Melford Town

Melford
Hall

	Ancient woods
	Secondary woodland
	Parks
	Plantations
🏰 ♂	Town, Church

0   1   2 Km

0   1/2   1 Mile

Fig. 18. Changes in woods and parks around Long Melford, Suffolk. This is an unusually well-documented area – for instance, there are four pre-1620 maps which cover almost the whole of it – but is otherwise a typical sample of Ancient Countryside. The small groves towards the north-west are shown on Plate XXIII. The extent of ancient woodland is not now as poor as the 1974 map shows: some of the woods which had then been made into plantations have reverted to woodland.

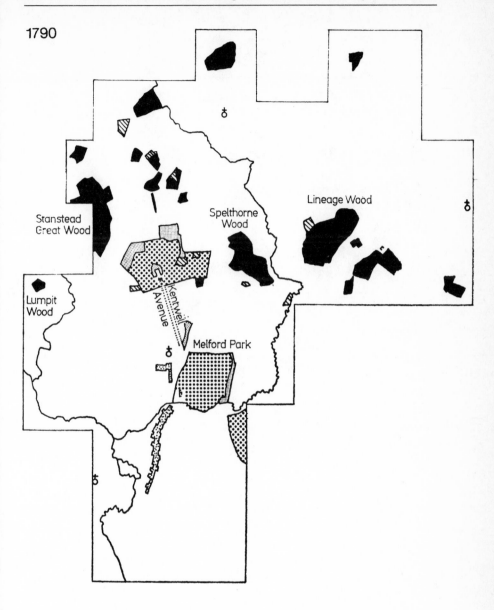

1790

Lineage Wood

Stanstead
Great Wood

Spelthorne
Wood

Lumpit
Wood

Kentwell Avenue

Melford Park

1945

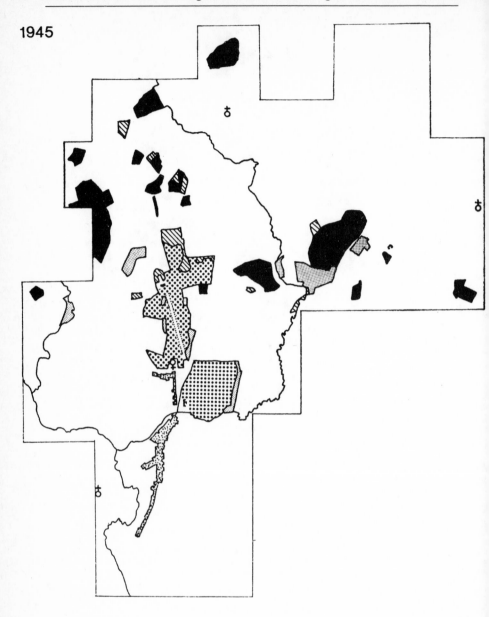

1974

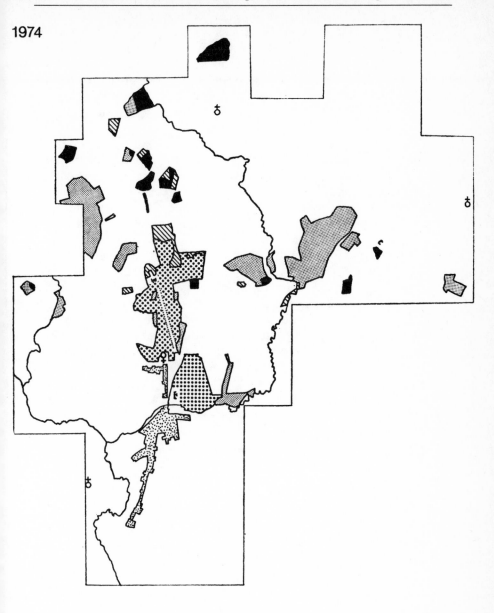

where there were any, were not radical innovations; many woods in 1900 differed only in detail from what they had been 650 years earlier.

In Eastern England, coppicing cycles lengthened and became more regular. In Hayley Wood, the seven-year rotation in the fourteenth century had lengthened to 10–11 years by 1584 and to 15 years by 1765.[83] This is entirely typical: before 1500 it was unusual to fell a wood less often than every nine years, whereas by the eighteenth century rotations of nine years or less were rare, and those of 15–20 years not uncommon. Logs were being produced instead of faggots.

The part played by timber in woodland varied. Both woodland records and the timbers themselves show that trees on the whole were bring allowed to grow bigger by the seventeenth century; but there were wide variations even between neighbouring woods as at Barking (Table 4). Trees continued to be felled in large numbers at long intervals: for instance at Little Bentley, Essex in 1598 there were ten woods, totalling 430 acres, with only 561 standard trees between them; Cowhey Wood was 59 acres (modern measure) 'wherin are but viij good tymber trees remayninge'.[85] Small standard oaks continued to predominate in some woods until the early nineteenth century, and can often be found in eighteenth-century buildings.

Eighteenth-century surveys of woods, mainly in Suffolk and Essex, show that by this time it was usual to fell a certain proportion of the timber trees at every fall of the underwood, according to a pre-determined plan, rather than irregularly as need arose. On big estates with many woods the coppice rotation was often arranged for the

Table 4.   Timber trees in Barking (Suffolk) in the 1600s

	Acres	Trees	All timber trees, 1607		Naval trees, 1608	
			Trees per acre	Cubic feet per tree	Trees per acre	Cubic feet per tree
Boyney wood	82	1640	20	19	48	34
Parkwood	14	160	11	17	6	25
Prestley wood	37	73	2	14	–	–
Tickley wood	4	40	10	19	–	–
Swineside wood (now Swingen's)	13	0?	–	–	–	–
Demesne lands*	–	149	–	13	–	50
Tenants lands*	–	109	–	20	–	–

Based on surveys of all the timber trees in woods and hedges in 1607, and of trees which James I, the owner, proposed to use on his Navy in 1608.[84]
* Presumably non-woodland trees.

estate as a whole, rather than for each wood separately as had usually been done earlier. In consequence a quite large wood might be felled all at once, as was Dodnash Wood (Bentley, S.E. Suffolk) in 1663, 1740–1 and 1761.[86]

Woodland provided income and capital, and unlike modern forestry did not involve the expense of planting trees. The only important cost, of maintaining the boundaries, was often passed on to the purchaser of underwood. For at least 600 years prices of trees, both timber and underwood, either remained steady or rose in real terms. In Eastern England, in the later middle ages, an acre of underwood at ten years' growth would have cost around 5s., and an oak-tree measuring 20 cubic feet would have fetched 2s. By 1830 the underwood would have cost £4 and the oak £5. Most of the difference, of course, was due to inflation. In real terms, the price of underwood rose only once, by about 75% between 1540 and 1553 – an age of colder winters, rising population and chimney-building, but with a stable area of woodland. (The *retail* price of firewood, especially in cities, was increased by greedy middlemen.) Prices of oak-trees rose more slowly. From 1510 to 1690 – the age of the Great Rebuilding – there was a rise of about 50% above inflation. From 1750 onwards the prices of oak timber and oak bark rose more rapidly, as we shall see in the next chapter. This is why, by 1830, the oak-tree cost more than the underwood. In 1800 a working man could have afforded less oak and less underwood than in 1400; but then he was worse off in most other respects as well.[87]

We think of woodmanship in economic terms because accountants and valuers wrote the surviving documents. But woods have social functions as well. A landowner may maintain a wood because he supposes it pays him; or because he has not the labour to grub it out; or because he does not want his tenants or neighbours to be cold, because he appreciates it as a pheasant-covert or an antiquity, etc., etc. The economic value of woods, plus the capital cost of destroying them, tended to preserve woodland against other land-uses from 1350 to 1850. Occasional woods were grubbed out when farming prospered, especially when it was subsidized by the government (p. 184), or when an individual owner happened not to like woodland. We can rarely ascertain why one wood survived and another did not.

Woods and heavy industries

One of the toughest of canards is the notion that woods have been largely destroyed by industrialists felling them to use the trees. Examples of one kind and another have been quoted from Roman times until World War II. Here I deal with fuel-using industries: tanning and shipbuilding are reserved for the next chapter.

Many industries used wood or charcoal as a fuel. For some it was essential, for others optional. Brickworks, for example, could use coal or reeds instead;[88] I do not know how the thousands of millions of bricks were burnt that rebuilt London after the Great Fire. The best-documented industry, and perhaps the biggest, was iron-smelting with charcoal. Ironmasters are said to have 'cut down' the woods of England between 1550 and 1700. These woods are supposed to have ceased to be woodland, leading to a 'timber famine', high prices, restrictive legislation, industries moving further afield, and even the invention of coke as a substitute for charcoal. Finally the ironmasters, having 'used up' the woods of England, committed economic suicide in the flames of the remaining woods of Scotland and Ireland. This argument is stated in general terms: I am not aware that a single named wood has been proved to have disappeared which would still be there had the iron-men not felled it.

This inverted pyramid of argument was overturned many years ago by the researches of M.W. Flinn and G. Hammersley;[89] here I can but summarize their main arguments and add a few of my own. The tip of the pyramid, on which all else rests, is the notion that *timber* trees were used for fuel and did not grow again. This is not true. Charcoal came mainly from underwood, and had to be made locally because it was too fragile to transport far. A blast furnace working on the basis of non-renewable fuel would have taken a few years to devour the woods within reach and would then have gone out of business. Furnaces were not such fly-by-night enterprises. Half the known sites remained active for at least fifty years and a third for more than a century, which they could have done only if their fuel had grown again. Ironworks were often set up by woodland owners to run on a continuous basis in conjunction with particular coppices, as in 1541 at Pickering, N.E. Yorkshire.[90] A regular 16-to-18-year coppice rotation was widely used for this purpose in West Yorkshire.[3a] Ironmasters who moved into Scotland were expanding their production, not abandoning England. The decline of the industry was not due to economic suicide – there is no evidence that the price of standing trees was ever more than a small part of the total costs – but to competition from Sweden with its better ores and cheaper labour. Coke was substituted because its labour costs were less, but over a long period: the last charcoal blast-furnace is still standing at Backbarrow in the Lake District.

Fuel-using industries lived near woods because ores and finished products were easier to transport than charcoal. Like all heavy industries, they disrupted local society and were unpopular. Industrialists, who had many bigger bills to pay than that for trees, could afford to buy up woods and to deprive local people of previously cheap fuel. Although they preferred not to waste labour on chopping up timber, they may have discouraged the growth of timber trees which took up space that might have been growing underwood. It is hardly surprising that politicians and the public should have been angry with industrialists and should have overlooked the distinction between harvesting trees and destroying woodland. Sixteenth-century legislation was no more than a half-hearted attempt to prevent this competition.

The tin industry around the Helford River in west Cornwall is an example. Tinning flourished in this area from about 1300 to 1750. Wildwood had disappeared long before; by 1300 the woods had been reduced to less than 2% of the land area, and were coppiced and fully used for purposes other than tin. The tinners at first used peat charcoal, but when they ran out of peat they bought up the woods and for a long time would have used up the entire wood production and more. Carew in 1602 refers to the 'intolerable price' of wood in Cornwall. Later the tinworks were converted to use imported coal, and the woods – which still exist – reverted to domestic uses.[91]

The theory that ironworks destroyed woodland derives much of its popularity from the great authority of John Evelyn, the seventeenth-century savant. Sixty years later, things ought to have got worse, but Evelyn was flatly contradicted by Daniel Defoe, who 'found that Complaint perfectly groundless, the Three Counties of *Kent*, *Sussex*, and *Hampshire*, ... being one inexhaustible Store-House of Timber never to be destroy'd ...'[92] Although Evelyn was much more learned, there can be no doubt that Defoe was right: the Weald, which Evelyn had had in mind, had lost its great woods in the early-medieval expansion of agriculture, long before the heyday of the iron industry. Yarranton, another polemical writer, claimed in 1677 that landowners around the Forest of Wyre were in the habit of planting new woods, 'knowing by experience that the Copice Woods are ready money with the Iron Masters at all times.'[93]

The theory that industries destroyed woodland fails to pass a simple test. If it is true, less medieval woodland ought to survive in areas where there was industry than where there was not. Exactly the opposite is the case. The woods did not disappear from the industrial Weald or Lake District, or the Forests of Dean or Wyre. It was non-industrial Norfolk, the land of agricultural innovation and prosperity, that lost three-quarters of its medieval woods between 1600 and 1790. In Wales the woods did not disappear from the industrial Cynon, Merthyr and Ebbw valleys until long after they had ceased to be used for charcoal; they did vanish from rustic Montgomeryshire. In Scotland the woods vanished from the agricultural Lowlands, but remain in the once industrial Loch Lomond and Appin areas. In Ireland some ancient woodland remained into the nineteenth century in counties such as Wexford and western Waterford which had had an industrial history, but not in rural Limerick or Tipperary. The survival of almost any large tract of woodland suggests that there has been an industry to protect it against the claims of farmers. As Hammersley puts it:

Ironmasters ... did not plough up woodlands or uproot them, neither did they nibble the young shoots; most of them wanted to protect their investment and maintain their profits, and that needed fuel for the future as well as the present.

Wales

The history of woodmanship was at first worked out for Eastern England, but it turns out to be repeated, with surprisingly little difference, all over Lowland England and largely in the Highland Zone as well. On the Helford River, Cornwall, the story of coppicing, woodbanks, wood-names etc. turns up in an oakwood environment and in a Celtic culture.

The documentary history of Welsh woodland has been related in detail by Dr William Linnard. Some parts of Wales, such as Monmouthshire, were like the more wooded English counties; against these must be set Anglesey, almost woodless, and the great extent of moorland. The general impression is of a land less wooded as a whole than England; but because nearly half Wales was moorland, woodland was more concentrated and more prominent in the *inhabited* countryside than in England.

The broad history of Welsh woods is not unlike that of English. There are many references to grubbing in the thirteenth century. W. Rees made a map of the southern half of Wales in the fourteenth century, showing the locations of 41 Welsh woods.[94] Comparing this with the Ordnance Survey of the 1830s, I find that 20 of the woods were apparently still there, and of the remainder 18 sites were farmland. The survival rate, about 50% over 500 years, confirms an impression that the forces of conservation were a little weaker in Wales than in England.

Linnard gives many scattered references to medieval woodmanship, to systematic coppicing (underwood prices were at least as high as in England), charcoal for industrial fuel, sales of bark, and thefts of timber. Timber is known chiefly from the accounts of royal castles;

more timber appears to have been sent from England to Wales than vice versa. Pannage of swine is often referred to, as befits a land of oakwoods, but died out, as in England, in the later middle ages. Woodland terminology is often a strange mixture of Welsh and English words, for example 'spring-goed' – Welsh *coed* 'wood' + English *spring* 'coppice'.

Many Welsh woods have woodbanks round them, and the remains of walls dividing woods from the moor. Woods in the past were evidently protected from grazing, not ravaged by sheep as too many are today.

Scotland

Despite the great work of M. L. Anderson on Scottish woodland history, our knowledge of the middle ages and earlier is still vague. Medieval Scotland seems in general to have been rather less wooded than medieval England; but it did have woods in parts of the Lowlands and Southern Uplands from which almost all trace has since disappeared. Scotland, like England, imported timber from Norway and Prussia.[95] One or two grants, such as that of 100 loads of hazel rods annually to Lindores Abbey (Fife) in 1250, imply extensive coppicing, but Anderson gives little evidence of woodmanship. Is this because Scotland had no woodmanship tradition, or because the documents were not kept or have not been found?

As we shall see in Chapter 6, fieldwork has gone some way towards solving this problem. The Dalkeith Oaks were undoubtedly a medieval coppice. As Dr Jim Dickson pointed out to me, Mugdock Wood north of Glasgow has woodbanks and giant coppice stools in the English manner. Scotland therefore did have an early coppicing tradition, but the evidence is poorly preserved and awaits investigation.

After the middle ages, coppicing is well recorded, notably in the oakwoods of the S.W. Highlands.[96] Their early history is unknown. From the seventeenth century these woods grew charcoal for iron-works, bark for tanning, and a little timber. They were highly organized and were coppiced on an inflexible rotation of 21–30 years. The longest-lived furnace, at Lorn (Argyll), went on until 1876 and maintained about 10,000 acres of underwood. As with many Welsh woods, both timber and underwood were predominantly oak. Attempts, not very successful, were made to remove underwood of other species, to thin the oak poles, and to introduce English oaks.

Birchwoods have probably been for centuries the commonest native woodland of Scotland. There is some evidence that the Highlands once had a birch economy like that of north Norway, everything – even roofs, wheels, tubs – being made of the tree.[97] Birchwoods, however, do not normally appear to be ancient woodland, and have no defined boundaries or proper names. Birches seem to invade moorland whenever reduced grazing allows them, but do not persist long in the same spot.

The famous 'Caledonian' pinewoods appear to have been uncommon by the time of the earliest documents; they had shrunk through prehistoric tillage and pasture or the growth of blanket peat. 'Legends' of great woods being burnt by warrior chieftains to consume their enemies, and never recovering, are unlikely to be historical: they are usually of late origin, and may have been inspired by prehistoric pine trunks buried in the peat. The pinewoods are usually said to have been 'discovered' about 1600, but the less remote ones are recorded in the late Middle Ages. 'Mamlorn Forest', identified with the still-extant woods of Glen Lyon (Perthshire), supplied ships' masts,[98] which normally came from pine-exporting countries. Mr Robin Callander tells me that the Deeside pinewoods were managed and conserved by the Bishops of Aberdeen. There is some evidence of losses of area, especially in Deeside, though most of the seventeenth-century pinewoods still exist. Pinewoods seem never to have had defined boundaries, and probably moved around somewhat as did birchwoods.

Sir T. D. Lauder in c.1830 found in Glenmore, Inverness-shire, giant rotten trees that had escaped felling: probably the very last time that this characteristic wildwood feature was seen in these islands.

Ireland

The history of Irish woodland is a succession of disasters. At all times there seems to have been less surviving than in England. Much of the woodland was in the south and west; the Irish Midlands were even less wooded than the English Midlands. Medieval cartularies show that woodland was not a normal possession of an Irish monastery as it was of an English one.

The Irish equivalent of Domesday Book is the Civil Survey of 1654–6. The records survive for rather more than half the country, and list many thousands of woods. Adding these up, and allowing for missing counties, I arrive at a total woodland area of 420,000 acres, 2.1% of Ireland, roughly one-third of the proportion in England at the time. The most wooded county, Clare, had 7% of woodland, similar to an average English county.[99]

Because of later disasters very little survives even of this, but there is enough to show that woodland once played much the same part in the Irish cultural landscape as it did in England. In County Waterford I find the remains of woodbanks, boundary pollards and giant coppice stools. On the other hand, the oakwoods of Killarney, which were very remote, seem not to have had defined boundaries or management.[100]

Viking and medieval Ireland certainly had a coppicing tradition. Excavations have revealed the immense importance of wattle-work in Cork and Dublin; whole buildings were made of it.[101] It implies woodland management on a large scale. One still sees the ghosts of Irish underwood on the under surfaces of concrete vaults in castles, in which are impressed the hurdlework forms that held up the newly-built vault while the mortar was setting. The Civil Survey sometimes mentions 'copps' or 'underwood', but many woods were described as 'timberwood': coppicing was already dying out. Timber-framing, as in much of England, was confined to cities. The Civil Survey lists many such 'cagework' houses, but as far as is known every one was demolished in the eighteenth and nineteenth centuries.

In general coppicing declined in Ireland so early that it has been sometimes claimed, against the above evidence, that it never existed. But it never died out quite completely; it was active this century in Counties Wicklow and Waterford. In Waterford I found a newly-cut coppice-wood in 1985.

Even the small area of woodland recorded in 1654–6 was, for the most part, to disappear during the eighteenth century. Except in Co. Waterford, it is very unusual to find a wood on the 6-inch Ordnance Survey of 1834–44 where there was one in the Civil Survey. In general, less than one-tenth of the Irish woodland of 1655 was still there 180 years later; the rest was ordinary farmland.

There were numerous complaints that woods were being destroyed by industries, especially English industries. These have been well chronicled by Dr Eileen McCracken,[102] but should be treated with the same scepticism as in England. A popular, but unlikely, candidate was the barrel industry, for example:

[The woods have been] very much wasted and spoyld by that plague of all good timber (*to wit*) pipe staves and barrell staves, &c. soe that ... this county will lament the loss thereof which might be imployed to more honourable uses ... If not timely prevented, it may be conjectured that the inhabitants of this nation must with Diogines live in tubbs for the choycest timber is imploy'd to that use.

Civil Survey, Co. Carlow

However, cooperage is a very specialized craft, using only the best oak-trees; most Irish woodland would have been useless, and it is inconceivable that a whole wood could have been turned into barrels. Nor can the export of a few thousand tons of barrel-staves a year have had much effect on 420,000 acres of woodland. Ireland, a big consumer of iron, had its own ironworks, but as in England these were permanent and must have come to terms with their woods.

The real destroyer of the woods was agriculture. From 1700 to 1840 Ireland had a fourfold rise in population. Every inch of possible land (and much that was impossible) was grubbed out and farmed. With ironworks in decline, cagework unfashionable, and plenty of peat for domestic fuel, there was no obstacle to reducing the whole country to the woodless state of the Irish Midlands. Even the last of the 'derry' islands in bogs, with very rare exceptions, was farmed. The Irish woods perished in the tragic population explosion that resulted in the Great Famine.

5

The woods in decline: post-medieval changes

The high Price of Coal ... undoubtedly tends to increase the Consumption of Wood for Fuel ... for though it is not large Timber which is consumed in that Way, but Underwood and the Branches of Trees, yet the additional Demand for Underwood renders it more valuable, and the Growth of great Trees, by which it is injured, is the more discouraged. The Inducement to the wasteful Practice of lopping Trees is, by the same means, increased ... In Consequence of the Improvement of Roads, and Increase of Inland Navigation, the Use of Coal has, of late, become more general than it formerly was.

House of Commons Journal, 1792, p. 281

The beginnings of modern forestry

So far we have been concerned with native or 'semi-natural' woodland rather than with trees that have been planted. Planted trees, as part of the orchard and garden tradition, go back well into Anglo-Saxon times and could well be derived from Roman gardening. As we shall see, planting trees in the landscape at large was not uncommon from the thirteenth century onwards, but nearly all the records relate to hedgerows and perhaps parks; they are not the beginnings of modern forestry.

As John Harvey points out, attempts to plant *areas* of trees, though rare, were made in the middle ages. For example, Abbot Godfrey of Peterborough in 1304 and 1311

in the eastern part of Cranemor [in Eye near Peterborough], from arable land planted a wood, and it is called Childholm. At Witheringtone [Werrington] he planted a wood where a wood had never been before, and surrounded it with a willow ditch.[103]

My earliest example, the only one that can now be identified and probably the only one of more than a few acres, is Soane or Bullock Wood, a 60-acre fragment of which still stands near Colchester. There is some evidence that around 1242 the site had been enclosed and sown with trees by the monks of the Abbey of St John, Colchester. The matter is not conclusive – it rests partly on a contemporary belief that the wood's name meant 'sown wood' (*boscus seminatus*) – and the wood is not now obviously recognizable as a plantation.[104]

In medieval England the planting of even a small wood was something to be recorded among the memorable deeds of a great abbot, rather than an everyday event. What the result was we do not know. The medievals would have been aware of natural succession, and might have appreciated that an unused field turns into an oakwood whether or not oaks are sown or planted on it. But in Scotland as early as 1457 a statute exhorted landowners to make 'all tennentis plant woodes'; and in the following century this appears occasionally to have been put into practice, although the sites cannot now be identified.[105]

In Tudor times planting *areas* of trees was a rare event, not adding significantly to the natural woodland. For example, Watling Wood (36 acres) in Sudbourne Park (E. Suffolk) is described on Norden's map of 1602 as 'A newe Wood full of yonge Settes'. English forestry, as a definite tradition, begins with Arthur Standish's *The Commons Complaint* in 1611, followed by other pamphlets in 1613 and 1615. These have a curiously modern flavour, consisting of an ambitious national planting plan, directions for how to carry it out, and speculation on how much the crop might eventually be worth. Being mainly exhortatory they are of little value as evidence, but some details of propagation and pruning seem to be derived from experience.

Standish is remembered for having influenced John Evelyn, the author of *Sylva* (1664), which was a best-seller, a standard work for 150 years, and the subject of endless plagiarism. Evelyn was a great scholar who combined a lifelong enthusiasm for trees with considerable practical experience and a mastery of English prose. His book is a mixture of woodmanship, horticulture, forestry and folklore, combining scientific experiment with popular mythology; much of the misinformation about trees that is still current today can be traced back to it. Although he records many woodmanship practices, he was most influential in the matter of plantations. Evelyn believed that woods were in decline, and that

nothing less than an *universal Plantation of all the sorts of Trees* will supply, and well encounter the defect.

In the seventeenth century plantations were still mainly a gentleman's hobby. Most seem to have been small compared with medieval woods; among the few known to survive are parts of Felbrigg

92

Great Wood, Norfolk, established by the Windhams.[106] As late as 1780 gold medals of the Society of Arts were often won by plantations of less than ten acres. In Scotland, and probably in Ireland, where planting was enjoined by statute, the area of plantations overtook that of native woods at some time in the eighteenth century; this did not happen in England until the twentieth.

Early plantations were not like those of today. They were intended to add to the woodmanship tradition, not to replace it. Most of them were coppices, made in imitation of existing woods by sowing or planting a mixture of trees such as 'mast of oke, beech and the chats of ashe, bruised crabbes'. Such planted woods, coppiced from the start, are unlikely by now to be distinguishable from other seventeenth-century secondary woodland. But there was a tendency towards planting for timber only, perhaps because Evelyn and other writers claimed that timber was in shorter supply than wood; and towards using just one or two species, often conifers or other foreign trees. Plantations and woods therefore diverged into different land-uses, each going its own way and often appearing separately in the records.

Planting coppices went on, at least in a small way, throughout the eighteenth century; forestry textbooks were still giving instructions for doing it in the twentieth century. It is often supposed that the woods of almost pure hazel, widespread in south and middle England, are all of planted origin. No adequate documentary or archaeological evidence has been published for this view. Against it there is a map of 1618 showing Cranborne Chase – that stronghold of hazel-woods – having almost all the woods that it now has, plus others that have disappeared, already organized as a system of coppices.[107] As we have seen, there is abundant evidence that hazel-woods are natural, going back to wildwood times. One may well ask why anyone planting underwood should specialize in hazel, a tree with which England has always been over-supplied.

A feature of the plantation tradition, still continuing today, is the existence of fashions in trees. Beech was a favourite of the eighteenth and nineteenth centuries – previously it had hardly been thought a timber tree at all – and was planted both within and far outside its native range, from Aberdeen to Cornwall. The majority of what are now often mistaken for natural beechwoods, especially on chalk, are beech plantations. In well-defined periods in the nineteenth century there were fashions for wych-elm, hornbeam, and (European) larch. In the twentieth there have been vogues for, successively, Scots pine, Corsican pine, hybrid poplar, and lodgepole pine. Some of these were grown for specific purposes, which (as human purposes do) often disappeared by the time the trees had grown.

The shipbuilding period

The British believe that the history of woodland has been dominated by the influence of the sea. Holland and Greece show that a nation with a proud seafaring history need not necessarily have had much woodland; but despite these examples we suppose that the supply of shipbuilding timber has been the reason either for the sacrifice of our ancient forests or for the maintenance of our ancient woods. Is this history or pseudo-history?

From the mid-sixteenth to the mid-nineteenth century, writers such as Evelyn foreboded, or complained of, a shortage of naval timber. From such general writings derives the traditional theory that ship-building was a steady influence down the centuries, touching nearly every wood and hedge in the land. But when we investigate the history of particular woods shipbuilding shrinks into merely one among many uses of timber. In the records of, for example, Hayley Wood, the Bradfield Woods, and Hatfield Forest the subject is not mentioned at all.

The fact is that as a big consumer of timber, shipbuilding was short-lived. There was not much technological advance down the centuries – the *Mary Rose* is essentially the same structure as the *Victory* – but the total tonnage increased enormously from 1750 onwards (Fig. 19).

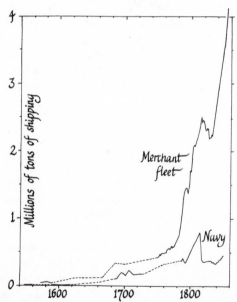

Fig. 19. Growth of the British timber-built navy and merchant fleet.[108] Broken lines indicate sparse information.

Merchant shipping expanded as trade became intercontinental. At each successive war there was an arms race which permanently increased the size of the Royal Navy, culminating the final escalation of the Napoleonic Wars. There are minor uncertainties about what exactly a ton of shipping meant, how much timber it took to build, and how long a vessel lasted; but the conclusion seems inescapable that as much timber shipping was launched in Britain between 1800 and 1860 as in the whole of history before 1800.

Except for masts (always imported), warships were built almost entirely of British timber, most of it oak.[109] Foreign oak was not much used until about 1803, and the Navy continued to rely on British oak until 1860. Our best ships were captured from the French, and some timber was re-used from older ships;[110] these factors will be offset by the practice of adding new timbers to an old ship to supplement rotten ones.* The size of the fleet therefore gives a rough idea of the rate at which shipbuilding consumed British oak. Shipbuilders, especially for the Navy, were supposed to use large trees, and had particular needs for natural bends for making curved timbers; for this reason oak from parks, hedges, etc. was preferred to that from woods. Some woods, such as those of Loch Lomond,[111] sold timber regularly to shipyards, but it was often claimed that oaks grown as standards between coppice were unsuitable.

Early complaints about shortage must mean poor organization or transport, or low prices offered, rather than lack of trees. Had there been the slightest physical difficulty in finding timber for the tiny fleet that defeated the Armada, it would have been utterly impossible to build the sixtyfold larger fleet that defeated Napoleon. Even such obvious sources as the New Forest and Dean appear not to have been touched by the Navy until well into the seventeenth century.[112] In the eighteenth century, the reports of parliamentary commissions do not portray an industry that was being driven to substitution, economy, or even to avoiding waste. Forebodings of crisis came from the Navy dockyards, which were short of money and had to buy trees cheaply; commercial shipyards paid the market price and had no difficulty in getting timber. Even so, no war was lost for want of shipping; the Navy continued to expand even after it had crushed the opposition at Trafalgar. Naval shipwrights could still afford to be pernickety about what timber they used and where they got it from, to indulge their prejudices against foreign oak or iron components, and to let timber rot in store before they used it. In 1808 it was proposed, not unreason-

* It is a popular myth that ships' timbers were re-used in buildings, even far from the sea. Building timbers tended to be re-used in buildings and ships' timbers in ships.

ably, to maintain even the then inflated Navy comfortably and indefinitely from 100,000 acres of plantations, less than a tenth of the
woodland area at that time, to be established for the purpose. Only
in 1809 did substitution begin in earnest with a large purchase of
Albanian oak from Ali Pasha, despot of Yannina; and only after 1815
did the Navy's prices for oak start to increase in real terms.

The market for oak-trees was affected less by the price of timber
than by that of bark. Oak bark – other trees will not do – has long
been used for tanning leather. Medieval accounts record sales of bark
as a by-product of felling timber; an unimportant by-product, since
the timbers of many pre-1600 buildings still have their bark left on.
The trade went on quietly until 1780, when there was a sudden boom
in leather which followed the same course as the contemporary boom
in shipbuilding. From 1780 to 1850 the tanyards were no mere users-
up of by-products but a gigantic industry, a much bigger consumer of
oak-trees than the naval dockyards and almost certainly a bigger
consumer than the merchant shipyards. The supply came mainly
from the historic oakwood regions of Scotland, Wales and Highland
England. Even in Lowland England, bark, as a by-product of timber
trees, came from almost every wood and hedge.[113]

What permanent effects has the shipbuilding era left? The 'tradition'
that it destroyed woods is implausible – only very rarely did a wood
consist entirely of suitable trees – and I know of no examples. The
dockyards had a wide, but by no means universal, influence on woodland. In Suffolk and Essex, even in 1810 (at the height of the supposed
timber crisis) only a very patriotic wood-owner would have sold oak
to the Navy, at less than 3s. a cubic foot delivered, for which other
purchasers would have paid 4s. In Highland Britain the dockyards
failed altogether to compete with the tanneries: tens of thousands of
acres of woodland were maintained as oak underwood, in which
timber production was sacrificed for a greater yield of bark. The two
industries together provided a use – or the hope of a use – for oak-
trees between 1780 and 1860, when imported conifers were replacing
oak in new buildings. This may have saved many woods: remarkably
little woodland was grubbed out during the Napoleonic Wars, despite
the high price of corn.

The price of an oak-tree was at its highest between 1825 and 1840
when it reached about $2\frac{1}{2}$ times its value (allowing for inflation) in
1690.[114] This abnormal price-rise, to which bark contributed rather
more than timber, encouraged landowners to grow oak. It hastened
the decline of the ancient coexistence between different uses of tree-
land, official contempt for which is illustrated by the passage at the
head of the chapter. In the royal Forests oaks were given precedence

over grazing. In some coppice-woods, in place of the traditional underwood with scattered oaks of various sizes, we find a close-set stand of oak (sometimes planted) beneath which a remnant of the underwood makes shift to survive. What to do with these woods is a problem still with us.

Change and stability in woods

The eighteenth century was an age of much tree-destruction. Woods were grubbed out by 'enlightened' landowners not only in Norfolk, but here and there throughout England. In the last chapter we saw what happened in non-industrial parts of Wales and Scotland, and the disaster to the meagre Irish woods. We shall later see what happened to wood-pasture and non-woodland trees. At the same time, a considerable but unmeasured acreage of new woodland was formed both by intention and default, especially in and around parks (Fig. 18).

Most surviving ancient woods still did their medieval duty of supplying local needs of timber and wood, largely unremarked by forestry writers but amply recorded in the humbler pages of surveys and woodsale accounts. Scores of Cambridgeshire, Essex and Cornwall villagers each year bought logs and poles from their local woods. Apart from a lengthening in the coppice rotation, hundreds of woods were much the same in 1900 as they had been in 1250.

Woodmanship traditions continued in full operation, were extended to new woods, and were even exported to America. The colonists of what are now the eastern United States, like their prehistoric ancestors in England, found a land largely wildwood, which they proceeded to convert into farmland. As in Neolithic England, some areas were set aside as coppice-woods. Most of the eastern States has now reverted to woodland and these coppices are no longer obvious, but careful search will find them in many places. The colonists did not get far with making woodbanks: there was unlimited woodland, and plenty of other things to do. I have found a few woodbanks in Massachusetts, but the best I have seen are in the tropical woods of Cumberland Island (Georgia), the work of eighteenth-century slaves.

Ancient woods sometimes changed in composition if not in area. For example in the middle ages elm, though common as a non-woodland tree, seems to have been relatively rare in woods.[115] From 1650 onwards elm became more important in the general countryside, became widely planted, and was well on its way to recovering the abundance that it had had before the Elm Decline. New elm woods became established by suckering from adjoining hedges, and existing woods were invaded by elm suckers (p. 135). This still goes on.

Sweet-chestnut is a southern European tree; pollen evidence and finds of charcoal show that it was introduced, almost certainly by the Romans, and has persisted. Records of *castanea* or 'chesteine' in the middle ages cluster in several of the areas where it is now abundant. In the Forest of Dean it was valued in the twelfth century for its nuts and possibly its timber. The famous Tortworth Chestnut in Gloucestershire (Plate XXI) is an enormous tree which may have begun in a medieval orchard. There are stools of similar size in several woods in S.E. Suffolk and N.E. Essex (Fig. 20). In 1769 ancient chestnut stools and pollards were cited by Hasted, the Kentish antiquary, in a controversy over whether or not the tree was native.[116] From the time of Evelyn chestnut has been appreciated for its excellence as underwood, and has been much planted; but it also grows readily from seed, and has invaded existing woods. The chestnut-woods that we now have are a combination of ancient woods, some of which may go back to Roman times; woods naturally invaded by

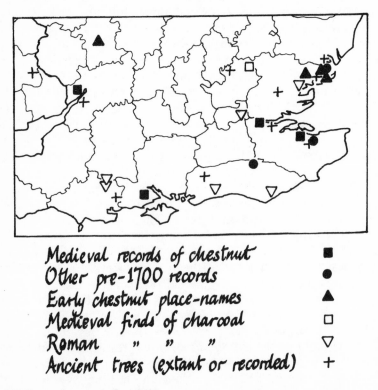

Medieval records of chestnut	■
Other pre-1700 records	●
Early chestnut place-names	▲
Medieval finds of charcoal	□
Roman " " "	▽
Ancient trees (extant or recorded)	+

Fig. 20. Sweet-chestnut before 1500.

chestnut; planted coppices on former non-woodland sites; and woods deliberately converted, we do not yet know how, to chestnut.

The decline of woodmanship

In the latter nineteenth century the earlier kinds of document fade away. The history of woods has to be traced from maps (especially the magnificent early editions of the Ordnance Survey at 1:2500) and from air photographs taken by Hitler's Luftwaffe in 1940 (p. 111).

Coppicing fell into decline; most woods ceased to be felled at some time between 1900 and 1930, although some were already neglected by 1870. The reasons have still to be critically studied. In the Chilterns, as early as the eighteenth century, coppices were replaced almost entirely by the practice of growing beeches for timber on the selection system widely practised in semi-natural forests on the Continent.[117] A beech coppice in the Chilterns is now a rarity. Elsewhere it has not been general for coppicing to be supplanted directly by a rival practice: woods in which coppicing ceased fell into neglect.

The decline of coppicing is connected with the loss of its ancient markets. Coal was at first mainly an urban fuel; it supplemented wood and charcoal but only gradually replaced them. In the mid-nineteenth century the coming of the railways introduced cheap coal to the countryside as well. Specialized wood industries, although dis-organized and having no spokesmen in high places, still showed remarkable vitality. Successive editions of *Kelly's Directory* reveal that in East Anglia the number of specialists in rakes, hoops and hurdles actually increased until 1908; they must have competed successfully with metal substitutes. A study of such trades in 1925 showed a welter of tiny and inflexible businesses cutting each other's throats; they had no control over their markets or their wood supplies, and most of them were to perish in the agricultural depression of the 1930s.[118]

The first nation-wide survey distinguishing coppice-woods was made by the Board of Agriculture in 1905. It showed them as covering 1.65% of England (about a third of the total area of woods plus plantations), 0.33% of Wales, and 0.12% of Scotland. Coarse as these figures are – who can tell when an abandoned wood ceases to be a coppice? – they are worth mapping (Fig. 21), for no better record survives since Domesday, and in all subsequent surveys the ancient woods have been split up among different categories and cannot be disentangled. Coppicing had already begun to retreat from the north, and was to continue to do so.

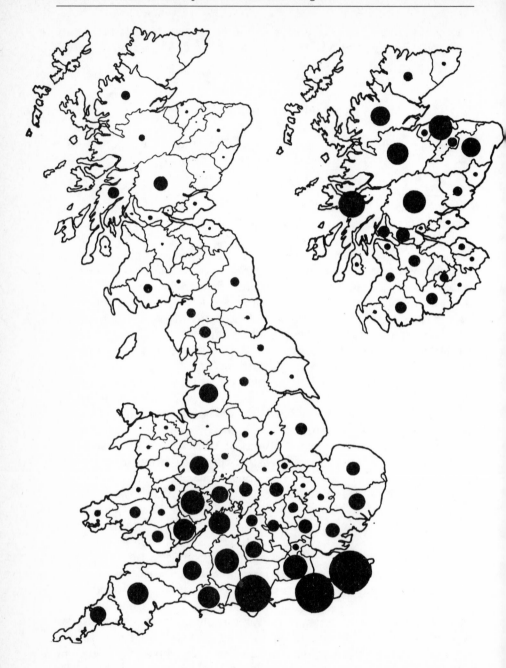

Fig. 21. Left, areas of woods regarded by their owners as coppices in 1905. Each black spot is ten times the area of coppice-wood in the county at the scale of the map. Right, area of natural woods in Scotland in 1845 shown on the same basis.[119]

A Scottish survey of 1845 separates 'natural woods' from 'plantations'. The former, although incompletely recorded, can be estimated as 0.91% of Scotland.

The impact of modern forestry

The first two centuries of forestry had little effect on existing woods. My earliest record of anyone planting trees into a wood is at Cawston (Norfolk) in 1612. A lease of South Hawe Wood required the lessee, in addition to the usual conventions of woodmanship, to

yearely and everie yere of the 14 yeres putt a good number of Sallowes in the vacant emptie places of the ... underwood ... so that the sayd vacant and emptye places may be well planted and supplied with wood ...[120]

This seems to be an isolated instance: most woods are as full of trees as they can hold, and any new trees planted among the stools perish through competition.

My first record of the destruction of an existing wood, and its replacement by planted trees, is in 1759, when 'a fresh plantation' was made of one of the coppices in Hatfield Forest, Essex. No details are given, but the attempt had some effect. By 1803 the wood was producing very little underwood, but timber trees being felled included beech and chestnut, which would not have grown there naturally. Another half-century later it had disappeared from the map; the other coppices, which were not replanted, are still there today.[121]

In Victorian times English forestry developed in three ways which were to have a profound effect on existing woods. It became assimilated – via the imperial forestry of India and Cyprus – to German practice; several great German foresters, such as William Schlich, worked in England. The commitment to plantations and to conifers thus became firmly established: there had been conifer plantations in Germany since 1368.[122] At the same time, foresters began to claim existing woods, as well as farmland or moorland, for their operations. Further, forestry acquired a theoretical basis, and in particular became thought of as a financial operation: it was thought possible to predict how much money a plantation would earn and to decide whether to invest money in trees or in, for example, the stock market. In those days of economic stability such calculations would not have seemed so wildly idealistic as they do today.

Nineteenth-century replanting of woods was more widespread than we might suppose from what now remains. A typical example is Birchanger Wood, Essex, a medieval wood which on the 1876

Ordnance Survey is shown as full of conifers. Remarkably few of these now survive; they died out in the 1930s, being replaced either by the regrowth of the existing stools or by self-sown birch or oak. An alternative fate is illustrated by the ancient woods of the Rhondda and other coal-mining valleys of South Wales. Earlier bards had lamented in song the apparent destruction of these woods by English woodcutters; but in fact the valleys, though industrialized, were among the most wooded parts of Britain until the end of the nineteenth century. Well over half the woods, however, then became moorland with scattered trees. A study of early Ordnance maps reveals a big replanting in the mid-nineteenth century; the woods that now survive are ones that escaped this change.

Foresters might have drawn the inference that, even on their own terms, they would do well to stick to moorland and farmland for new plantations, and to leave the ancient woods alone. However, forestry is an art in which, because of the long time-scale, failures tend to be forgotten, not learnt from, and thus later repeated. Academic foresters continued to work out the profitability of plantations on the most favourable, rather than the most probable, outcome. Forestry had, at last, a 'sound theoretical basis' which was preferred to any analysis of what it had actually achieved.

The first half of the twentieth century

There was a further decline in what was left of the traditions of woodland conservation. In the nineteenth century the nation had got into the habit of obtaining its cellulose by plundering other countries' wildwood. When this activity was interrupted by German submarines the Government's reaction was to encourage the growing of conifers at home, a policy put into effect by the Forestry Commission founded in 1919. Most of the new planting was on moorland or heath, but it was decided that ancient woods, too, were suitable places for growing conifers. This decision to treat existing woods as moorland, and the failure of academic foresters to recognize them as a distinct land-use, were to discourage any attempt to revive woodmanship.

This attitude to woodland was, alas, the parting gift of the British to Ireland. The last one-fifth of one per cent of the ancient Irish woods that survived into the twentieth century has been sought out and coniferized with even more enthusiasm, and with more success, than the woods of England.

A great deal of timber was felled to meet the sudden needs of two world wars. Probably even more was felled in the social upheavals between the wars, when a quarter of England is said to have changed hands in four years and landowners often needed capital suddenly. It is a vulgar fallacy that these fellings led to much diminution of woodland. As anyone can see by comparing successive Ordnance Survey maps and air photographs, the years 1914–1950 were a time of unusual *stability* of woodland. Outside South Wales, and apart from a few woods that happened to be in the way of airfields, it is hard to find a single ancient wood present in 1914 that was absent in 1950. By no means all these woods had been felled; in those that were, wartime fellings made up for what had been a time of unusually *little* felling since 1860. Often, as in Hayley Wood, felling oaks saved the medieval underwood from destruction by too much shade. Ancient woods, of course, grew again: for example Monks' Wood near Huntingdon, 'devastated' by clear-felling in 1918, became a National Nature Reserve in 1953. Even plantations, when felled, normally turned into natural secondary woodland.

Natural and semi-natural events have left their mark on the woods. In 1908 a new disease, oak mildew, appeared from America, and possibly in consequence oak no longer grows readily from seed in woods: an oakling may be less tolerant of shade if it has mildew to contend with as well.[123] From 1916 to 1924 an unprecedented plague of caterpillars struck oaks throughout Europe; in Hayley Wood at least a quarter of the oaks died of repeated defoliations, and are still lying about. The Dutch Elm Disease epidemic of the 1970s had some effect on woodland elms, though there are many more survivors than outside woods; traces of the earlier epidemics of the 1930s and of 1826–60 are now hard to find.

In the last seventy years birch, which had been uncommon in the lowlands throughout historical times, has become one of the commonest trees. It has invaded woods after felling and has formed secondary woodland on derelict fenland, felled plantations, and unused wood-pasture (p. 130). The parallel expansions of sycamore, chiefly into highland woods, and of *Rhododendron ponticum* in the south and west, go back into the last century. The rabbit, escaped from semi-domestication in the eighteenth century, became locally destructive of underwood; but the consequence of its sudden decline through myxomatosis in the 1950s was the growth of great areas of 'scrub', i.e. young woodland, on what had been old grassland and heath. The increase of grey squirrels has rendered the future of hazel precarious.

'The years that the locust hath eaten'

In 1945 there were thousands of woods which still had continuity with their medieval vegetation; there was to be a brief revival of coppicing. The next thirty years were a time of unprecedented destruction of ancient woodland, in contrast to the active conservation or slow decline of the previous thousand years. This time it was not a matter of felling trees which would grow again, but of converting sites to other uses. When I wrote the first edition of this book in 1975, I had grown used to tracing a wood or hedge through seven centuries, and on going to the spot to being just in time for the dying embers of the bonfires in which it had been destroyed.

In 1975 I estimated that at least a third of the ancient woodland had been destroyed in a mere thirty years; an estimate which I later revised to nearly half. For a typical example, George Peterken and Paul Harding, going through Rockingham Forest, Northamptonshire, wood by wood, showed that 42% by area of the ancient woodland which remained in 1946 had lost its characteristics by 1975, almost entirely through being replanted with conifers or grubbed out altogether.[124] A similar story could be told of nearly every sheet of the Ordnance Survey: of Dorset, the steep oakwoods of mid Wales, the Wye gorge, the Forest of Wyre, the hilltop woods of the Welsh Border, and the romantic lichen-hung corkscrew oaks of the deep valleys of Dartmoor and Bodmin Moor. The long arm of destruction reached from the Lizard Peninsula to remote Argyll. As much ancient woodland was attacked in 28 years as in the previous 400 years.

The bulk of the loss was to afforestation, followed by agriculture; quarrying, housing, roads and industry accounted for only small acreages. Ancient woods were regarded by politicians as vacant land which farmers or foresters ought to do something with. It was thought that every available acre – including acres that we did without in the dark and hungry days of World War II – was needed to grow food; nobody noticed that this policy was being overtaken by the success of plant breeders in growing more crops per acre.

Trees, by their very nature, cannot be brought within the scope of modern financial prediction. By the time the trees have grown, the purposes and philosophies on which the predictions were based will be obsolete, and the records of what was spent on establishing the trees will have been thrown away. However, human nature being what it is, politicians and economists persuaded themselves that every tree has cost a definite amount to establish and has a single, ascertainable monetary value; and that it is possible, by calculation, to set off one against another and to ascertain (or, in practice, to forecast) whether a particular mode of growing trees is profitable. In the 1960s any financial calculation commanded instant respect, regardless of whether the data were sound or the methods meaningful. As late as the 1970s the politics of forestry were dominated by Victorian ideas of cost-benefit analysis, which were still thought to provide the 'hard economic facts' on which to decide what to do with ancient woodland. Conservationists, far from challenging the calculations, continued to believe them after economists and foresters had lost their confidence.

Pursuant to those 'hard facts', about one-third of the ancient woodland of Britain was replanted, nearly always with conifers. To do this it was necessary to get rid of the trees that were already there and to prevent their regrowth from competing with the planted trees. The existing trees were dug out with bulldozers, felled, ring-barked or poisoned (usually in combination); even, in one moment of enthusiasm, 2,4,5-T was sprayed from a helicopter.[125] The ground vegetation might flourish for a few years, but after the conifers closed in, their dense evergreen shade should have made it impossible for anything to grow under them and should have reduced the original vegetation to remnants along rides. This is what was supposed to happen: what did happen is discussed in Chapter 11.

6

What woods now mean: a guide to field-work

Ancient banks will be rounded, and consolidated by centuries of drumming rain, and of baking sun.
They may be worn down, but they will not be crumbled by modern traffic, either two-wheeled or four-footed.

*   *   *

Where such banks are continuous, they will be slightly rambling in alignment, and their corners and turns will be gradual and rounded.
Ancient banks will be broad, as a general rule.

Heywood Sumner, The ancient earthworks of the New Forest (1917)

'If only these trees could speak' – but they do speak, if we listen

Methods of woodland archaeology are akin to those used in the study of churches and other standing buildings. Woods, like buildings, may have been in constant use for many centuries, and have accumulated natural changes and deliberate alterations.

With woods, as with buildings, only part of the evidence is primary, simple and direct. Detailed maps, and the absolute dates from counting the annual rings of living trees, go back (for woods) some 400 years. Most other evidence involves a greater or lesser amount of circumstantial interpretation of the kind usually employed by archaeologists. The objective is to investigate in what respects features such as earthworks and vegetation patterns are historically determined and can be used to construct chronologies. This may be based on written evidence: as for instance by comparing woods with a continuous documented history since the Middle Ages with others known to have originated in the eighteenth century. Or it may depend on internal evidence, particularly that provided by alterations: as when a wood contains earthworks of two types which intersect in such a way as to prove that one earthwork was made first. A combination of written and internal evidence may be called for with a wood which, though known to be medieval, partly overlies the ridge-and-furrow produced by ancient ploughing. Once a chronology has been established from woods which have a good historical record or contain clear evidence of alteration, it can be applied to interpreting others which are not so favoured.

The woodland archaeologist should make simultaneous use of as many lines of inquiry as possible. An argument involving vegetation and earthworks is generally more convincing than one based on vegetation alone. Investigators who confine themselves to written evidence sooner or later run into the Scylla of pseudo-history; those confined to field evidence are caught by the Charybdis of circular argument. Even in the best-documented wood there is always something more to be learned from fieldwork.

Names of woods

In England every wood has a name, which may be as old as the names of the surrounding villages and hamlets. Wood-names often have the same characteristics of Anglo-Saxon and Norse language and grammar that we find in settlement-names, and show that the woods themselves were already separated and named in that distant period when such forms were in common use. Wayland Wood, Norfolk, anciently *Wanelund*, is an example of the Old Norse *lúndr*, a grove or sacred grove;[126] any wood called Lound or Lownde is likely to go back to Viking times. A wood now called The Frith or Free Wood or Beare Wood is almost certain to be pre-Conquest, from Anglo-Saxon *fyrhþ* or *bearu*. The Old English *lēah* can mean a wood as a clearing, and has given rise to some of the many woods called Hayley (hedge *lēah*), Brockley (badger *lēah*), Smilley (small or narrow *lēah*), Trundley (circular *lēah*), etc.; but let us beware of other woods named after nearby settlements derived from *lēah* meaning 'clearing'. Anglo-Saxon case-endings, dating from when English was an inflected language like Latin, are preserved in the old spelling of Felshamhall Wood (Fig. 17b). *Ffelshamhalle* is, as its name implies, the wood 'at the Felsham corner' (*hale*, dative case of *halh*, 'corner') – the corner nearest Felsham of Bradfield St George parish.

The Norman-French language is represented by *coppice*, otherwise spelt *copse*, which implies a particular form of management. The synonym *tailz*, now sometimes turned into Taylor's Wood, appears in modern French as *taillis*, 'underwood'.The Anglo-Saxon equivalent is *hrīs*, as in Royce or Rice Wood. The later English word is *spring*, commonly used of any coppice-wood. A coppice compartment within a wood can be called a *fell, sale, cant* or *hag*. *Hurst* can mean any isolated wood, especially one on a hill (e.g. Hearse Wood, formerly Herstwood, in Great Saxham, west Suffolk), but is sometimes applied to series of defined copses or springs attached to parks or commons, like the 'hursts' in Sutton Coldfield Park, Warwickshire. A wood that was itself common land gives rise to the name Manwood or Mangrove.

Any wood called Monk Wood, Prior's Wood or Nuns' Wood must date from before 1536. A Mincing Wood must be pre-Conquest, for it preserves the Anglo-Saxon word *mynecen*, 'nun'.

Apart from *Spinney* (a wood of thorns) and *Carr* (a wood of alders) early wood-names seldom tell us much about the composition of woods. A wood consisting of a particular tree is implied by the Anglo-Saxon ending *-ett*; but names like *Birchet* and *Oket* are much less common than their French equivalents *Biolet* and *Chesnaye* or the German *Birchat* and *Eichat*.

Many woods are named after the village, hamlet or farm to which they belong. For example the name of Man Hall, a manor in Little Chesterford, Essex, has been transmuted into *Emanuel* Wood which overlies its remains. Some woods, now called after parishes, had names of their own in the middle ages: Hinderclay Wood and Pakenham Wood, W. Suffolk, used to be called *Stanberowe* and *Leinðenhale*. Where woods are numerous they tend to be named after their owners or tenants, but such names are not kept up to date; Peverel's Wood near Saffron Walden, Essex, is still called after a family last heard of in the parish in Domesday Book.

Wood-names that indicate recent origin include Plantation (or Plantin), Cover, Jubilee Wood, Furze (or Firs) Wood, and Hundred Acre Wood (an ancient wood of that size would have had a more distinctive name). Occasionally these are re-namings of ancient woods.

A few wood-names are known in the extinct Cornish language. Merthen Wood, a great wood on the Helford River, was once regarded as three woods called Coesenys (Island Wood), Coose-Carmynowe and Cosabnack. Welsh wood-names are disappointing, being too often named after adjoining farms. An exception is Coed Ffyddlwn, 'Beeches-grove Wood', near Abergavenny, one of the most remarkable ancient mountain beechwoods in Britain. It is a sad consequence of Scots and Irish woodland history that very few woods survive with Gaelic names. Occasionally the wood survives but not the name: for example Portlaw Wood (Co. Waterford) is part of the Great Wood of Kilconish.

I   A Suffolk limewood, with big stools of pry (small-leaved lime) underwood of 30–40 years' growth since last felled. The smaller stools in the foreground, also of pry, were cut last season and have since made one year's growth. Groton Wood. *April 1974*

II   Coppicing in progress. Note the stacks of cut wood (here mainly ash, hazel and alder) awaiting transport; the standing underwood in the background; and the scatter of timber trees, which are mainly oaks and vary in age, size and branching pattern. This scene has changed very little since at least the thirteenth century. Felshamhall Wood, Suffolk. *January 1976*

III   A moderately large ash stool immediately after felling. It has been so treated every ten years or so throughout its life. Felshamhall Wood, Suffolk. *W. H. Palmer, 1971*

IV   Underwood in the first summer after cutting, showing two months' regrowth of sallow and alder. Felshamhall Wood, Suffolk.
15 August 1986

V   Underwood of ash and lime (pry), five years' growth. The timber trees, exceptionally, are pry also. Shrawley Wood, Worcs.
May 1985

VI   A giant ash stool, at least 800 years old. It is all one tree, which through centuries of cutting has grown into a great ring, with a hollow centre; it now bears about twenty stems around the margin. Paynsden Wood, Quendon, N.W. Essex. *May 1971*

VII   Medieval (or earlier) woodbank exposed by felling the underwood. Note the width, rounded profile and external ditch. Felshamhall Wood, Suffolk. *March 1973*

VIII   Oxlip, a plant of ancient woodland, which has been stimulated hugely to flower by coppicing. Hayley Wood, Cambs. *April 1987*

IX *Above:* Wattle-work filling a panel in a medieval timber-framed house. The rods, of about seven years' growth, are of lime (pry), and have had their bark removed for use as fibre. Lavenham, Suffolk. *May 1988*

X *Left:* A big oak. This tree is exceptionally large and old for an oak in a wood: it is middle-aged (about 260 years old). In the fourteenth century this would have been an outsize, and specially valuable, tree.

XIX   Not a wood, but a field full of pollard oaks. Fields with many trees are a speciality of the Breckland edge, and are differentiated from woodland on maps back to the sixteenth century. Risby, Suffolk. *April 1980*

XX   Pollard elms at Knapwell, Cambs. *May 1979*

XXI   The Tortworth Chestnut (Gloucestershire), already a famous ancient tree in 1704. *April 1977*

XXII   A wood attacked by fallow deer. The tree foliage ends abruptly at a browse-line 4 ft 1 in. (1·22 m) above ground. An overgrown ash–maple–hazel wood; ground cover sparse, because the deer have eaten the oxlips and other tasty plants. Hayley Wood, Cambs. *May 1984*

XXIII   Part of the parish of Long Melford, Suffolk. Typical Ancient Countryside with numerous large and small woods, irregular and often small fields, and scattered farms. The area shown measures about 1 × 1 mile; its historical development can be followed in the maps of Fig. 15. Most of the features shown are of medieval origin. A map of 1613 depicts the great wood to the left and the cluster of groves in the middle and top of the photograph almost as they are now, as well as the majority of the hedges. The groves differ in their vegetation to a remarkable degree, as can be seen to some extent in this picture. The park and groves at the bottom date mainly from the late seventeenth and early eighteenth centuries but incorporate earlier hedges and field trees. Recent changes, though not quite as severe as in much of Suffolk, have included the replacement of the great wood by a plantation and the destruction of some of the hedges. *Cambridge University Committee for Aerial Photography*

Maps and surveys

The medievals could, on occasion, measure the areas of woods with surprising accuracy, and therefore had it in their power to make accurate maps; but as far as I am aware the earliest maps to show the shapes of woods begin about 1580. These maps depict parishes or parts of parishes – occasionally single woods – at scales of 1:10,000 or larger. They should be sought, in the first instance, in county record offices. Maps of all periods vary from diagrammatic to highly accurate; late ones show no appreciable improvement on good early ones. The accuracy of any map can be checked by using features that survive in modern maps and aerial photographs.

The frontispiece shows part of a huge map of the parish of Earl's Colne, Essex, made at a scale of 1:4750 by Israel Amyce in 1598.[127] The wealth of detail is typical of some of the earliest reasonably accurate maps. Compare the outline of Chalkney Wood with the modern outline (Fig. 22a).

The art of making small-scale maps, at one inch to the mile (1:63,360) or smaller, developed much more slowly. Few county maps earlier than 1750 are of any use to the woodland historian – except for the tiny counties of Rutland and Middlesex, which are sometimes drawn on a large enough scale for individual woods to be shown. The big county maps, by cartographers such as Rocque, Chapman and Greenwood, of the period 1750–1820 often leave out known woods (especially those away from roads), and their wood outlines, when checked against contemporary large-scale maps, often prove to be wildly inaccurate. Successive maps of this type often copy one another.

The Ordnance Survey began work on England in 1795. The survey drawings – the originals are in the British Library – often contain details which are not on the published maps, although the field boundaries are fictitious. Early Ordnance Survey maps share the deficiencies of their private contemporaries, but there was a rapid improvement after 1820. The large-scale Ordnance Survey, at scales of 6 and 25 inches to the mile, began in Ireland in 1824 and did not finish Great Britain until the 1880s. These wonderful maps, which purport to show every hedgerow tree, are the zenith of cartography in the British Isles. They should form the base for any study of modern woodland topography. Recent Ordnance Survey maps cannot compare in detail or accuracy with those of a century ago.

Verbal surveys, which go back well into the middle ages, often define the location as well as the names and sizes of woods. The perambulation of Hatfield Forest in 1298, for instance, mentions only one wood, Rowewode, and there is still a Row Wood at precisely that

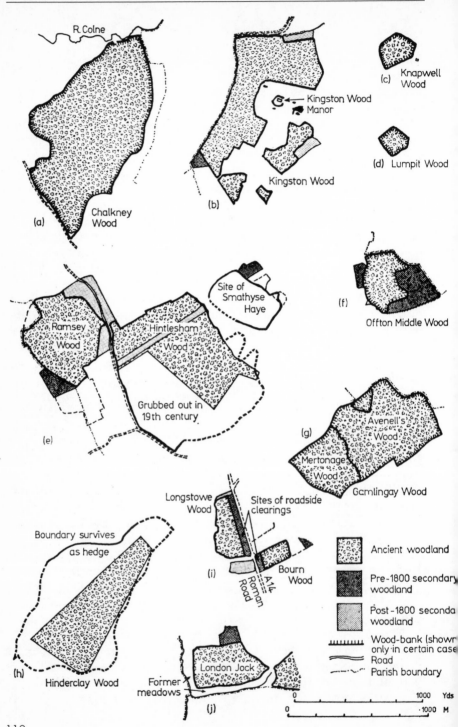

(a) Chalkney Wood — R. Colne

(b) Kingston Wood — Kingston Wood Manor

(c) Knapwell Wood

(d) Lumpit Wood

(e) Ramsey Wood — Hintlesham Wood — Site of Smathyse Haye — Grubbed out in 19th century

(f) Offton Middle Wood

(g) Avenell's Wood — Mertonage Wood — Gamlingay Wood

(h) Hinderclay Wood — Boundary survives as hedge

(i) Longstowe Wood — Sites of roadside clearings — Bourn Wood — Roman Road — A14

(j) London Jock — Former meadows

Ancient woodland

Pre-1800 secondary woodland

Post-1800 secondary woodland

Wood-bank (shown only in certain case

Road

Parish boundary

0   1000   Yds

0   1000   M

point on the boundary.[132] Abuttal surveys, which list each field on a farm giving the acreage and what it adjoins on the north, south, east and west, enable us to ascertain the positions of woods in relation to landmarks such as churches, rivers and parish boundaries. The best of these, such as the survey of Leaden Roding (Essex) in 1450,[133] are nearly as detailed as maps.

Early aerial photographs, sometimes going back to the 1920s, are by now a historical record. The most valuable is the great survey of much of Britain, flown by the Germans in World War II, and now in the United States National Archives in Washington.[134] These record the state of coppicing of hundreds of woods. It took our enemies to make, and our allies to preserve, a proper record of what was still, in many places, a medieval landscape.

Fig. 22. Medieval woods and later alterations. The original boundary of each wood, whether extant or surviving as a field boundary, is a thick line; a thick broken line shows an original boundary that hs disappeared altogether. No account has been taken of attempts at coniferization.
(a) Chalkney Wood, Earl's Colne, Essex. Sinuous outline unaltered since before 1598 (Frontispiece).[127]
(b) Kingston Wood, Cambridgeshire. Complex zigzag outline, almost unaltered since before map of 1721,[128] with moated manor-house (probably on site of an independent Anglo-Saxon settlement) in the middle.
(c) Knapwell Wood, Cambridgeshire, first recorded *c.* 1130, (d) Lumpit Wood in Glemsford, Suffolk, first recorded 1251: very small but complete medieval woods with great boundary banks and boundary pollards.
(e) A trio of woods at Hintlesham, Suffolk, with complex sinuous and zigzag outlines, mapped in 1595[129] and since altered both by addition and subtraction. The strip of secondary woodland across Hintlesham Wood marks a 'prospect avenue' cut through it in the landscaping period.
(f) Middle Wood in Offton, Suffolk. Although there is no early map, the woodbanks strongly suggest two additions to the original very sinuous outline. It was called 'middelwode' *c.* 1300, but seems even then to have been the only substantial wood left in the parish.
(g) Gamlingay Wood, Cambridgeshire. Unaltered since map of 1601.[130] From Anglo-Saxon times there were two manors in the parish, with the wood divided between them; the dividing earthwork still exists, but has had no function since the manors were amalgamated in 1599.
(h) Hinderclay Wood, Suffolk. A medieval wood reduced to a straight-edged shape by encroachments; eighteenth- and nineteenth-century maps show the original boundary.
(i) Bourn and Longstowe Woods, Cambridgeshire, with trenches on either side of the Roman road between them.
(j) London Jock, a wood in Widdington, Essex, almost unaltered since map of 1635;[131] avoids streams on two sides.

111

Sites of medieval woods

Ancient woods are not distributed at random about the countryside. In East Anglia and Essex the majority are on high ground, usually on hilltops or broad ridges; they are often visible from one another. In N.E. England they are in ravines and on steep valley sides, especially if wet. In Wales they occur either high on valley sides, just below the boundary of the moor, or on less steep ground which is irrigated by springs. In Ireland they are often on patches of specially rocky terrain.

Woods tend to survive, not so much on sites that are good for growing trees, as on sites that are bad for anything else – according to medieval or earlier ideas of land capability. No ancient woods are to be found on river terraces, fens or flood-plains, all of which were much too valuable as meadow. Woods survive on small tracts of land that were too steep, wet, rocky or infertile to cultivate. (In East Anglia it is the hilltops that are wet.) *Large* tracts of poor land tended to become moor or heath.

Ancient woods tend (with many exceptions) to be in remote places, on parish boundaries and often in the farthest corners of parishes. They usually occur away from villages, but often have single houses attached. These may be mere woodwards' cottages, but sometimes there is a substantial moat: the 'moat-in-a-wood' is a definite type of medieval settlement in Eastern England (Fig. 22b).

Medieval woods seldom abut on rivers or large streams (unless very steep-to), or on main roads. Streams are avoided (Fig. 22j) because well-watered land was so valuable that even the narrowest strip of it was worth making into meadow. Main roads are avoided because, in an age of crime, landowners were encouraged to remove trees, bushes and earthworks from alongside roads which might give cover to highwaymen. In 1284 a statute laid down that underwood and wood-banks be removed for a distance of 200 feet from main roads.[135] A number of such clearings, called **trenches**, still survive, for example along the A1 north of Huntingdon and along the main roads into Canterbury. In Bourn and Longstowe Woods (Cambs) a murder was committed on the A14 in *c.* 1280; trenches were made in the hope of preventing a repetition;[136] the woods have again encroached on the road but the thirteenth-century woodbanks remain (Fig. 22i). Edward I, on his campaigns in Wales, took 1800 woodmen to cut down woods alongside main roads;[137] I have found a possible survival of such a trench at Coed Allt-y-rhiw north of Bridgend, Glamorgan. The presence of a trench proves that both the road and the wood are older than 1300, but the converse does not hold: Dunmow High Wood

(Essex), a well-documented medieval coppice, comes right up to a main Roman road with no trace of a clearing.

Shapes of woods

When investigating an unknown wood one begins by walking the boundary. This at once gives an impression of the age of the wood and of any alterations which there may have been.

The earliest maps show beyond doubt that many wood outlines were exactly the same (to within a few feet) 400 years ago as they are now. Changes, if any, have involved adding or subtracting definite areas. Almost every wood on an early map, if it survives at all, has retained at least part of its ancient boundary. Many a wood has not changed at any point since the sixteenth century. Where a wood has increased in size, the old boundary nearly always survives as an internal earthwork. Where part of the wood has been grubbed out, the old boundary often remains as a hedge or a soil mark running across fields (Fig. 22h).

Ancient wood boundaries – those shown on the earliest maps, or specified in medieval documents – have characteristically irregular outlines of two types (Fig. 22a, b). Some are **sinuous**: the boundary straggles across country in a series of curves, changing direction every few yards. Some are *zigzag*, with abrupt corners at rather longer intervals. With practice, these outlines can be used to pick out possible ancient woods on the 1:25,000 map.

These outlines are part of the beauty of woodland in the landscape, but are definitely not the product of the æsthetic movement. Many of them are in places where they cannot be seen. Although landscape designers sometimes imitated such shapes when setting out groves in parks, eighteenth- and nineteenth-century wood boundaries run characteristically in straight lines, or less often in formal circles, ovals and kidney-shapes.

Early wood-margins tend to avoid streams and other natural features, and seldom pay regard to drainage considerations. They date from an age when the landscape was hewn out on the ground rather than in the draughtsman's office, and when the countryman saw no purpose in straight lines. In Planned Countryside the outlines of medieval woods sit awkwardly among the straight-edged fields that enclosure commissioners had to fit in round them. In Ancient Country-side wood outlines are often even more erratic than the boundaries of the adjoining field.

Many wood outlines go back to a very early period. Sinuous outlines may have been determined by having to pass round individual big trees, for instance if a tract of wildwood was being divided into wood-pasture and coppice-wood. Zigzag outlines may result from successive small intakes of farmland. A re-entrant angle may represent the point at which some Anglo-Saxon laid down his twybill after a year's assarting, never to return because of pestilence or the Danes.

A perfectly straight edge usually means a wood boundary later than 1700. There are a few exceptions: in Dodnash Wood, E. Suffolk, the straight edges appear on a map of 1634[138] and have earthworks of medieval type. An intermediate type of outline, with broad regular curves lacking the small-scale irregularities, may date from the sixteenth or seventeenth centuries.

Boundary earthworks

Nearly all woods more than 100 years old have some kind of earthwork round the edge. Typically this consists of a bank and ditch, the bank being on the *wood* side. As we have seen, coppice-woods have had boundary earthworks since the Anglo-Saxon period. They exist in several types, whose interrelations can be established from wood boundaries known from written evidence to be of different dates, from boundaries left behind by the enlargement of a wood, and from the intersections of banks of different dates.

Medieval wood boundaries have relatively massive banks and ditches – at least 25 feet in total width – partaking of the characteristics of ancient earthworks quoted at the head of the chapter. (The unusually substantial bank around Norsey Wood, Billericay (Essex), even has a name, The Deerbank.) Profiles vary (Fig. 23): the normal shape is rounded, but there is a broad flat type which seems to go with woods attached to early deer-parks. Woodbanks follow all the sinuosities and zigzags of the boundary. This is why even complex outlines are so stable, for any straightening-out involves a lot of earth-moving to efface the bank. Where a bank turns a sharp corner there is a *corner mound* formed by the earth cast up from both sides of the ditch.

Occasionally a known early wood margin has only a ditch, for example the wood mysteriously called Canfield Hart in Great Canfield, Essex. Dr Richard Gulliver finds that ancient woods in the Vale of York usually lack woodbanks.[138a] Sometimes the bank is reversed, which indicates that the boundary has once been that of a park (p. 161, Fig. 23d).

Woodbanks formed in later periods are progressively less massive

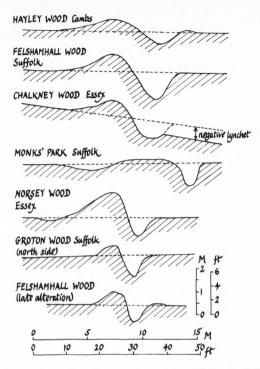

Fig. 23. Measured profiles of woodbanks. Hayley and Felshamhall Woods: medieval boundaries on level ground. Chalkney: medieval boundary on a slope. Monks' Park: one type of deer-park boundary, with remains of internal ditch. Norsey: derived from park boundary. Groton and Felshamhall: boundaries created by seventeenth- or eighteenth-century encroachment on medieval woods. The wood side of each boundary is on the left. The vertical scale is exaggerated twofold.

and more acute in profile. They continued to be made into the nineteenth century – by which time the typical wood-margin, like the field hedges of that period, is perfectly straight, with a small ditch and bank of triangular profile bearing a single row of hawthorns.

Outlines and earthworks can be used to reconstruct the history of alterations to a wood for which there is no precise documentary evidence. Fig. 22f shows an embanked wood of very irregular shape inside later additions; a document of 1628 suggests that the large eastern addition to the wood had already taken place. Multiple banks and ditches around a wood tell of successive encroachments of the wood on adjoining land, particularly roads. Road-narrowing, politely called 'purpresture on the highway', is a time-honoured, and still by no means obsolete, method of winning an extra strip of land. In one Suffolk wood I have counted five successively diminishing parallel

115

banks between the wood and what is left of the lane alongside!

Where a wood abuts on arable land there is often a change of ground level – a *lynchet* caused by ploughing and sheet-erosion moving earth towards, or away from, the boundary. It is most often seen on sloping ground on light soil, and is more pronounced the older the wood boundary. Usually we have a 'negative lynchet' where soil has been moved away from the wood (Fig. 23c). Where a field lies up-slope from a wood we may get a 'positive lynchet' of soil accumulated against the woodbank.

Woodbanks extend at least from Scotland to Normandy and from East Anglia to Ireland. In stone-wall country they may be replaced or supplemented by walls, but often with evidence that the bank came first. Cheddar Wood (Somerset), for example, has a woodbank revetted with a stone wall (and now left behind by expansion of the wood); the work has been left unfinished in such a way as to prove that the wall was added to an existing bank. In South Wales I sometimes find that the moor-wall (the boundary between moorland above and woodland or farmland below) runs through the wood; this appears to mean that the wood has encroached on to the moor, though so long ago that the wall no longer marks any obvious change in the wood.

Woodbanks are a more eloquent record than any document of the value of woods in the middle ages. Woodland was precious, and people spent thousands of man-hours on defining and defending it. The perimeter bank round a big wood might seem a reasonable investment, but equally massive banks surround small woods and fractions of woods – taking up, on occasion, as much as one-sixth of the entire area of the wood.

Internal woodbanks

Woods have internal banks. Some of these, as we have seen, may be from much earlier periods; others record the division between two contiguous woods, or the subdivision of a wood between owners. A typical example is Eversden Wood, west Cambridgeshire, in which we can trace three stages of subdivision (Fig. 24). The wood (of 123 acres) was first divided, at some time before the Norman Conquest, between

Fig. 24. Eversden Wood, Cambridgeshire. (a) Wood as it is now, showing internal woodbanks, pollards, ridge-and-furrow, moats, ponds and the non-conforming system of modern rides. The north corner has been grubbed out. (b) Interpretation using documents. The seventeenth-century names of the Great Eversden sub-woods are shown in capitals; the later names in lower-case.

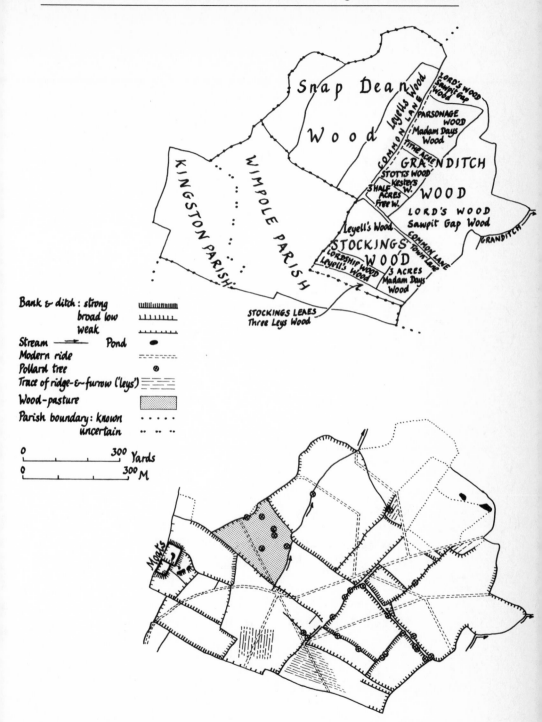

Bank & ditch: strong
                 broad low
                 weak
Stream ——→   Pond
Modern ride
Pollard tree
Trace of ridge-&-furrow ('leys')
Wood-pasture
Parish boundary: known
                  uncertain

0   300 Yards
0   300 M

the parishes of Great Eversden, Wimpole and Kingston. Next the Eversden share was subdivided into three parts separated by lanes, regarded as separate woods and named Snap Dean, Granditch and Stockings Woods. These were then further divided into thirteen sub-woods, named mainly after their owners ('Madam Day' etc.). Similar subdivisions happened in Wimpole and Kingston. Some of the sub-woods were grubbed out for a while and ploughed, forming ridge-and-furrow; one had a double moat with a house; pollard trees in another indicate a wood-pasture period. All the boundaries are marked by massive woodbanks with old pollard trees on them. The earliest relevant document, the Eversden glebe terrier of 1638, indicates that the period of greatest subdivision was then past and the cultivated areas had reverted to woodland. By the mid-nineteenth century the whole wood was again in one ownership, and a new grid of rides was made ignoring the old divisions.[139]

Woodbanks are the main evidence for what seems to have been a general social progression. The very big estates of the Anglo-Saxon period were divided into manors and 'subinfeudated' into sub-manors and split into single farms. At each stage the wood was subdivided as well as the land. The greatest subdivision seems to have been at, or just after, the time of the Black Death. After this a slow succession of takeovers built up the big estates again and re-amalgamated the woods. In the woods of S.E. Essex the consolidation was begun by the monasteries and is still not quite complete.[140] At Eversden there are a few documents to give us some names and dates, but even without them we could work out most of the story from the archaeology.

Subinfeudation did not happen everywhere. The three woods of Hayley, Gamlingay and Eversden are of much the same size and close together. Little Gransden always remained in one unit: there are no division-banks in Hayley Wood. Gamlingay Wood has one internal bank; the estate was divided in two before the Conquest and reunited in 1599. Eversden Wood was divided into at least twenty parts.

Occasionally woodbanks come to an end in the middle of a wood; this reminds us that making them was very hard work, and was sometimes left unfinished.

Ponds, pits and dells

There are, or were, well over a million ponds and depressions in England and Wales;[141] there has been little systematic study of their origin. Certain well-defined kinds of dug pit – gravel-pits, brick-pits, marl-pits, bell-pits or drifts (for coal), ochre-pits – sometimes happen to occur in woodland. But ancient woods are full of hollows for which there is no such artificial explanation. In East Anglia, which is particularly rich in ponds and dells, they are much more numerous per square mile in ancient woodland than in the rest of the landscape.*

Woodland ponds challenge our British presumption that the original state of the land surface was smooth and that ponds and dells have been made by people digging. On the contrary, the land surface, as the glaciers left it, may well have been as full of depressions (made, for example, by masses of melting ice) as New England is today. A concentration of such hollows may be one of the obstacles to cultivation that caused particular sites to be set aside as woodland. Hollows are less noticeable outside woods; the shallower ones have been ploughed out, and the deeper ones are indistinguishable from other kinds of field pond.

Anyone finding a pond or dell should ask 'What has happened to the contents?' If a pond or pit was deliberately dug because it was wanted, there will be a corresponding mound of spoil somewhere near at hand. (A bomb-crater is a neatly circular hole, with the displaced soil forming a mound all round, and with no trees older than 1915.) Where a pit was made by digging out some mineral, we have to ask what the mineral was, how the digger knew it was there, and where are the ramp and track by which he took it away. Natural depressions do not have corresponding banks† – there never were any contents – and their rounded contours contrast with the sharp edges of all but the oldest artefacts. With few exceptions they are older than any artificial earthwork. A pond that cuts through ridge-and-furrow is unlikely to be natural.

Other surface features in woods

We do not plough woods and seldom dig in them. They tend to preserve all the earthworks and other surface features that there have been on the site since it became a wood. Some of these features are related to the wood as such, others to what may have been happening before it became a wood. Faint earthworks are best looked for in February, when the ground vegetation has died down and worms have eaten the more palatable fallen leaves.

---

* The silt of woodland ponds may contain a pollen record, and should not be dug out.
† Except for the crater-like hollows called *pingos*, which are unlikely to be in ancient woodland.

Woods often contain small ditches. The little branched ones with no banks, meandering among the trees, may be natural, the ultimate twigs of the branching system of rivers and streams that covers the country. Artificial drains are straighter, incorporating earlier earth-works and ponds which serve as sumps. Their occurrence is haphazard, and they appear to be mostly post-1750.*

Sawpits and charcoal-pits were usually temporary and filled in after use. Where they survive, they should be looked for where they would not fill with water. Sawpits should be rectangular, like a churchyard grave; charcoal-pits should be round. Charcoal-*hearths* (for charking wood in an earth-covered stack above ground) should be looked for in woods with industrial histories. A hearth is a circular platform, about 30 feet across, scooped into a hillside. Under the leaf-mould will be found pieces of charcoal, from which the species of wood can be identified using a microscope.

Almost any kind of non-woodland earthwork can be found in what is now a wood: hillforts (especially along the Welsh Border), linear defensive ditches, barrows, 'Celtic' fields, trackways and Roman roads, castles, deserted villages, moats and hedgebanks. The connection may be accidental, but often the earthwork may have brought the wood into existence by making a bit of land uncultivable. For example, a remarkable wood-pasture, with giant pollard oaks, has developed on the Iron Age hillfort of Wallbury near Bishop's Stortford. Many small groves in arable country are nineteenth-century pheasant-cover plantations; but some of them contain barrows or moats. Trees on a moat, as we shall see, may be an integral part of its history.

Some features are compatible with pre-existing woodland. The ancient mine-workings of the Forests of Dean and Wyre, and the 'hammer-ponds' and industrial reservoirs made by damming valleys in the Weald and Black Country, may often have been formed inside existing woods. But many types of 'non-woodland' earthwork can only have arisen on open land. When they occur in a wood they prove that the site is secondary woodland, and set a limit to its possible age. *Ridge-and-furrow* is the round-topped parallel undulations which result from long-continued ploughing. Classic ridge-and-furrow was made by ploughing strips in medieval open-fields;[142] the ridges are typically 11 yards wide by 220 yards long (but with some variation), and gently curving, often with a 'reversed-S' double curve. Where the ends of the ridges abutted on a wood there is an intervening headland

---

* Most farm crops, originating as they do from steppes, will not grow without good drainage; from time to time some farmers have supposed that drainage must be good for native trees too.

on which the plough was turned. Ridge-and-furrow is widespread, but not universal, in former open-field districts. It was also imitated in enclosed fields, sometimes as late as the nineteenth century; late examples tend to be narrow and straighter. If correctly identified, it proves secondary woodland, but its absence does not prove that a wood is primary.

Terraces on hillsides may be *strip-lynchets*, made by prehistoric to medieval cultivation. But there are also terrace-like structures produced by landslips, where part of a hillside suddenly gives way, rotates and comes to rest in a tilted position (Fig. 25). Landslip terraces are crescentic, with concave profiles; they often slope back into the hillside. Slopes liable to slip tend to be avoided by farmers and left as woodland. There are magnificent examples in the Ironbridge Gorge, Shropshire, but I have seen them in many places where there are steep slopes with strata of clay lubricated by springs.

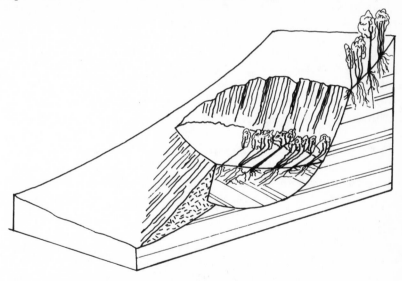

Fig. 25. The terrace produced by a rotational landslip.

The soils of ancient woods are usually more complex than those of the surrounding fields. The original soil profile has been less affected by erosion than in the cultivated landscape, and has not been mixed by ploughing. Woodland soils tend not to be derived from the underlying bedrock, but to preserve thin surface layers of materials such as *loess* – a fine silty material deposited by great prehistoric dust-storms. The inverse of woodland ponds are *sand-lenses* – pockets of sandy material often abruptly different from the surrounding clay. Woodland soils,

121

especially acid soils, may have much to say about the history of woodland versus heath: a heathland episode may create an iron pan in the soil which persists even if the site becomes woodland. Acid soils also preserve pollen.[16]

The historical meaning of plants and animals

Every wood is a complex series of communities of plants and animals. Such communities are constituted, for instance, by the trees and shrubs; the flowering-plants and ferns growing on the ground; the birds and other larger animals; the mosses and lichens growing on trees; and the armies of fungi and creeping things which live off rotting logs and leaves. These interdependent plants and animals reflect the history of the site to varying degrees.

The simplest historical link results from *continuity*. A new wood does not suddenly acquire all the woodland flora and fauna. Some get there within the first few years; others, incapable of travelling long distances or of getting started at all, may still be missing centuries later. Conversely, heath converted to woodland does not suddenly lose all the characteristic heathland species. A second historical link depends on *management*, for instance on the effects of coppicing, pollarding or grazing. Historical links may also depend on *development* – the alteration of the habitat with time: for example the different development of soils under trees and in fields.

Not all organisms are useful as historical indicators. I shall deal chiefly with flowering-plants, including trees, which have been well studied and will mean something to the general reader. Others have studied insects, slugs, snails, spiders and mosses which go with old woodland, but only specialists will make much of these.[143] Lichens present a contrast to flowering-plants, which will be discussed under parks. Mobile creatures, such as most mammals and birds, should be able to settle down in any suitable habitat; their historical significance, if any, can only be indirect.

Woodland structure

The structure of a wood tells us what has gone on during the lifetime of the present trees. It can easily be appreciated by the amateur, who can recognize coppiced or planted trees without much botanical book-learning – although to understand the finer points is an art which grows with experience.

The shape of a tree that has been coppiced – a stool base with two or more main trunks – is normally unmistakeable in all coppiceable trees, except for hazel, woodland hawthorn and sallow which grow naturally into such a shape. Coppice structure is still perfectly plain in many woods last cut more than a century ago. The evidence still remains even if the wood has been 'singled' by cutting out all the poles but one on each stool. It is not equally common in all ancient woods. The stools can be destroyed (though seldom completely) by grazing, replanting or elm invasion. A few ancient woods never had a coppice structure. Occasionally one can confuse sparse coppice stools with casual regrowth from the stumps of timber trees. The first generation of oaks or beeches arising on heath or downland may branch at the base, especially if bitten when young, and can be mistaken for coppice stools.

Pollarding is not a normal woodland practice, but was done to create distinctive, long-lived trees as landmarks. Pollards and stubs are a regular feature of wood boundaries, both external and internal. Usually they are on earthworks, but sometimes a row of stubs ('cant-marks' in Kent) defines an otherwise unmarked internal boundary. Pollards which make no sense as boundary markers indicate an episode of either wood-pasture or trees standing in a field. Beeches have sometimes been planted as boundary markers where beech is not native (e.g. in Great Ridge wood west of Salisbury).

To decide whether a wood has been planted we first look for trees in rows, but these are not very easy to identify with certainty. A single tree-row may be due to chance alignment or to natural establishment along a ditch or ride-edge. Occasionally a regular pattern may be imposed on the vegetation by features such as ridge-and-furrow. Even air photographs are often misleading, and should not be trusted without confirmation. They may fail to show up tree-rows known to exist. Or they may give the optical illusion of rows that are not really there; this most easily happens with slightly oblique photographs taken in sunshine, when the shadows and the apparent tilt of the taller trees seem to line up into rows. The absence of rows does not prove that there has been no planting. Nor does their presence prove that the wood is *merely* a plantation: it may contain trees surviving from before the plantation or arising since.

A minimum limit to the age of a wood is normally given by the age of the oldest trees. Annual rings can sometimes be counted in dead trees, or in the stumps or abandoned branches of trees felled long ago. Much of the story of Hatfield Forest can still be read in the rings of oaks felled in 1924 and left lying. However, trees can be older than the wood in which they grow, as when a park or common, or a field with trees in it, turns into secondary woodland. These old trees are often pollards. Burnham Beeches (Bucks) is a good example.

In many woods the oldest trees are coppice stools. The age of the poles tells us when the stool was last coppiced; sometimes we can find the half-rotten stumps of the previous crop of poles, which tell us how long the last rotation was. The age of the stools themselves (pp. 14–15) is a guide to the minimum age of the wood. Hazel is less informative than other species. Giant stools indicate ancient woodland – in many woods in Wales, Scotland and Ireland they are the best evidence of age – but not every ancient wood has them. Stools seem usually to die through being overshadowed by timber trees. Woods such as Bradfield, in which underwood has normally predominated over timber, may have many big stools. In other woods the giant stools may have all but disappeared through nineteenth-century planting of oak for timber.

Stumps and dead trees may reveal much about the last two centuries. For instance, if a known ancient wood has a poorly-preserved coppice structure, this may be accounted for by the stumps of an unusual number of standard trees which once shaded the underwood. Dead trees, or trees showing recovery from damage, may record the effects of lightning, caterpillars or diseases. Or they may result from natural competition, as when oak is overtopped and gradually killed by beech or elm (p. 135).

Planted and wild trees

Planting covers a wide range of activities. At one extreme it may consist of burying acorns where they fall from the tree, giving them a slightly better chance than if they had remained on the surface. It is perhaps unimportant to distinguish a wood so treated from one managed by felling alone. At the other extreme planting may consist of grubbing out a wood and growing spruce on the site. How do we detect those forms of planting which, though significant, are not so drastic as to efface the earlier vegetation?

Non-naturalized trees such as horsechestnut, 'Norway' spruce, or 'commercial' poplars in a wood will always have been put there. With lime, the planted tree is nearly always the hybrid 'common' lime, not the native pry (p. 21). It is more difficult to determine the planting of native trees such as oak and ash, or to tell with naturalized species – e.g. sweet-chestnut, sycamore, and (in Scotland) beech – which are the planted trees and which are their children.

Oak, the most often planted native tree, consists of two species.

Until recent years pedunculate oak was preferred by planters to sessile, especially in Scotland. Not only planting, but the various other ways in which mankind has favoured oak down the centuries, such as allowing new woodland to form, tend to favour pedunculate oak more than sessile.

In Lowland England, where the oaks of most ancient woods are all pedunculate, they are nevertheless exceedingly variable. The trunk may be straight, curved or corkscrew; smooth or burred; the branches and twigs may be spreading or erect; the foliage even or clustered; the leaves may fall as early as October or as late as January; and occasionally there are such bizarre features as bright scarlet shoots in August. Most of these variations are known to have existed down the centuries. They appear to be due to heredity more than to the environment or age of the tree. These irregularities represent the natural variation of a wild species, maintained since prehistory. Oaks raised in nurseries, in contrast, tend to be all the same, the progeny of trees selected for modern (or what were once modern) ideas of timber quality. In a minority of ancient woods the oaks are clearly an intrusion: all of the same age, often mid-nineteenth century, all cast in the same genetic mould with straight trunks and an even, moderate amount of burr formation. Often they are in regular rows and set so close as to interfere badly with the underwood or with each other. Yet even in such woods we find the occasional deviant tree, older than the others, to show that the suppression of the wild oaks was not quite successful.

Similar variations can be used to distinguish wild populations of ash, hornbeam, lime etc. To visit the Bradfield Woods or Hatfield Forest is to realize that much of what one reads of the branch and twig architecture of trees is derived from 'perfect' specimens in plantations or arboreta: wild trees may look quite different.

Often more than one tree was planted. Where the oaks in a wood are nursery-type, an early large-scale Ordnance map may have conifer symbols to show pines or spruces that were planted with them. Often the conifers have disappeared by now, although careful search may find dead remains or the occasional survivor.

Kinds of ancient woodland

Every ancient wood is uniquely different from every other. Usually a wood does not consist of just one kind of tree, or of the same mixture of trees throughout. For example, Tarecroft Wood in Rivenhall, Essex, has patches of seven kinds of woodland within its 16 acres (Fig. 26). These variations, for the most part, are expressed in the underwood

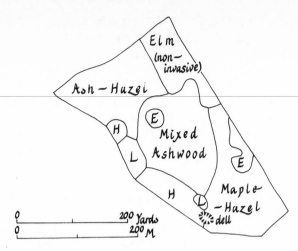

Fig. 26. Types of woodland in Tarecroft Wood, Rivenhall, Essex. E: invasive elm. H: hornbeam. L: lime (pry).

rather than the timber trees, which are usually oak. Underwood stools are long-lived, and it is they that make the difference between one sort of woodland and another. Standard trees come and go, and result from the arbitrary decision of woodmen which trees to treat as timber.

To classify British woodland is a very difficult task. Several attempts have been made, but it will be many years before all kinds of woodland have been described, and many more years before there is any agreement on what they mean. Are we to base our work on the trees, or the herbaceous vegetation, or do we try to include both? (There is a tendency for particular plants to grow under particular trees – but it is not a strong tendency, and an impossibly large number of combinations of trees and herbs exists.) The forthcoming woodland volume of the *National Vegetation Classification*, which places more emphasis on herbs, is a deeply learned work, three times the length of this whole book; yet it manages to define only 53 types of woodland, many of which are recent.[144]

To the historical ecologist the trees are the essential part of a wood, and the only part about which we have historical records. In Table 5 I try to give a manageable list of the tree communities so far recognized in British **ancient** woodland. The list of 54 types of woodland is not as long as it might be, for some types are demoted to variants; including all variants, rare tree communities yet to be identified, and distinctions between related communities yet to be drawn, the total is likely ultimately to reach 100. I cannot hope, within one chapter, to define them all. The purpose of the list is to give some indication of the richness of detail in native woodland, and of its geographic variation.

Table 5.   A summary of kinds of ancient woodland in Great Britain
Partly based on the work of G. F. Peterken. These are 'stand types', which very often do not comprise a whole wood. Many variants can be recognized of these listed.

LOWLAND PROVINCE

Wet ash–hazel wood	Abundant, especially E. Midlands and East Anglia (e.g. most of Hayley Wood); variants with aspen, hawthorn or blackthorn
Mixed hazel-wood	Abundant
Pure hazel-wood	Widespread, especially on more sandy soils
Wet maple–hazel woods	Frequent in East Anglia, Essex, E. Midlands
Dry ash-maple woods	Mendips; otherwise thinly scattered
Maple-woods	Widely scattered, chiefly in clayey Forests (e.g. Wychwood); frequent in N.W. Essex
Limestone ash–hazel woods with wych-elm	Widespread; also on chalk in S. England
Wet ashwoods with wych-elm	Scattered from Somerset to Yorkshire; outliers in Wales
Ashwood on acid soils	Suffolk and Essex, rare
Limewoods with maple	Chiefly Mendips, Lincs, East Anglia
Limewoods with ash	Local but widespread north of the Thames; also Mendips; outliers in Wales and Lake District
Pure limewoods	Local but widespread, e.g. Worcs, Norfolk
Oak-limewoods	Rare but widespread
Valley alderwoods	Widespread as ribbons along streams within other woodland types
Spring-fed alderwoods	Widely scattered; frequent in S. England
Plateau alderwoods	Rare (e.g. Bradfield Woods, Suffolk)
Acid beechwoods with sessile oak	S. England, rare
Ditto with pedunculate oak	Chilterns, S.E. and mid-south England
Dry oak–ash–beechwoods with lime and wych-elm	Mid-south England, rare; outlier in S.E. Wales

Damp oak–ash–beechwoods with wych-elm	Mid-south England
Oak–ash–beechwoods with maple	Cotswolds, Chilterns, mid-south England
Acid oak–ash–beechwoods	Mid-south England
Maple–hornbeam-woods	Mainly N.W. Essex
Hornbeam–ashwoods	E. Anglia, S.E. England
Hornbeam-woods with hazel	Mainly N.E. Suffolk and S.E. Norfolk
Pure hornbeam-woods	Commonest ancient woodland within 30 miles of London
Acid hornbeam-woods with sessile oak	Mainly Herts and S. Essex
Hornbeam-woods with sessile oak on chalk	Darenth Wood, Kent
Chestnut–limewoods	Essex, rare
Chestnut–hornbeam woods	S.E. Suffolk, E. Essex, S.E. England; abundant but often not ancient
Chestnut–oakwoods	Ditto, less common
Clay oakwood	Hatfield Forest (otherwise not ancient)
Lineage elmwoods	Mainly S. Suffolk, N. Essex
Invasive elmwood	Abundant in E. Anglia, Essex, E. Midlands; elsewhere widespread but of small extent; extends into Highland Zone

OAKWOOD PROVINCE (Highland England, Wales, south and middle Scotland and south Scottish Highlands)

Oakwoods (sessile oak)	Commonest type from Cornwall to Scotland; outliers in Lowland England and the Caledonian Province; also Ireland; variant with holly
Oakwoods (pedunculate oak)	Scattered from Devon to N. Scotland; occasional outliers in Lowland Zone
Oak-hazel wood	Widespread, but seldom abundant, from Cornwall to N. Scotland
Valley ash–hazel wood	Lower slopes, from Cornwall to N. Scotland; also in Ireland (rare)
Valley wych-elm woods	Fringes at bottoms of slopes, from Devon to Scotland; outliers in Caledonian Province; also Ireland (rare)
Limestone hazel-ash woods	Thinly scattered in N. England and Scotland; also Ireland
Limestone ash–wych-elm woods	Scattered from Devon to Scotland

Ash–wych-elm woods on heavy soils	Shropshire and Herefordshire
Limestone limewoods	Mainly Wye Valley and Lake District
Limewoods with sessile oak	Wales and Lake District, rare
Valley alderwoods	Abundant in Wales and Lake District, but often not ancient
Slope and springline alderwoods	Widespread but local
Bird-cherry woods	Scattered as ancient woodland; outlier in Norfolk
Acid ash–beechwoods with sessile oak	S.E. Wales; occasional outliers in S.E. England
Limestone ash–beechwoods	Wye Gorge
Mountain beechwoods	Confined to S.E. Wales

CALEDONIAN PROVINCE (middle and western Scottish Highlands)

Pinewoods with birch	Throughout province
Pinewoods with oak	Eastern, rare
Birchwoods	Widespread, often not ancient
Hazel–birchwoods	Scattered in north and east of province

Most variation is natural. The geographical distribution of many woodland types is exactly related to the provinces of the prehistoric wildwood (Fig. 8). It is often possible to relate a particular woodland type to some aspect of soil variation: for example, alder goes with springs, maple with clay. Where ancient woodland lies on ridge-and-furrow, the ridges are often maple–hazel and the furrows ash–hazel. Some changes from one type to another within the same wood are gradual, others abrupt; either kind of change is irregular, eschews straight lines, and disregards rides and ownerships.

Artificial variation, due to the destruction of natural underwood and the successful planting of blocks of different trees, is obvious where it occurs. The boundaries are usually abrupt and straight, coinciding with rides, fences and ownership boundaries. The planted trees may be genetically distinct, or of the wrong species for the soils or geography. Hornbeam is the common tree of ancient woods in all ownerships in a well-defined region around London, and in a second well-defined region in East Anglia. Outside these regions it is very rare in ancient woods. However, hornbeam is to be found in certain people's *plantations* all over England. Why anyone should plant hornbeam is a mystery, but there was a fashion for it in the early nineteenth

129

century, which is quite unrelated to the tree's occurrence in ancient woods.

Many types of woodland have their own separate histories. Lime-woods are an example. Lime (pry) is well-documented: people took notice of it because it produced bast for fibre. It was also a tree of delight and romance. From being the commonest tree of the wildwood of Lowland England, lime has shrunk to being still the commonest tree of *ancient* woods in certain small and sharply-defined areas of England, such as in Suffolk and Essex (Fig. 10), or in Shrawley Wood (Worcs) and its neighbours. From most of England it is totally absent. Why this should be so is a mystery, but it is known that lime retreated mostly before the Anglo-Saxon period and has not changed much in the last thousand years. Chalkney Wood, one of the Essex limewoods, is well documented in an account-book of 1603–12.[145] Parts of the wood consisted entirely of 'prye'; parts were of pry and other trees including ash and hornbeam; parts contained no pry at all. This is just how pry is distributed in Chalkney now; it is a gregarious tree and occurs as patches of pure limewood rather than mixed with other species. Lime appears, as we have seen, in place-names, including a number around Shrawley. I have found the underwood – with bast duly removed – in a medieval house in Lavenham (Plate IX). Evidence for historic lime comes from all the possible directions, and most of it is exactly congruent with the behaviour of the tree today.

Although woodland types are often stable, they are not always static. Much happened unrecorded in prehistory and the early historic period. There can be little doubt that much of what is now hornbeam-wood, beechwood and chestnut-wood was originally limewood. One of the best historic chestnut-woods is Stour Wood near Harwich (belonging to the Woodland Trust), yet this still has a few surviving lime stools.

Elm, birch and ash have increased. The elms we shall deal with later. Birch had its heyday in the early post-glacial period. In later prehistory it was squeezed out by more competitive and longer-lived trees. In the last hundred years it has returned on a large scale. This probably began with secondary woodland on heaths, fens and derelict land. Birch colonizes such places and produces wind-blown fruits which drift into ancient woods. Traditional woodmanship might not have favoured birch, but it has been helped by the fashions for growing abnormally large numbers of oaks and then felling them, and later for planting conifers which often die. Both practices damage the underwood and make room for birch, which is now increasing even on clay soils on which it was once thought incapable of growing. Ash has recently increased in many woods from Shropshire to Somerset and Huntingdonshire. In the Mendip 'ashwoods', for example, there are some ancient ash stools, but most of the ashes are no older than the last coppicing but one. The woods are really hazel-woods and limewoods now turning into ashwoods. The change began at different dates, and there is no obvious change in management to account for it. Woods have a life of their own, and we should take warning not to guess at facile explanations of similar changes in prehistory.

E. W. Jones and G. F. Peterken have kept watch on marked plots in Lady Park Wood, in the Wye gorge, since 1945. The wood was last cut partly in 1943 and partly in 1902. In the 1970s there were quite big changes. Beech, which had been increasing in dominance, was set back by drought, windblow and the crumbling of cliffs. Much elm was killed by Elm Disease. It is expected that ash and perhaps lime will increase in consequence.[146] However, this wood seems to be unusually unstable, both from its topography and from having so much beech, a 'catastrophist' tree which tends to come and go in response to unusual extremes of weather. Madingley Wood, Cambridgeshire, in which D. E. Coombe has been taking fixed-point photographs since 1951, has changed much less. A few overtopped maples have disappeared, and the occasional big ash has collapsed, but the general character of the wood – maple–hazel invaded by elm – is unchanged. My own observations suggest that long-uncoppiced woods in Eastern England behave like Madingley Wood more often than like Lady Park.

Floras of ancient and recent woodland

It is observed that woods with a long history, and especially ancient coppices, often have a richer flora than recently established woodland, and contain certain characteristic plants which the latter lacks. Continuity, management and development all contribute to the difference. An ancient wood will either have inherited species from the wildwood, or – if secondary – will have had sufficient time to acquire all but the least mobile plants. A recent wood will have acquired only those plants which readily colonize new sites, or which survive from the previous land-use.

The plant communities of an ancient wood will have had perhaps a thousand years in which to come to terms with management, often with the mixed-coppice practice which provides a sequence of habitats favouring a rich and complex flora. The continual cycle of felling and regrowth provides homes for plants with varying requirements for shade; the mixture of tree species ensures that some areas, for instance under ash trees, will always be suitable for species that cannot stand heavy shade. In recent woodland, or plantation, all parts tend to be evenly and often densely shaded. There are also soil differences. A friend of mine who tried, as an experiment, to plant an imitation of an ancient wood found that he could get the trees to grow, but failed with the herbaceous plants. The site, having been a field, was too fertile for a wood: there was no way to prevent nettles and cow-parsley from smothering the woodland herbs.

I shall resist the temptation to draw up a rule of thumb for woods like the well-known 'one shrub species per century' for hedges. A wood acquires plants faster and less evenly than a hedge. The plant list for a wood is liable to be disturbed by (for example) soil variation, neglect or continuance of coppicing, presence of woodland grassland on rides etc., and by how long one spends looking for them. Poolthorn Covert in N. Lincolnshire, dating from 1797, had a much richer flora[147] – though not in plants specific to woodland – than the hursts of Sutton Coldfield Park, Warwickshire.

Individual species characterize woods with particular types of history. Let us examine a well-known example, the Oxlip, *Primula elatior* (not to be confused with the 'false' oxlip, a hybrid between primrose and cowslip). This is confined in Britain to a well-defined area in Cambridgeshire, Suffolk and Essex. Within this area oxlip occurs in practically every wood known on documentary or topographical grounds to be ancient. It often grows in great abundance, but is hardly ever to be found outside such woods. In several places this plant has spread into secondary woodland adjoining a primary wood; observations at Hayley Wood indicate that it does so at the rate of some 4 feet a year. There are many secondary woods, some of them more than 350 years old, that fail to contain it. Oxlip is extremely rare in hedges; in Hayley Wood there used to be 4 million oxlip plants, yet not one has been found in the hedges abutting on the wood, some of which were already 'antient' in the early seventeenth century.[148]

Other plants behaving as oxlip does, over a wide geographical area, include woodland hawthorn, service, herb Paris and lily-of-the-valley. Small-leaved lime, a living link with Mesolithic wildwood, is strongly associated with ancient woodland and seldom grows in hedges. (One very occasionally meets a hedge of solid lime – there is a famous example in Shelley, Suffolk – but then finds that the hedge is the 'ghost' edge of a grubbed-out wood.) David Allen points out that ancient woods often have special kinds of bramble (for those of us who can identify them).

From a careful study of the Lincolnshire flora G. F. Peterken has identified 50 plants more or less confined to primary woodland, including such a common species as wood anemone.[149] Such plants now find difficulty in colonizing new sites, but can survive indefinitely in existing sites. Among possible reasons may be mentioned climatic changes which prevent them from setting good seed; changes in woodland structure; and the extinction of animals which once dispersed the seed. But above all, for two thousand years our woods have been discontinuous. Plants can no longer move in short stages through wildwood; to reach a new site involves a jump across farmland.

We must use the method with caution. Plants vary their behaviour from one part of the country to another. Although most of the species mentioned are associated with ancient woodland all over England, this is not always so. Dog's-mercury, for example, is a good indicator of ancient woodland in the Midlands, where it spreads very slowly into hedges; in Suffolk it is in innumerable ancient hedges, and I cannot believe that each of those hedges has successively been the edge of a wood. Even the more exacting woodland plants occasionally survive, though they do not increase, outside woodland. A railway cut off a corner of Hayley Wood in 1863 and made it into grassland; oxlip, bluebell and anemone have survived for 126 years out in the open. This perhaps explains the occasional records of oxlip in wet meadows. In Britain it is on the edge of its geographical range. It has little power to colonize new sites, but survives with tenacity where it already grows, provided it is protected from grazing, ploughing and the competition of ranker herbs. It grows in woods because it needs protection, not shade; it benefits spectacularly from coppicing (Plate VIII). Occasionally, as in meadows and along railways, it lives under the protection of the scythe rather than the axe.[149]

Evidence from indicator plants, therefore, should be based on a suite of species rather than a single one. Where possible it should be based on their behaviour in the same region, not extrapolated from other parts of Britain. To make a regional list of ancient-woodland plants, one should begin with those plants that grow in woods known to be ancient, but not in hedges.

The flora of recent woods consists mainly of plants that have no particular connexion with woodland but are widespread in hedges and other habitats. In much of England (except limestone country), ivy is uncommon in primary woods except round the edge; it is very common in secondary woods. Ivy gets in in the early stages of forming a wood and may persist for centuries; it does not readily colonize existing woodland, and so may mark out areas that have been added to a primary wood. (Americans will note that poison-ivy, a similar but unrelated plant, does just the same in the eastern States.)

Management and woodland flora

Coppice-woods have had years of light followed by years of shade, going back in cycles through all history. The magnificent and spectacular displays of woodland flowers, for which England used to be famous, are the result. Primrose, oxlip, anemone, bluebell flourish in the years of light; they also need years of shade to suppress the tall grasses and other non-woodland plants which would overwhelm them outside woods.

Coppicing plants are gloriously unpredictable, and each wood has its specialities. The wetter parts of Hayley and Hardwick Woods are yellow with countless oxlips in the second and third springs after felling. Norsey Wood in south Essex has one of the greatest concentrations of bluebells in the world. In the Mendip woods there is the miraculously brilliant blue *Lithospermum purpureocaeruleum*. These plants survive the shade years in an attenuated form, but flower in profusion in the years of release. Many other plants wait as buried seed between coppicings. In Chalkney Wood red campion and wild raspberry are completely killed by the shade of tall lime and hornbeam, but come up in tens of thousands after each felling. Wood-spurge can wait 125 years.

Long periods of continuous shade, combined with a heavy fall of tree leaves that do not rot, may produce a poor flora even in an ancient wood. Evergreen monocultures of conifers or rhododendrons are particularly unkind to the ground vegetation; hawthorn and sycamore are not much better.

In Sutton Coldfield Park a poor woodland flora is attributable partly to unfavourable dominant trees, continuous oak and holly. The beechwoods on the acid soils of the Chiltern plateau, though largely ancient, have for some 200 years been carefully managed to produce timber only. They now have a plantation-like appearance with miles of tall beeches, beautiful but monotonous, varied only by a few oaks and the occasional giant wild cherry. Ground vegetation is very sparse; underwood is almost non-existent, except around wood edges and near internal banks where there are hornbeam (probably originally planted as a shade-bearing boundary hedge), whitebeam, etc. Immediately outside the woods are fields and lanes with ancient hedges full of different trees, shrubs and herbs. Although the woods are sometimes on poorer soil, the abrupt contrast between the plantation-like woods and the wood-like hedges must be mainly due to past management encouraging the densely shading beech.

Woodland elms

Wych-elm, though distinctive of a number of different woodland types, does not have a special behaviour. The other elms in woods display a complex interaction between human activities, woodland ecology, and elm reproduction. There are six ways in which suckering elms can get into woods:

1. By having been on the site ever since it was wildwood. This is possible but rare: suckering elms in wildwood were probably on flood-plains, where no ancient woodland survives.
2. By planting – known examples are rare.
3. By invasion of farmland, an elm hedge broadening into a belt of woodland – common.
4. By an elm hedge, planted next to a wood, suckering into the wood – common.
5. By natural seedlings arising in an existing wood. This could happen only rarely, when the weather and the state of the underwood were both favourable; but it is important because it may give rise to new sorts of elm. Many small elm clones round wood edges started in this way.
6. By suckering from elms originally planted round a settlement – common.

One can learn much about a wood's history by mapping the elms in detail, deciding where each clone came from, how quickly it has advanced, and whether there are any remains of trees that grew on the site before the elms. The most interesting are the settlement elms, especially in East Anglia and Cornwall where elms are common and variable; they give us our one opportunity of direct contact with the varieties of plants that grew around habitations now deserted. (Elm Disease is not an insuperable difficulty; many woodland elms are still alive, and where the big trees have died new suckers are usually springing up.)

What stinging-nettles say

The stinging-nettle is one of a group of plants that indicate a fertile soil; others are elderberry and goosegrass (*Galium aparine*). Nettles are greedy for phosphate, and their roots are inefficient at getting it.[150] Some soils are naturally rich in phosphate; but most ancient woods are on soils too poor to support nettles, which generally indicate places where phosphate has been artificially accumulated.

Man is a phosphate-gathering animal. All crops contain phosphorus: every consumer of wheat, faggots or sheep is transporting phosphate from the countryside at large into built-up areas. Little of this ever goes back whence it came. Phosphate accumulates particularly in bones and ashes. Most of it goes to feed the nettles in gardens and on middens, and much of it awaits the Last Trump in country churchyards. Especially in alkaline soils, phosphate persists in the ground. At Stockton (Wilts) the earthworks of a deserted Romano-British village extend into Stockton Wood; the phosphate still nourishes nettles after 2000 years. Not that nettles necessarily indicate secondary woodland: some countrymen have long had the habit of throwing rubbish into the nearest grove, and phosphate may come from the geology or be dropped by a big starling-roost. Nevertheless, an area of nettles in an otherwise nettle-free wood usually has a story to tell.

Three complex woods

These examples illustrate how to combine the evidence of documents, earthworks, flora and vegetation. All three woods contain ancient secondary woodland, so that a previous land-use has to be taken into account.

Overhall Grove, west Cambs (Fig. 27), 42 acres, lies between Boxworth and Knapwell, among the most interesting of the shrunken medieval villages of the east Midlands. It belongs to Cambridgeshire Wildlife Trust. The steep site contains springs, one of them called the Red Well. The wood is mainly of elm, of about six clones of the East Anglian group, with scattered oaks (some of them immense) and big stools of ash and maple. It is full of earthworks. A formidable moat, almost on the scale of a castle mound, stands inside a doubly-ditched 'bailey' with artificial ponds. There is a second enclosure, and also various woodbanks, hedgebanks and ridge-and-furrow.

This is an ancient wood: a map of 1650 shows it almost as it is now, the internal features having already been forgotten. The earthworks prove it to be secondary woodland except perhaps for the narrow, very wet middle part. The big moat represents the manor-house of Overhall, documented in the thirteenth century but abandoned by the mid-sixteenth at latest. Badgers have excavated pottery of from early to late medieval date. The outer earthwork may be older.[152]

Although there is a history of coppicing, the flora is poor, totally lacking such plants as dog's-mercury and hazel, common in nearby primary woods. Surprisingly, this is an oxlip wood, which suggests

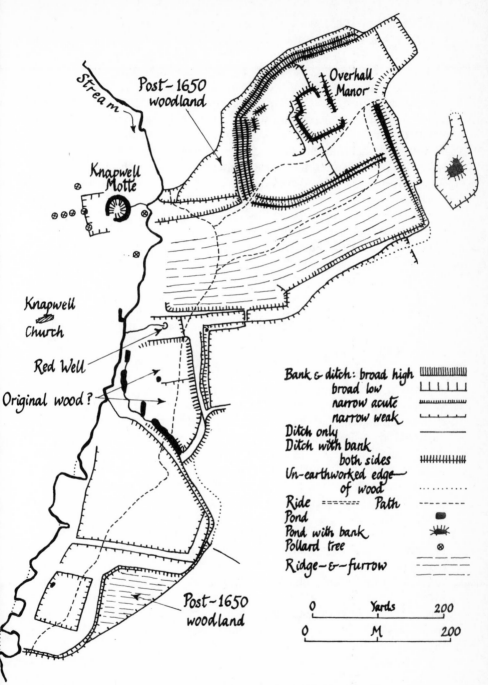

Fig. 27. Overhall Grove in Boxworth, Cambridgeshire.[151]

137

that the middle of the wood may always have been woodland. (Grange Grove, $\frac{3}{4}$ mile away, with a very similar history, has neither oxlip nor mercury.)

The elms may well have originated by suckering from those growing around the manor. They are of an aggressive kind; they have invaded most of the wood and the fringes of the adjoining fields. The oaks and ashes remain from a pre-elm wood. The wood has ground-elder and white deadnettle, both of them garden relics, not woodland plants. The moated site and most of the wood are ear-high in stinging-nettles, whose vigour testifies to all the phosphate still in the soil from the high living of the 'Hobridges or Boxworths', lords of Overhall.

Overhall Grove is probably of fifteenth-century date, formed by the late-medieval recession in the East Midlands. Ash and maple, followed slowly by oxlip, spread from the original nucleus. Elms, suckering out from the moat, gradually filled up the site and invaded the ashwood. Since 1978, many of the elms have died of Elm Disease, giving ash a chance to return.

Buff Wood (Fig. 28), 40 acres, is not far away. It overlies part of the shrunken village of East Hatley; its complicated earthworks include two moats and four areas of ridge-and-furrow. It can be traced back to the Hundred Rolls of 1279, but has evidently grown bigger since then. It appears to have reached almost its present shape by 1650; documents indicate that it had been in divided ownership like Eversden Wood.[153] The original wood is a mixed-hazel and maple–hazel coppice with much aspen, very like Hayley Wood nearby. It has oxlip, dog's-mercury, woodland hawthorn, herb Paris and many other plants of ancient woodland.

The secondary woodland areas nearest the original wood are almost indistinguishable from it in vegetation, as we might expect after more than 300 years of direct contact. They too have very large ash and maple stools. But they have ivy and spurge-laurel (a secondary wood-land indicator in the East Midlands). Towards the moats there is no indication that the woodland has ever been anything other than elmwood.

Elms are represented by at least 29 clones, mostly distinct, covering much of the total variation of British elms. (Many are eclipsed by Elm Disease, but suckers remain.) Different elms have got into the wood by succession, invasion from hedges, seed and planting; they have invaded the secondary wood and much of the original wood, and where they meet they compete or interpenetrate in various ways. In the area of the old village the elms are particularly complex: within the moats are ten clones, some of them in specific positions as though

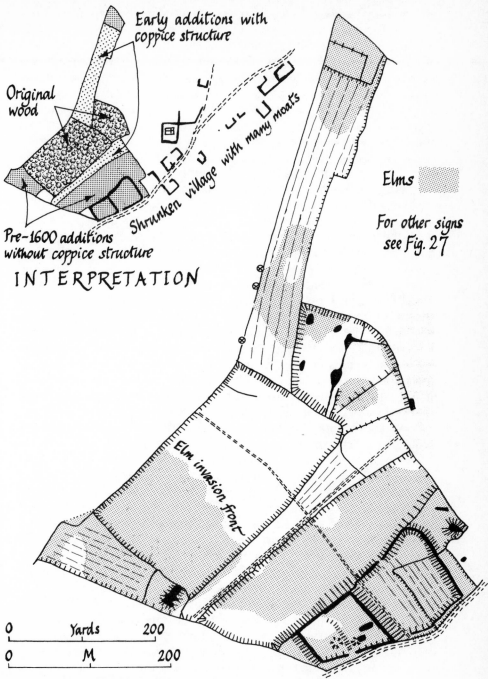

Early additions with coppice structure

Original wood

Pre-1600 additions without coppice structure

INTERPRETATION

Shrunken village with many moats

Elms

For other signs see Fig. 27

Elm invasion front

0   Yards   200

0   M   200

Fig. 28. Buff Wood in East Hatley, Cambridgeshire.

representing hedges planted by the moat-dwellers. One moat and part of the other are covered with vigorous nettle-beds.

The later history of Buff Wood involved a little planting: a few rows of hybrid poplar, the occasional common lime and Huntingdon elm were inserted, while some unsuccessful beech, larch and spruce still soldier on. The wood is a monument to the fashions and the optimism of the Victorian forester. The last addition to the wood was in the 1860s, and for a century one could see one hybrid between primrose and cowslip, a vestige of the previous pasture.

The wood has belonged to Cambridge University Botanic Garden since 1955. It is one of the longest-running examples of 'conservation coppicing.' It has both primrose and oxlip, and is a famous wood for the hybrid between them. It has one of the richest floras of any middle-sized wood in Britain – richer than Hayley with three times the area. It has been the scene of much of the ecological research from which we have learnt how woods work.

Groton Wood, 50 acres, belongs to Suffolk Wildlife Trust. It lies on the yellow, acid loess of south Suffolk, on which neither oxlip nor ridge-and-furrow occurs. There are two very distinct parts. The northern third of the wood (Fig. 29) is surrounded by a massive, sinuous, partly double, evidently early woodbank (Fig. 23), except on the north side where there is a straight, much less substantial boundary. Its only internal features are two faint streams. The southern two-thirds has only slight boundary earthworks, but is criss-crossed with a tangle of low banks and ditches, and contains many pits and ponds.

Earthworks show that the present outline of Groton Wood, although known to date from before 1778, cannot be its original shape. The original wood is the northern third, which has been truncated on its north side and enlarged on the south, where some of the internal features are probably the hedgebanks of former fields. This is abundantly confirmed by the vegetation. The northern wood is dominated by huge stools of small-leaved lime, accompanied in wet hollows by an elm of the Lineage group. The southern part has small, irregular, scattered coppice stools of ash, hazel, etc. and also many small clones of cherry. Lime is strongly associated with primary woodland, and cherry with wood margins and secondary woodland.

Indirect references to lime in Groton go back to 1279. Henry VIII confiscated 'Growton wood' from Bury St Edmund's Abbey in 1544 and bestowed it on Adam Winthrop; the area, 37 acres, fits with the present northern wood plus two 'Wood Fields' adjacent which were, until recently, bounded by a sinuous hedge with massive lime stools in it. The alterations to the wood therefore probably happened between

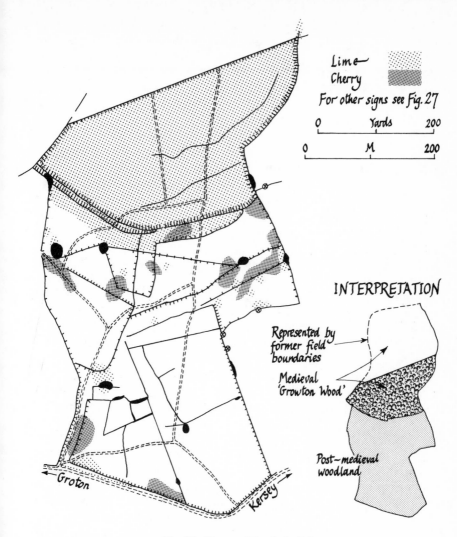

Lime
Cherry
For other signs see Fig. 27

0   Yards   200

0   M   200

INTERPRETATION

Represented by
former field
boundaries

Medieval
'Growton Wood'

Post-medieval
woodland

Groton

Kersey

Fig. 29. Groton Wood, Suffolk.

then and 1778. I am tempted to attribute the enlargement to John Winthrop II, who sold Groton Wood when in 1631 he went off to found the State of Massachusetts; he had previously been the co-author of a pamphlet advocating woodland conservation.[154]

The boundary of lime does not quite coincide with the old woodbank but overlaps it by a few yards. Elsewhere in the southern wood there are occasional lime stools, often on banks. Here we are seeing what happens when lime is presented with an exceptionally good opportunity for colonization, a new wood formed adjacent to an existing lime-grove. Lime seedlings are not uncommon in Groton Wood in some years, but seldom grow into trees. Few of them have done so more than 25 yards outside the old boundary, and some of these may already have been there in field hedges.

Dalkeith Oaks: Scottish woodmanship

Six miles south-east of Edinburgh stands Dalkeith Palace, with a wonderful deer-park formed by walling off a neck of land between the gorges of the North and South Esk rivers. It is a unique landscape of mighty oaks, glamorous with bizarre shapes and long-dead upper boughs.[155] I have worked out much of its history with certainty from annual rings.

There are two generations of old oaks. The younger date from the mid-seventeenth century, and are maidens – not coppiced or pollarded. The older oaks have trunks dating from between 1580 and 1617, and are either multi-stemmed or have big gnarled bases.

What we see today is evidently the remains of a coppiced oakwood not felled for nearly 400 years. It would once have been an ordinary wood, but the site happened to be chosen for a park in the early seventeenth century, perhaps in connexion with the building of a previous palace. Since that time it has not been felled, and the coppiced oaks have gradually, but still not completely, been replaced by younger trees.

A wood left so long uncoppiced would itself be unique, but the Dalkeith Oaks have a more important meaning still. Some of the stool bases are 10 feet across, and would already have been giant stools in 1617. The age of the stool, added to the age of the tree since last felling, takes us back at least to the time of King Robert the Bruce. It is therefore possible, *on the evidence of trees still alive*, to settle the question of whether Scotland had a medieval coppicing tradition, which we left in Chapter 4.

7

Trees on commons: the wood–pasture tradition

By Langley Bush I roam but the bush hath left its hill
On Cowper Green I stray tis a desert strange and chill
And spreading Lea Close Oak ere decay had penned its will
To the axe of the spoiler and self interest fell a prey
And Crossberry Way and old Round Oaks narrow Lane
With its hollow trees like pulpits I shall never see again
Inclosure like a Buonaparte let not a thing remain
It levelled every bush and tree and levelled every hill ...

John Clare, *Remembrances*
[the Inclosure is that of Helpston, Peterborough, in 1809]

The practice of using the same piece of land for trees and grazing animals is to be found all over the world, and presumably goes back to prehistoric times. Wood-pastures, often managed by burning as well as grazing, were operated by Red Indians in favour of deer and buffalo.[25] While woodland itself may involve some conflict of interest, if only between timber and underwood, the conflict between the two elements in wood-pasture is more severe. The more trees there are, the less abundant and the worse will be the pasture; the more animals graze the pasture, the more difficult it becomes to replace the trees. This conflict has been resolved, or stabilized, in various ways on commons, in parks, Forests, hedges and farmland.

In England the simplest form of wood-pasture is the **wooded common**. A common is a piece of land on which certain of the local inhabitants have **common-rights**, most often of pasturage for cattle and sheep, but sometimes of woodcutting and other things. The land itself, and often the trees, belong to the lord of the manor. Wooded commons are only one among many other kinds of common. In Wales

143

and Ireland there is a tradition of private wood-pasture, and of having ribbons of woodland along streams within pasture-fields; little is known of the details of how these functioned.

History of wooded commons

Archaeologists can only by rare chance identify the products of wood-pasture; most of the evidence has to come from documents. Several Anglo-Saxon charters refer specifically to wood-pasture commons, for instance:

and here are the pastures of swine, four *mansiones*: in the place called Boganora, at Hidhurst in the wood, and on the wood-pasture common (*communi silva pascuale*, 'common pasturable wood') called Palinga Schittas.

Charter of the exclaves of Felpham, W. Sussex, 953.
(*Mansio* is some kind of unit of settlement; Palinga Schittas may be the wood-pasture called The Mens in Kirdford (Fig. 31);[156] Idehurst and [Little] Bognor are nearby hamlets.)

We have seen that pasture (for unspecified beasts) and pannage are used to describe some woods, especially the bigger ones, in Domesday Book. By the thirteenth century wood-pasture had much declined, though not everywhere. As late as 1305, a tenant of Great Horwood (Bucks), accused of not ploughing his lord's land as he should have done under the terms of his tenancy, was able to get away with the excuse that his plough-oxen were grazing in the manor woods, and he needed three days' notice to round them up.[157] The decline of wood-pasture is partly due to conversion to other land-uses. Assarting for agriculture is well documented, though on a small scale. Other wood-pastures were converted to parks or coppices. Where, as at Shipdham (Norfolk), a large Domesday pannage record coincides with a large thirteenth-century coppice-wood, it is likely that the wood was converted to coppicing before its structure had been too far damaged by grazing. In the Hallingburys (Essex) the lords of the two manors appropriated two-thirds of the wood as their own, private, embanked coppices; in return, they left the tenants in sole possession of one-third as a wood-pasture common (Woodside Green), an arrangement which still operates (Fig. 37).

An early wood-pasture often turned into a treeless common because the livestock gained the upper hand and grazing was sufficient to prevent trees from replacing themselves. Thorpe Wood, Norwich, is probably a typical example of what happened to a Domesday pannage wood.

Domesday Book says that Thorpe had a wood 'for 1200 swine', one of the largest assessments in Norfolk. Thorpe Wood was bestowed on the bishopric of Norwich by Henry I in 1101. In the 1140s it was the scene of the bizarre and sinister affair of 'St William of Norwich'; contemporary accounts show that the wood then extended over the present Mousehold Heath as well as its later site on the steep slopes above the river (Fig. 30). Herbert de Losinga, first bishop of Norwich, wrote a letter to his woodward which is the earliest record of an interest in woodland conservation on the part of an individual:

As to making a present of Thorpe Wood to the sick or anyone else, I gave you no orders, nor did I give nor will I give any; for I appointed you the custodian of the Wood, not the rooter up of it. To the sick, when I come to Norwich, I will give as I did last year, not logs of wood, but money ... Guard the Wood of the Holy Trinity, as you wish to be guarded by the Holy Trinity, and to continue in my favour.

The Bishop evidently appreciated the value of a large wood adjacent to an important city. His concern probably arose from grazing rights which he could not control. The development of Mousehold Heath, which he tried to postpone, is first recorded in 1156 by Pope Adrian IV, who refers to 'the Heath with all its wood.' By 1236 we find a reference to 'the part of Thorpe Wood which was covered with oaks' in contrast to the heath part of the wood. A new state of stability was reached with managed woodland on the southern slopes, while the gravelly plateau was heathland with common-rights for sheep, cattle and pigs.[158] This appears in late-medieval perambulations and six-teenth-century maps and views. A little grove, with real woodbanks, was still maintained to give colour to the dedication of the chapel of 'St William in the Wood'. Wood-consuming installations nearby included the Bishop's lime-kiln and the Lollards' Pit, 'where men are customablie burnt'.

Both the Wood and the heath have since been eaten away by enclosure-act farmers and expensive builders. The Wood of the Holy Trinity is now reduced to steep fragments, drastically planted with exotic trees. In the 1960s a few pollard oaks, ancient beeches, and the occasional stool of small-leaved lime lingered on. Woodbanks still surround the site of St William's Chapel. Mousehold, like most heaths, suffers badly from lack of grazing, lack of rabbits, and the efficiency of the Fire Brigade. Most of the once-glorious heathland has now turned into undistinguished oakwood and birchwood, and trees have even been *planted* on the remainder.

How wooded commons worked

Wood-pastures are less stable ecologically and socially than coppices, but not all commons lost their trees. At Minchinhampton (Gloucs),

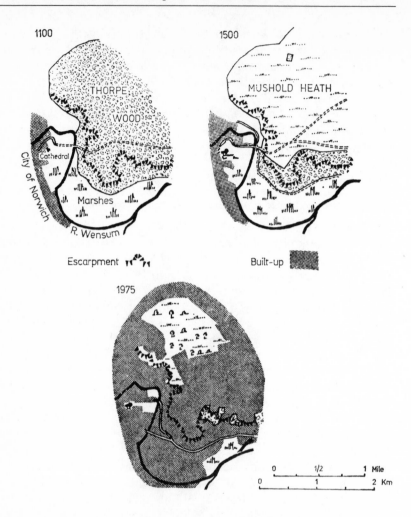

Fig. 30. Development of Mousehold (Mushold) Heath, Norwich.

for instance, there were some 2000 acres of woods, some privately owned, all subject to various common-rights both of wood and pasture. The woods were jealously protected by the medieval courts of the manor against over-exploitation by any of their users. They were still flourishing in 1538, and most of them were still there when the system finally broke down in the seventeenth century.[159] Even without such regulation, grazing was not always intensive or continuous enough to prevent trees from regenerating. When grazing declined, as on many commons nowadays, trees could increase. Commons that were normally woodless sometimes grew thorns: at

146

Little Gransden (Cambs) the sixteenth-century villagers cut 'busshes and trees of about the bignes of a mans legge' on Langland Common.[160] Even if grazing afterwards increased, the thorns might give protection to saplings of other trees growing up among them.

Where a common had trees, these were most often pollards, in order to prevent the livestock from getting at the young shoots. Woodcutting rights might belong to all the commoners, or some of them, or the lord of the manor, according to local custom. Often the pollard shoots belonged to the commoners but the bollings to the lord. Coppicing was difficult on a common: a few commons (as at Minchinhampton) had a compartmentation system, whereby a coppice-wood was felled and then removed from the common until it had grown again, but this was too favourable to the lord to be widely accepted. In Gernon Bushes (Essex), adjacent to Epping Forest, management for underwood may have gained the upper hand quite recently: the common is covered with dense dark pollard hornbeams, both younger and more recently cut than in the Forest itself.

Wooded commons today

Wooded commons are rarely preserved. Commons were a target of the enclosure movement in the late eighteenth century, especially the bigger commons which were the ones that more often had trees. Once a common was enclosed it was destroyed, with a few exceptions: on part of Little Baddow Common (Essex) the coppice stools and pollards still stand on a soil so poor that it was not worth-while grubbing them out. Even where a common survives, its historic features are often obscured by secondary woodland.

Commons, wooded and unwooded, have a distinctive shape which is very different from the shape of woods. They have a straggling, concave outline (Fig. 31), funnelling out by 'horns' into the roads which cross the common. Commons are surrounded by houses which front on to the common and back on to their own private land. The shape of a common is that of a piece of land which it is no one person's duty to fence. The boundary earthworks are merely the ditches of the surrounding fields. Where a wooded common adjoins a wood, the woodbanks belong to the wood and face towards the common: for example Woodside Green (Fig. 37).

The differences between woodland and wood-pasture are illustrated in the hornbeam hills above Hertford, where a stretch of Ermine Street, a main Roman road, survives as a broad green lane between woods (Plate XIV). The woods (where not devoured by modern

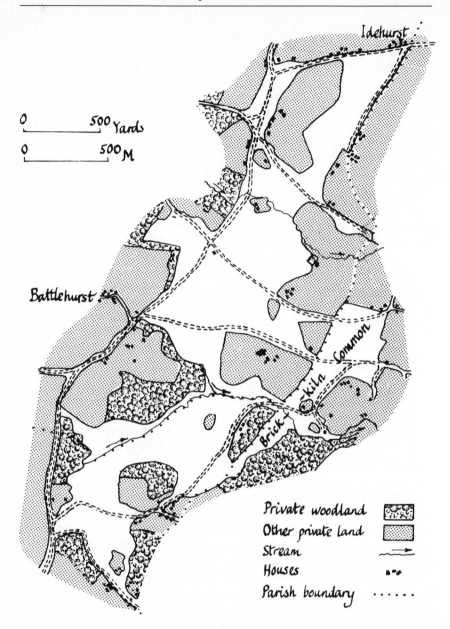

0 _____ 500 Yards

0 _____ 500 M

Idehurst

Battlehurst

Brick Kiln Common

Private woodland

Other private land

Stream

Houses

Parish boundary

Fig. 31. The Mens, Sussex: a large wood-pasture common with straggling concave outlines, bordered by houses, funnelling into the roads which cross the common, and joining up with another common in the next parish. There are many enclaves of private land, including woodland. (Compartment boundaries within the common are excluded.)

148

forestry) consist of hornbeam *stools* with timber trees of both species of oak. There is a woodbank on each side of the road, bearing hornbeam *stubs* remaining from a hedge that once kept out animals passing along the road. The roadway itself counts as wood-pasture; in it are hornbeam *pollards* – which the livestock could not reach up to – plus thorns and timber oak trees.

In Ancient Countryside, particularly East Anglia, the smallest commons are greens or *tyes* of an acre or two, with two or three cottages, at the junction of three or four roads. Greens come in all sizes above this: often they are interconnected, as in the magnificent series of greens, much of which still remains, rambling across six parishes around Long Stratton, Norfolk. There is a continuous range of sizes up to Epping Forest, which in social terms is the largest green of all. Chapman & André's map of Essex in 1777 (which, like other early county maps, is more detailed and reliable for commons than for woods) shows the Forest in its ancient state, with a straggling, convex outline and hundreds of boundary houses (Fig. 35).

Ancient woods and some greens (though probably not the small tyes) have a common origin in remnants of wildwood. The wooded commons of Middlesex, which even in the eighteenth century covered much of the county, continued a strong wood-pasture tradition going back to very large swine-entries in Domesday Book. Around Fressingfield in Suffolk, which has long been a very woodless area, the many Domesday pannage-woods appear to have turned into large greens, some with wood-names like Gre*shaw* and Al*wood* Green.

Even where a wooded common is on a wildwood site, it does not follow that it is primary woodland in the sense that an ancient coppice may be. Continuity of vegetation is more difficult to establish for wood-pasture. If a wood loses its trees, it ceases to be a wood and disappears from the record. A common is more likely to lose its trees and, if it does so, does not cease to be a common; the wood-rights may still be documented even if they cannot be exercised. If grazing relaxes, trees may unobtrusively return.

The majority of woodland on commons is less than a century old. Embedded in it there may be pollards, often of oak or hornbeam. A special characteristic are beech pollards. Burnham Beeches (Bucks), Felbrigg Beeches (Norfolk) and Frithsden Beeches (Berkhamsted, Herts) are famous groves of ancient beech pollards on former commons on very acid soils – the typical habitat of native beech before it became a tree-planters' tree.* (It has been claimed that Burnham

* The similar magnificent beech pollards of Blaenavon and near Abergavenny (Gwent) appear to belong to the Welsh wood-pasture tradition.

Beeches arose in the seventeenth century on what had been a nearly treeless common;[161] there are, however, some oak pollards of much earlier date, including the venerable Druids' Oak.) Other ancient trees are less frequent. Elms are abundant in the field hedges around Essex and Middlesex commons, and fringe the boundaries of commons, but are rare in the commons themselves – a striking instance of the effect of different management on a palatable tree.

Grazing combined with shade is very bad for the woodland flora: a heavily-used wood-pasture consists of grassland plus two or three species of tree. In the Lake District, Wales and Ireland, where many ordinary woods have been exposed to grazing in recent decades, the more exacting woodland plants – ivy, violets, primrose, the woodrush *Luzula sylvatica*, etc. – are often confined to small cliffs or undercut stream-banks, where the livestock cannot get at them. Cliffs as refuges for palatable plants can be found elsewhere, notably in the Avon Gorge, Bristol, with its wood-pasture history and its great lime-trees and curious whitebeams growing on the cliffs.*

In compensation, the ancient trees of wooded commons provide a wealth of habitats for the more exacting birds, lichens and insects. Many of the best commons are, alas, in places now too rain-polluted for lichens; an exception is The Mens, now one of the finest reserves of Sussex Wildlife Trust.

* The supreme example is Crete, an island over-grazed probably for millions of years, with its hundred goat-proof gorges and soaring cliffs famous for a magnificent flora.

150

8

Parks:
private wood-pasture

The same Manor of Redgrave is A manor within whiche ... there is A park wt dere in the same ... the herbage of the parke there is not above valued....
Lytel Coppies nyghe the parke conteyneth 15 acres.
Freyth Coppies conteyneth 44 acres.
Redgrave Wood conteyneth 45 acres.
In the parke be 30 acres thyn sett with pollyng[a] okes and hardebeme[b] growing by parcelles....
                    [Detailed census of the coppices follows.]
The sprynge[c] ... of 30 acres not valuyd because the wood ys old ... which once fallen shall never be any wood agayne.

Valuation of part of the Suffolk estates of
Bury St Edmund's Abbey, c.1540[162]

[a] pollard   [b] hornbeam   [c] 'spring', that is the regrowth of underwood.

The word *park* has meant many things down the centuries. The Anglo-Saxon *pearroc* was any piece of land within a fence. Later it meant a place for keeping deer; then the outer, less formal part of the grounds around a gentleman's house; and now it is where one airs the dog amid geraniums and begonias. These meanings are not as distinct in practice as one might expect. The earliest meaning survives in Cornish and Welsh place-names. The landscape and recreation aspects of parks already existed in the Middle Ages, and several medieval parks have turned into municipal parks.

The deer-park tradition

The classical meaning of *park* in Great Britain is an enclosure for semi-wild animals. The tradition goes back to ancient Crete and Persia.

It was well developed by the Romans in Italy; Columella describes keeping red and roe deer, wild pigs, fallow deer or gazelles in wooded enclosures within walls or wooden pales. If there were parks in Roman Britain they did not outlast the Empire. The Anglo-Saxons had no fallow deer; parks and Forests are both conspicuously absent from their perambulations.

Parks are a monument to the Normans' interest in deer-farming, but the fashion began to penetrate England just before the Conquest. An Anglo-Saxon will, dated 1045, mentions a 'deerhay' which was later known as the Great Park of Ongar (Essex). By 1086 the fashion had progressed a little farther: Domesday Book mentions 35 parks, including Ongar. These would have contained native red and roe deer. Shortly after this, the wood-pasture tradition was transformed by the introduction of the fallow deer, an oriental beast which reached Europe via Minoan Crete, ancient Rome and probably Norman Sicily. This new deer, easier than the native species to keep in a confined space, prospered in England in the twelfth century, and became the most important beast of the medieval chase. Then, and for long after, it was confined to parks or concentrated in royal Forests, and did not roam the countryside as it does now. Its introduction was a new means of exploiting land, not unlike the cattle ranches of Texas. Some parks contained, as a few still do, other deer or the mysterious 'wild' white cattle; we also hear of hare-parks and swine-parks (for wild boar, extinct as a free-living animal by the later Middle Ages).[163] On the Earl's Colne Map of 1598 (Frontispiece) Chalkney Wood bears the inscription:

Chawlkny woodd In wch woodd the Erles of Oxenforde in tymes paste bredd and mayntayned wyelde Swyne And in the reigne of kinge Henry the eight John then Erle of Oxenforde caused them to be destroied for the greate damage and hurte the Contrie susteined by them.

Medieval parks

Parks proliferated in the twelfth century. From the thirteenth century onwards we have a more or less systematic record from 'licences to empark' – a kind of planning permission for a new or enlarged park. Parks reached their heyday about 1300. I estimate, from the lists of myself and others in eight well-studied counties, that there were then about 3200 parks in England, covering nearly 2% of the country – roughly one park to every four parishes. Anyone could have a park who could afford it. It was a status symbol of the whole upper class, of gentry and ecclesiastics as well as nobility. Wales and Scotland, lands of petty Forests, had few parks; there were a handful in Ireland.

The deer of Forests were at liberty to stray on to surrounding land, but those of parks were confined by a deer-proof boundary. Fallow deer are as strong as pigs and more agile than goats; they were confined by a *park pale*, a special palisade of cleft-oak stakes, whose maintenance was very expensive in labour and in the best timber. An alternative might be a hedge, or a stone wall – even where the stone had to be brought some miles.

Ongar and other very early parks have a characteristic compact outline with rounded corners (Fig. 32) which suggests economy in fencing (like the costly burglar-proof fences round prisons today). A sign of a very early park is that the parish boundaries deviate to follow the park outline; this makes the park earlier than *c.* 1180, when parish boundaries became frozen and could no longer be altered to accommodate changes in land ownership. Later parks were often small or awkwardly shaped, perhaps because it was difficult to acquire the land, and were often short-lived. We often hear of parks of 30 acres or even less, which must have been impossibly expensive to fence or maintain. A park was a rich man's privilege – a valuable one, since it kept him in fresh meat over the winter – and a not-quite-so-rich man's status symbol.[163]

Whatever the original habitat of the fallow deer may have been, the medievals thought of it as a woodland animal. Many records of parks specify woodland. They were not all wood, for they often included heath, grassland and arable, but their distribution (Fig. 33) closely follows that of woodland in Domesday Book. Parks were thickest on the ground in well-wooded Hertfordshire, and very few in poorly-wooded Lincolnshire and Leicestershire. By 1300 something like one-quarter of the woodland of England was within parks. Deer, biting the young shoots, were one of the causes of shrinkage of woodland. (There were a few moorland and heath parks, such as Julian Park in Egton near Whitby.)

Parks were seldom 'set aside for hunting'. Slaughter of deer for the pot could seldom be called hunting, except by courtesy; and parks were no exception to the medieval practice of multiple uses for the same piece of land. Some of these land-uses might remain from the previous history of the site, for it was seldom possible to find a vacant piece of land to empark;* and usually there were trees as well as grazing.

Many small parks were formed by emparking the whole of an existing wood; but we occasionally hear of treeless parks. Deer were

---

* To buy out and empark a whole village is a post-medieval practice.

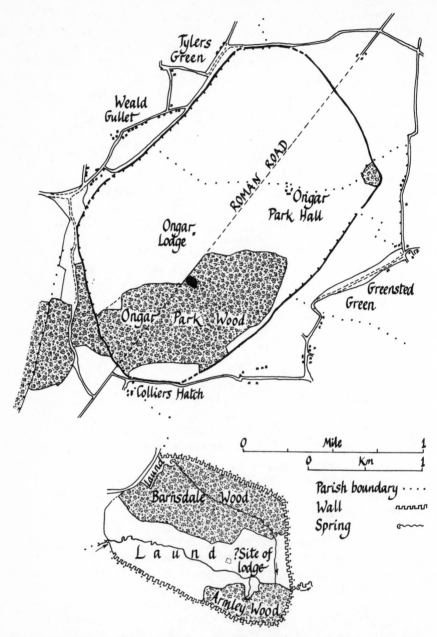

Fig. 32. Early parks. Ongar Great Park, Essex is shown as it survived until *c.* 1950. Parish boundaries are shown, as is the fragment of park boundary which still exists in the south-west. The rest of the park perimeter survived as a hedge (thick line). Barnsdale Park, Rutland has woods, launds and site of a lodge; it is shown as it survived *c.* 1850 (it is now partly drowned in Rutland Water).

154

not usually in practice the only, or even the chief, object of management: we often hear of cattle and sheep in parks, and sometimes of arable, meadow or common grazing. Surveys show that parks and woods were associated in the medieval mind, but were not the same thing, for example:

The wood
Item there is one park which contains in all sixty acres by estimate, part of which is $29\frac{1}{2}$ acres of arable land in the launds of the same park which are included in the total of arable land ... the pasture is worth 10*d*. per acre.
Item there is a wood called grischaue [later Greshaw Wood, now vanished] which contains 100 acres by estimate ... from which the underwood of 25 acres together with the herbage are worth 40*s*. per annum. . . .

Ely Coucher Book, 1251, entry for Pulham, Norfolk[59]
[see also the park at Barking, Suffolk, p. 59]

Woods
In the great wood 260 acres by estimate, in which can be made every year 600 faggots, worth 8*s*. (at 16*d*. the hundred). The agistment in the same is worth £2 per annum.
In the wood called lenynge 90 acres, one-sixth part of which each year is 15 acres which are worth £2 12*s*. 6*d*. at 3*s*. 6*d*. per acre.
Le Speltne is 80 acres by estimate, one-sixth part of which each year is worth £2 7*s*. 10*d*. at 3*s*. 6*d*. per acre.
In the little park 60 acres and the wood is worth £1 10*s*. per annum at 3*s*. per acre. [*sic*]
Cutting thorns in various places is worth 12*d*. per year.
Pannage of pigs worth 6*s*. 8*d*. a year.
Total £9 6*s*. 0*d*. a year.
Pasture ... [among other entries] 5 acres ... in the little park in the laund ... 2*s*. 6*d*. a year.

Abbot Tymworth's survey of Long Melford, Suffolk, 1386[165]
[see Fig. 18]

At Long Melford there were two ordinary woods, Lenynge and Spelterne, later Lineage and Spelthorne Woods, coniferized remains of which still exist. Each wood was supposed to be felled on a normal six-year coppice cycle. The Great Park had been a third wood: earlier and later documents call it Elmsett. (Its site is now occupied by the sixteenth-century Park Farm.) In 1386 it produced only a trivial amount of wood each year, but a bigger income from 'agistment', the letting of grazing land to outside farmers. The wood appears not as acres of underwood but as hundreds of faggots, which would have come from pollarding sparsely scattered trees. The Little Park, in contrast, was mainly woodland felled every six years, but of slightly less quality than the other woods. It also contained a *laund* – a word commonly used for treeless areas within parks.

The *Ely Coucher Book* shows that such arrangements already existed in the previous century. The parks at Pulham and Barking had launds. At Pulham the laund was under the plough, and since arable

Fig. 33. Medieval parks.[164] Each dot represents about 400 acres at the scale of the map, rather bigger than the average English park. The boundaries of the Highland Zone and of the Scottish Lowlands are shown.

farming can hardly have coexisted with deer on a mere 60 acres there cannot have been any deer in the park at the time. Even so, the return from the 'wood' part of the park was in the form of pasture, which implies only scattered trees. Greshaw *Wood*, in contrast, although much bigger, was a normal wood cut every four years. The deer themselves are never given a value in such surveys, and often are not mentioned. In medieval England – as in Texas and other States today – it was improper to buy or sell venison, which was therefore priceless. Valuers were interested in everything about a park except its *raison d'être*.

A woodland park was self-contradictory, and its life precarious. At Barking, the tiny park of 1251 still survives as one of the many small 'Park Woods' in which only the name remains as a record of a brief attempt to set up a deer-park. There were two ways to maintain a wooded park for a long period. The underwood could be given up and replaced by scattered pollards and big timber trees. This had evidently happened to Pulham Park, and to Long Melford Great Wood after it became a park. As we have seen, such **uncompartmented** wood-pasture was the usual practice on wooded commons.

Alternatively, deer and wood might be combined in a **compartmented** park, consisting of coppice compartments and launds. Each coppice was felled on a longish cycle, and then fenced for the first few years, until the underwood had grown big enough for the deer not to harm it much. Launds were grassland or heather areas in which the deer could feed and be caught; any trees in them would be pollarded. Barnsdale Park (Fig. 32) is a simple example. In Monks' Park, part of the Bradfield Woods, which has been a normal coppice-wood since the fifteenth century, there are internal woodbanks from its earlier history as a deer-park which imply a system of four coppices and four launds (Fig. 17). This park, dating from *c*. 1130, was one of the first generation of fallow-deer parks. A grand example of the type is Sutton Coldfield Park, surviving miraculously in the midst of the Birmingham conurbation, with its enclosed 'hursts' – embanked woods, formerly coppiced – around a great open plain of grassland and heath ramifying between the hursts. This park, three miles by two, was bigger than many Forests, but had a compact, un-Forest-like, outer perimeter.

Besides pollards, the open parts of medieval parks had oaks and other timber trees, which were allowed to grow bigger than those in woods – it being more difficult to replace them. In 1274 royal officials came to Stansted Mountfitchet (Essex) and confiscated 80 oaks valued at 4*d*. each from Hasishey (now Alsa) Wood, while the trees that they took from a nearby park were worth six times as much each.[166] Parks provided many of the outsize trees for structures such as King's College Chapel, Cambridge, and, in a later period, the large or specially shaped timbers used by shipbuilders.[167]

Tudor parks

The idea of parks as beautiful landscape is not an eighteenth-century invention. The medieval park was often a utilitarian deer-farm, a long way from the owner's house; the parkers did their business from a lodge in the middle of the park. But there were exceptions, particularly at the top of the social scale. King William the Bad of Sicily built a palace, La Zisa, in the midst of the wondrous park of Palermo; and Henry I did likewise at Woodstock (Oxfordshire) and Henry III at Clarendon (Wiltshire). Remoter parks, too, could have their moments of pleasure and romance. Did not the monks of Butley (Suffolk) in 1528 take the Queen of France for 'a picnic under the oaks with fun and games (*joco et ludo*)' in their newly-acquired Staverton Park?[168]

The park tradition declined in the later middle ages. Historians have neglected its revival in Tudor times, which forms a link with the well-known parks of the eighteenth century. Parks at this time were more used for ceremonial hunts than before or since, but they had landscape and deer-farming aspects too.

Henry VIII was a greater hunter than any of his predecessors. He took almost no interest in Forests, but in his later years he developed a mania for parks, and hunted in them. He created at least seven parks, including the present St James's, Regent's and Hyde Parks, and two parks which formed the landscape for Nonsuch Palace. He made Cardinal Wolsey give him the two great parks of Hampton Court, and relieved Cranmer of seven of the parks of the Archbishops of Canterbury. In 1537–9 the king created Hampton Court Chase, the largest park there has ever been, whose pale included 10,000 acres of land and four villages.[169]

Hunts were huge, spectacular and ceremonial, with a gory kill often enacted at an appointed spot where visiting dignitaries had assembled in a **standing** or observation tower. The Master of the Toils, whose duty was to transport live deer, found himself one of the chief officers of state and a very busy man.

The landscape aspect of parks had been revived by Henry VII and Cardinal Wolsey, with their parks that formed the setting for Richmond and Hampton Court Palaces. There was some formal planting: Nonsuch Palace was later to be famous for its Privy Garden,

Wilderness and Grove of Diana. But it is to Henry VIII that we owe the most distinctive feature of the English park tradition: the 'pseudo-medieval' park with its appearance of antiquity, given to it by the incorporation of old trees from the landscape before the park. A survey of Nonsuch Parks in 1650 records some 11,000 trees. Many were proposed to be felled for the use of Cromwell's navy; 200 were to be spared, because they were 'a speciall ornament', the loss of which would 'very much impayre the magnificence' of the palace; and many were 'ould decayed pollards'.[80] Such trees could not have grown up in the 110 years since the making of the parks. It is clear from the survey, and from early pictures of the palace, that the site had been a typical piece of Ancient Countryside, with small woods and many pollards and hedgerow and field trees, most of which remained as features beautifying the parks.

Hunting was a sport of later kings and queens down to Queen Anne; even Cromwell took a passing interest. Queen Elizabeth was the mightiest hunter of all English sovereigns. Like her father, she was still in the saddle in the last year of her life. Although she did not keep up all his parks, she often invited herself to hunt in her subjects', and her example set a fashion. Sometimes a medieval park was continued, as at Bradgate (Leics). Sometimes a new park was made next to a disbanded medieval one, as at North Elmham (Norfolk). At Long Melford (Fig. 18) the two monastic parks in remote places were discontinued, and a new park was made around Melford Hall in *c.* 1590; the manor of Kentwell acquired a park in the next century. Many new parks were of the 'pseudo-medieval' kind: their groves were formed by dissecting woods, their big trees were already there in fields and meadows, their avenues and lines of trees were made out of pre-existing tree-lined lanes and hedges. This is proved at Melford by maps made before and after the emparking. Both Melford Hall and Kentwell still have 'dodderel' oaks, now grown to baobab-like dimensions, from the pre-park landscape; Kentwell also has a wonderful lime avenue, a formal feature dating from *c.* 1676.

Georgian and Victorian parks

After Queen Anne the hunting tradition developed in other directions. Deer-farming, though it still continued, was overtaken by a revival of the landscape tradition. Eighteenth-century parks are now thought of as the supreme achievement in emparking as an art-form indeed of the whole English landscape. Although this is partly true, we now think more highly of these later parks because more of them survives, and because they were the work of professional landscape designers who wrote books and had much to say for themselves. But these designers, such as William Kent (1684–1748), Charles Bridgeman (?–1738), Lancelot Brown (1716–1783) and Humphry Repton (1752–1818), were well aware of the lineage within which they worked.

Brown was widely celebrated and criticized by his contemporaries as a destroyer of Stuart features and a creator of new ones. It is easy to suppose a 'Capability Brown' park to be entirely Brown's creation, and even to credit the master with transforming wide tracts of country-side. Writers often suppose that he 'laid out' landscapes out of nothing, and marvel that his patrons were content to plant trees the effect of which would not be seen in their lifetimes. This comes from confusing gardens with parks. Landscape gardens are small and relatively formal areas, transformed so often that early examples seldom survive. With parks the scale was much larger, and the operations slower and more expensive. The object was not to transform entire countrysides, but to enhance an existing landscape by judicious alterations. The tradition was that venerable trees should give dignity and continuity to a gentleman's seat. It was not enough to plant trees and wait for them to grow: an 'instant park' was needed, with an air of respectable antiquity from the start. Repton explicitly appreciated the beauty of ancient trees:

The man of science and of taste ... will ... discover beauties in a tree which the others would condemn for its decay; he will rejoice when he finds two trees whose stems have long grown so near each other that their branches are become interwoven ... Sometimes he will discover an aged thorn or maple at the foot of a venerable oak; these he will respect, not only for their antiquity, being perhaps coeval with the father of the forest, but knowing that the importance of the oak is comparatively increased by the neighbouring situation of these subordinate objects ...
Observations on the Theory and Practice of Landscape Gardening, 1803

The parks themselves show that much of Brown's and Repton's work involved limited alterations to a Stuart landscape: removing an avenue, adding a lake here, bisecting a wood there, and planting a belt of trees round the boundary. At Heveningham (Suffolk), until that house recently fell on evil days, Brown's 'before and after' drawings were hanging on the wall, showing pollards and what were already 'ancient thorns' which he preserved; and one could look out of the window and see these still there in the park.

Victorian parks are much less well known than Georgian. Deer-farming continued: in 1867 there were deer in 325 English parks.[170] There was a fashion for exotic or bizarre trees. A Victorian (or Victorianized) park is known by its giant horsechestnuts, its London planes, its copper beeches, its Wellingtonias (a fabulous, newly-discovered tree, introduced in 1853), and its ragged *Abies grandis* or *nordmanniana* towering above the coverts.

Parks as they are now

The prototype of all parks at Ongar survived largely intact, although disused, until most of it was tragically destroyed *c*. 1950. At Borough Green (Cambs) Domesday records a 'park of woodland beasts', the remains of whose massive earthworks still exist in Park Wood.

Occasionally a medieval park survives in working order. At Moccas (Herefordshire) the fallow deer, cattle and sheep share the grass beneath oaks and ashes whose slow growth sees the centuries slip by, and which in their bizarre shapes, textures and colours express the strange beauty of extremely aged trees. This Arcadian scene is completed by the cleft-oak park pale and the brackeny mountain behind. (Despite recent research its history remains mysterious.)

It is rare for a complete park to survive out of use. An example is Sutton Coldfield and its woods. Staverton Park still has 4,000 amazing medieval pollard oaks, and some of the mightiest hollies, birches and rowans in the country. Most medieval parks survive either incorporated in later parks or as fragments: a boundary earthwork, a boundary hedge (as at Hatfield Park, next to Hatfield Forest), a significant deviation in a parish boundary, a 'Park Wood', or a mere name such as Park Lane or Lodge Farm. Park boundary earthworks often have a bank with an *internal* ditch (Fig. 23).

Where an ancient park is still a park, it is often possible to sort out the stages in its development, and to discern the trees and other features of the original deer park behind the overlay of the landscaping period, Victorian conifers and pheasant coverts, or recent municipalization. For example, the ancient oaks and the High Lodge of the medieval royal park of Woodstock Palace are embedded in the eighteenth-century Blenheim Park.

Parks, like commons, seldom have many of the flowering-plants characteristic of ancient woodland, and for the same reason. The native trees of parks are likewise more limited than in woods, though one occasionally finds the more exacting species such as small-leaved lime. However, ancient parks excel in the special creatures that go with ancient trees (p. 16). Dr Francis Rose has listed 73 lichens, plus several mosses and liverworts, that grow on old trees and are correlated with ancient wood-pasture in the same way as some flowering-plants are indicators of ancient woodland. They seem to be derived from wildwood; they require plenty of light and little disturbance. Many of

161

his best sites, including the supremely rich Boconnoc (Cornwall), are parks.[171]

Time has dealt hardly with Henry VIII's enterprises. Of Nonsuch Palace and its parks the very site was lost. In the London parks, funds for maintenance have seldom been short, and everything of Henry's time has long been cleared away. Only his Great Standing, built in 1543 in a short-lived park carved out of Epping Forest, stands as a last survivor of his courtly timber-framed buildings; its function has been so far forgotten that it is called 'Queen Elizabeth's Hunting Lodge'.[172]

The earliest pseudo-medieval parks of which trees survive include the sixteenth-century Melford Park, and the early seventeenth-century park at Earlham, Norwich (now the University of East Anglia), with its medieval village earthworks. The avenue of Kentwell Hall tells a story: it was once a more formal feature than it is now, with pleached limes cut every year, but when this went out of fashion the trees were allowed to grow up. They are now mysterious and awesome, with their immense height, the pollard-like effect of the early pleaching, and the bizarre galls produced by generations of mistletoe.

Landscape parks have been much studied as regards what their creators said about them, but their real history is still little known. The researches of John Phibbs, going over parks tree by tree, tell a much more complex story than contemporary documents reveal. Wimpole Park (Cambs) was begun about 1700 and was worked on by most of the great names in landscaping: Bridgeman, Robert Greening, Brown and Repton. It contains trees of the appropriate dates, and others which are both earlier and later.[173] Phibbs found a group of distinctive, exceptionally tall East Anglian elms right in front of the house, with annual rings going back to the 1630s; these, and other groups of elms, were the trees of the lost village of Old Wimpole, preserved through all the successive re-landscapings. Even greater complexity has been found in the park at Woodhall (Herts). It is a delight of parks such as Heveningham to come upon an ancient pollard, of surrealist shape and improbable bulk, made a feature of the Capability-Brownery.

Sometimes deliberately, sometimes by accident, emparkers preserved samples of many earlier landscapes. These often survive very well because the original burst of prosperity, in which the park was made, was followed by a long period of decline in which there was no money to spend on keeping the park tidy and fashionable. The making of Dalkeith Park (p. 142) gave us almost the only clear evidence of medieval coppicing in Scotland. Ickworth (p. 196) and Sotterley Parks conserve what had previously been 'average' seventeenth-century

Suffolk landscapes with their hedgebanks and hedgerow and field trees. Most big parks contain the site of at least one deserted village or hamlet. Felbrigg Park (Norfolk) perpetuates one of the finest examples of a beech wood-pasture common. The magnificent ancient oaks and beeches of Windsor Forest survive in Windsor Great Park. Almost the entire Forest of Hatfield (Essex) was saved for seventy years by inclusion within a neighbouring park. Historians and ecologists owe an immense debt to the landscape-park tradition.

9

Wooded Forests: the king's wood-pasture

10 July 1256. The king sends Richard de Caundover and William de Caundover, his huntsmen, to take five harts for the king's use in the king's forest of Mendip; and W. de Plessetis, the keeper of the said forest, is ordered to admit them for this ...
The king sends William Luvel and Henry de Candover, his huntsmen, to take 12 bucks for the king's use in the king's forest of Selwood ...

14 June 1251. Order to the keeper of the forest of Brehull that he should provide in the same forest ... three bucks, of the king's gift, for the use of the two sons of Sibilla Giffard, about to graduate at Oxford in the dialectic arts.
> [Brehull is Brill near Oxford, meaning Bernwood Forest. Sibyl Giffard was a friend of the king, to whom he often gave oaks and deer. One of her sons was to become Chancellor of England.]

2 December 1238. To the Sheriff of Essex ... to cause 120 bucks and does that the king ordered to be taken alive in the Forest of Essex for the use of the Count of Flanders to be carried in carts to the Thames and to cause Reynold Ruffus ... to have a ship to carry them to Flanders.

29 May 1250. Order to Wilfred de Langele, justiciar of the Forest, that he should let Bertram de Crioll, warden of the king's castle of Dover, have 60 oaks in the king's Forest of Kingswood outside Colchester for repairing the buildings of the said castle; Mr John, carpenter of the said castle, wants to choose them for that work.

13 June 1231, Order to Richard de Muntfitchet to let Helen of Winchester, once the king's nurse, have two old *robora* [dead pollards] in the outwood of Havering [i.e. Hainault Forest] for her fire, of the king's gift.

Letters of King Henry III[175]

We owe the word *forest* to the mysterious Merovingian Franks, who lived in north-east France after the fall of the Roman Empire. Its original meaning is unknown. The medievals thought it signified a region outside (Latin *foris*) the ordinary laws. The learned brothers Grimm, of *Grimm's Fairy Tales*, conjectured a place of fir (Old High German *forha*) trees. Both guesses are still related by modern etymologists, but there is really nothing to be said for either: scholars clutch at any straw sooner than admit ignorance.

The word may originally have meant land covered with trees, but it soon came to mean a region subjected by the king to special laws concerned with preserving game. This latter idea, and the word, became widespread in Europe long before they reached England. Throughout our Middle Ages *a Forest was a place of deer, not necessarily a place of trees*.

Forests are first heard of in Britain in Domesday Book, where the word certainly implies deer, not trees. In Anglo-Saxon times the king was the first among equals; although he honoured huntsmen, and sometimes hunted himself, he pursued only wild deer on the same terms as any other landowner. William the Conqueror introduced the un-English doctrine that all land ultimately belongs to the Crown. It was part of the king's new, supreme, status that he had *the right to keep deer on other people's land* which lies at the heart of the Forest system.

Forests evidently began in England about 1070. They had been developing for some years by 1086. The setting-up of the system is mentioned in William's obituary in the *Anglo-Saxon Chronicle*. Domesday records about 25 Forests, including the New Forest, Dean and Wychwood; it is clear, from the details given of alternative land-uses, that others, such as Sherwood, Epping and Ashdown Forests, belong to a later date.

Forests are well documented in easily accessible records, and scholarly works about them are too numerous to list. These include, for example, the many books by C. E. Hart on the Forest of Dean, the books of C. Tubbs and R. J. Putman on the New Forest, the account by R. Grant of the Forests of Wiltshire, D. Pam's story of Enfield Chase, C. R. Young's book on Forest officialdom and laws, and J. M. Gilbert's book on Scotland.[112,175-7] (Not all these writers pay due regard to fieldwork.) Forests are also the most prolific of all fields of pseudo-history, and are responsible for nearly half the popular misunderstandings of the landscape.

Forests as institutions

The Forest system grew under Henry I (1100–35). Probably this was a new development after the introduction of fallow deer, which would have enabled him to set up Forests in places where there were not deer already. Many Forests, such as Epping and Sherwood, are first heard of in the twelfth century, and the legal bounds of others were enlarged. There was a third phase of afforestment under Richard I (1189–99) and his successor King John. This brought the number of Forests in England to about 143, of which some 90 were the king's and the rest belonged to the greatest nobility.[178] The increase in Forests and their corrupt bureaucracy caused friction between the king and the nobility, and was one of the abuses curtailed by Magna Carta (1215). After this Forests began to decline.

The word Forest was a legal term – a tract of land within which the **Forest Law** operated and people could be prosecuted before Forest courts. We now use the word to mean the physical Forest – the area of wood-pasture or other roughland on which the deer actually lived. Nearly always the **legal Forest** was much wider than the **physical Forest**: Forest Law protected deer not only when they were in the Forest but also, to some extent, when they strayed outside. Lands which were legally, but not physically, Forest included ordinary farmland, private woodland, villages and towns (e.g. Colchester). In medieval documents the two meanings are usually not differentiated – the reader would have known which was meant – but sometimes the physical Forest is specified by the words *coopertura foreste*, 'covert of the Forest'. This is a most important distinction, and scholars have drawn a wholly false picture of medieval England by overlooking it. They have taken the perambulations which defined the Forests in legal terms, have worked these out on the map, have assumed that they represent the actual extent of the Forests, and have compounded this blunder by the further error of assuming that all Forests were wooded. Hence the pseudo-historical belief that medieval England was very wooded. When it is said that Waltham Forest once covered 60,000 acres, of which the present Epping Forest is only 6,000 acres, most of the difference is due to a change in the meaning of the word and not to actual encroachment.

English Forests could be wooded, like Epping, Wychwood or Alice-Holt (Hants), although few were *entirely* woodland. They could equally be heath, with or without scattered woods, like Sherwood or Wolmer (Hants). Many Forests were moorland, like Dartmoor, Exmoor and some 25 Forests in the Pennines. There were a few fenland Forests, like Hatfield Chase (S.E. Yorkshire), although most fenland was too valuable to waste on deer.

The location of Forests was determined not by the terrain – though, except in a few merely nominal Forests, some kind of roughland had to be found for the deer – but by where the king had lands or palaces. The biggest concentration of Forests was in the London–Oxford–Dorset triangle, where the king had up to 15 palaces in which to consume the deer (Fig. 34).

A Forest was not the king's absolute property, nor was it 'reserved

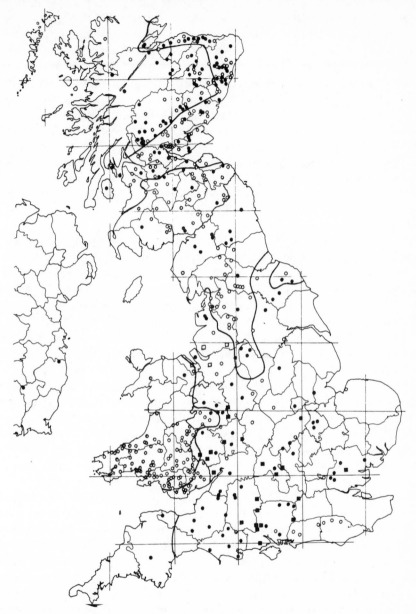

Fig. 34. Medieval Forests. Black points: royal Forests (i.e. those whose Forestal rights belonged to the English or Scottish Crown). White points: private Forests. Squares: Forests mentioned or implied in Domesday Book. The circles have an area (at the scale of the map) of 20 square km or 5000 acres, which would be a typical size for an English (physical) Forest. Not all the Scottish Forests operated at the same time. From numerous sources mentioned in the text and bibliography.

to the king for hunting' as we are so often told. All land, even roughland, in eleventh-century England belonged to someone and was used. The king's deer were added to, and did not replace, whatever was already going on.

The king had *Forestal rights*: the right to keep deer, to slaughter them, to appoint Forest officials, to hold Forest courts, and to pocket the fines inflicted. Already in Domesday Book there were a few Forests whose rights belonged to very great magnates such as the Earl of Chester. These private Forests (sometimes, but not consistently, referred to as *chases*) were always a minority. A Forest was the supreme status symbol.

Forestal rights did not necessarily include ownership of the land. The landowner had the soil, the timber and wood, and the grazing, except where these were subject to common-rights. Most physical Forests were also commons: specified commoners had rights to grazing and sometimes to wood or timber also.

No record survives of setting up a Forest. This would have involved defining the legal bounds – in effect, putting up notices saying 'This is a Forest' – and appointing administrators. There would also usually have been the practical matter of introducing deer.

Everyone 'knows' that Forests were places where the king's deer were protected by 'harsh laws and savage punishments'. This factoid is based on the *Anglo-Saxon Chronicle's* claim that the Conqueror blinded the slayer of hart or hind. Some obscure statutes of the twelfth century mention confiscation of the offender's testicles as well as eyes.[177] But medieval legal documents seldom mean what they say. In not a single actual court proceeding are these Byzantine penalties ever mentioned, let alone exacted. Offenders were in practice fined, imprisoned, outlawed or pardoned. The Pipe Rolls show that already by 1150 the main effect of Forest Law was to provide revenue.

In the Forest system we enter a bureaucracy that the modern mind cannot easily cope with: a never-never world of perquisites and sinecures, of courts that try offences committed so long ago that the participants are dead, and of nearly as many officials as deer. The top Foresters were the two Justices of the Forest on This (or That) Side of the Trent. Under them were the keepers of Forests in the various counties, keepers of individual Forests, justiciars, verderers, regarders, riding-Foresters, foot-Foresters, and 'boys'. Some Forest offices were hereditary, and others became negotiable assets. Hence there was a parallel hierarchy of deputy Foresters. In proportion to their dignity the Foresters received deer, wood and other perquisites; the deputy Foresters did the work if any.

The Anglo-Normans set up well over a hundred Forests in Wales;

in the south these were thicker on the ground than in any part of England.[94] Most were private, and had a shadowy existence; they were operated by marcher lords out of a taste not so much for venison as for the status symbols of English royalty. Surprisingly, this did not apply to Ireland, where only three Forests are known.

Scotland, also a status-ridden land of lords, had more Forests than England. The earliest known is the non-royal Forest of Paisley (Renfrewshire). The system did not decline as in England, but was renewed all through the middle ages and beyond. By 1500 there were or had been 180 Forests, almost all in the eastern half of Scotland.[95,98] In later centuries Forests spread into the Scottish Highlands, where moorland Forests are still operated to this day.

Forest land-uses

The belief that the sites of all Forests were chosen for being wooded is clearly wrong; but was there a *tendency* for Forests to be wooded, as there was with parks? Almost every Forest contained *some* woodland within its legal bounds (except Dartmoor and Exmoor, where the bounds were drawn so as to exclude the surrounding woods); but most parts of medieval England had at least a little woodland, and Forests were not unusual in this respect. In the Weald and the Chiltern plateau, the two most wooded parts of England, Forests were few and mostly not royal. The rest of this chapter deals with **wooded Forests** – those having more woodland than the surrounding country. These comprised rather under half the Forests of England and of Wales, and probably fewer still of those of Scotland.

The beasts of the Forest were four: red, fallow and roe deer, and wild swine. These, and these alone, are constantly mentioned in royal correspondence; they are carefully differentiated, with separate Latin words for the sexes. Fallow were much the commonest in England; red deer were mainly in moorland and heath Forests, but thinly scattered in wooded ones also; roe were rare. Wild sows and boars were confined to the Forests of Pickering (N.E. Yorkshire) and Dean, and became extinct in the 1260s; they were honorary deer, and are never confused with escaped tame pigs.*

Another part of academic folklore is that medieval kings were

---

* In Somerton Forest (Somerset) hares were officially regarded as deer, as were 'wild bulls' – probably related to the 'wild white cattle' still surviving in Chillingham Park (Northumberland) – in Windsor Forest. Claims that wolves and various other animals were beasts of the Forest are pseudo-historical.

'passionately fond of the chase'. Kings' biographers feel constrained to repeat this phrase, but how much evidence is there for kings hunting in person? In Anglo-Saxon times King Edmund the Magnificent, hunting from Cheddar Palace, had been saved by a miracle of St Dunstan from blundering into Cheddar Gorge. William the Conqueror 'loved the high-deer as if he were their father'. William II, and two of his nephews, met strange deaths by hunting accidents (or were they accidents?) in the New Forest. But then the records fade away – except for Edward II, the playboy king, reproached by his contemporaries for spending too much time in the field.[169] John Cummins has written a wonderful book on the symbolism and pageantry of the medieval hunt, but most of his evidence derives from France and Spain.[179] In England the ordinary working king could hardly hunt four days a week in ninety Forests. A royal hunt was nearly as full of meaning as a coronation, and about as rare.

The king hunted by proxy. Henry III and his successors have left hundreds of letters, filed in the Close and Liberate Rolls, ordering their professional huntsmen to slaughter specified deer in Forests (less often parks) for the table royal. A typical example is quoted at the head of the chapter. Medieval kings were great eaters of salt venison, especially at feasts. For Christmas 1251 Henry III had 430 red deer, 200 fallow, 200 roe, 200 wild swine (from the few then surviving in the Forest of Dean), 1300 hares, 395 swans, 115 cranes, and thousands of other beasts and birds, besides salmon and lampreys. These were carted to York and stored by the king's lardiner, the chief magnate of the city.

The king also gave away deer, either as carcases, or as permissions to hunt, or alive for stocking parks. Deer were feasting animals, and were given to celebrate consecrations, weddings and pregnancies. In an average year Henry III took 607 fallow deer: half for his own table, one-third for the feasts of his friends, one-sixth alive. He took 159 red deer, 45 roe, and 88 wild swine.[178]

The king owned trees on about half his Forests. By law, every other landowner within a Forest was supposed to get the king's permission for felling trees, but in practice this was done only for unusual fellings; there is not, alas, a file of felling licences for the routine coppicing of every private wood within a legal Forest.

The king took timber from his own Forests for work on his castles and palaces, and gave trees to favoured subjects, but he rarely sold timber. Most records are of small numbers of rare and specially valuable outsize oaks (as we saw at Gloucester, p. 55).

When the king had underwood in a Forest he used small amounts on his works, but most of it was sold. Henry III tried to organize his wood-producing Forests commercially: he had professional sellers of the king's underwood, such as Peter de Neyreford and Nicholas de Rummeseye, appointed in 1255 'for the relief of the king's debts.' He encouraged the charcoal iron industry in the Forest of Dean. Sales and grants of wood specifically excluded timber.

Wooded Forests, like parks, might be compartmented or non-compartmented. When the king sold wood, he ordered newly-felled areas to be fenced to protect the regrowth from browsing cattle and deer, wherever local custom allowed him to do so. Forests that were divided into a system of coppices and *plains* (unfenced areas) included Rockingham (Northants), Wychwood, Hatfield and Writtle (Essex), Grovely Forest and Cranborne Chase (Wiltshire).

Landowners and commoners appear in the record chiefly when they infringed Forest Law and came before the courts. Offences were of three kinds. 'Trespasses against the venison' – stealing the king's deer – could attract imprisonment or big fines, especially for organized poaching gangs. The defendants included surprisingly many knights and clerics: for example the Precentor of St Paul's Cathedral, convicted on several poaching charges in 1277, had a taste of jail and was fined £2. The ordinary individual snaring an occasional deer for the pot seems rarely to have come before the courts, and when he did was pardoned. 'Trespasses against the vert' comprised damage to the deer's habitat by 'abuse' of grazing or woodcutting. These were punished by fines, or by confiscating the animals – later redeemed for a fraction of their value.[180] Many 'fines' are no more than the value of the grazing or wood involved: the courts were evidently used as a convenient method of collecting revenue from grazing rents or casual woodsales. 'Assart' consisted of appropriating part of the physical Forest to private use: the offender was normally allowed to keep his assart on payment of a fine and an annual rent. Some Forest regulations were particularly well adapted for gathering fees from those who refused to observe them: for instance, the regulation that dogs be *expeditated* by cutting off part of one of the animal's feet lest it run after the deer.

What the king got from his Forests varied from one to another. From Dean he had minerals, underwood, timber, red and fallow deer, and wild swine, but few Forests produced more than two of these. From all the Forests together (wooded or not) he had less than a thousand deer a year, a few hundred big oaks and pollards, and some thousands of acres of underwood. These were not an intensive use of at least half a million acres of physical Forest. We must not be misled by the emphasis of the written record into supposing that the Crown had a dominating interest. It was landowners and commoners, who preserved few records, who did most of the grazing and woodcutting.

The king's rights over most Forests were limited by local bylaws, and Forest Law needed the cooperation of local people to put it into effect. The fines were worth having, although there was an army of Forest officials to be paid.

Forests were of more than merely economic value to the king. Medieval kings were poor, and their authority depended on the power to make gifts of a kind that money could not buy, such as deer and giant oaks. Forest Law, used with caution, was a means of oppressing the nobility (though medieval kings usually respected scrupulously the rights of their humbler subjects). An expandable hierarchy allowed the king to bestow honorific sinecures. Chaucer served his country well, but not in battle, and so was not eligible for knighthood; his reward was to be made under-Forester of an obscure Somerset Forest.

Forests in later centuries

The Crown's interests in deer and in the Forest laws waned in the later Middle Ages. At Hatfield, for instance, the king relinquished the landowning rights to Isabel, great-grandmother of Robert the Bruce, in 1238, and the Forestal rights to the Dukes of Buckingham in 1446. The other parties in Forests fought out their conflicts much as they did on any large common.

The Tudors' interest in hunting, with few exceptions, did not extend to Forests. Queen Elizabeth, however, took some interest in the trees on those dozen or so Forests where they still belonged to her. She commissioned Roger Taverner in 1565 to survey them; his reports, giving acreages, numbers of timber trees, and even details of under-wood, were the first of a series of such surveys which are a most valuable historical source.[181] But her Forest administration was poorly organized,[182] and she made less profit out of wood and timber than her private neighbours would have done.

The Stuarts did revive hunting in Forests. James I often hunted in Enfield Chase from his newly-bought palace at Theobalds.[176] Charles I made a last attempt to restore Forest Law, imposing huge fines on offenders and welcoming lump sums offered by landowners to contract out of the Law. Usually the commoners were too strong for him, but some Forests were privatized, such as a third of Neroche (Somerset).

After 1600 disputes over common-rights in Forests became ruffianly. Rioters took weapons and firebrands to Hatfield Forest and Enfield Chase. Other Forests, notably Waltham Chase (Hants), became noted for armed gangs of poachers and highwaymen. This led directly to the Black Act of 1723, the most ferocious of all English statutes, which created fifty new capital crimes. Indirectly, political opinion came to disapprove of Forests, which were represented as 'the nest and conservatory of sloth, idleness and misery'.[183]

The remaining Crown-owned Forests were encroached upon by modern forestry. Acts of Parliament were passed to allow other interests to be overridden, and between 1660 and 1700 some 11,000 acres of Dean and 1400 acres of the New Forest were enclosed and planted. The object, to make the Navy relatively independent of other supplies of shipbuilding timber, might have been achieved had the plantations been cared for and had the Navy stopped growing. In the event, the Forest of Dean supplied only about 3% of the oak used by the Navy from 1762 to 1817;[184] more timber came from Forests such as Hainault, where it had grown naturally. But the precedent had been set for plantations which in the nineteenth century were to destroy most of the native vegetation of Alice Holt and Bere (Hants), Dean, Parkhurst (Isle of Wight) and Delamere (Cheshire), and were to eat up nearly half the New Forest.

Forests, like other land with multiple uses, were a particular target of the enclosure movement. Most of the surviving Forests were privatized, and with rare exceptions destroyed, by Enclosure Acts between 1777 (Enfield Chase) and 1857 (Wychwood Forest). Much of what survived these disasters still remains, though often replaced by conifer plantations or spontaneous birch woodland.

Forests as they are now

As an institution, only the New Forest survives in something like its medieval form. The Verderers still regularly hold the modern equivalent of the Courts of Swanimote and Attachment, although by a historical inversion they are now appointed by, and uphold the rights of, the commoners and other interested parties; the rights of the Crown have devolved on the Forestry Commission. A shadow of the ancient administration, and of the common-rights, lingers in Dean and Epping.

The coppice element in Forests was neglected early by the Crown, which never revived Henry III's organization for selling wood. The medieval coppices in the New Forest and Dean fell into decay by the seventeenth century, although numerous woodbanks remain in the former.[185] Pollarding, too, was discouraged in the belief that it conflicted with the timber interest. Many pollards survive in the New Forest, though apparently not cut since the practice was prohibited in 1698. But coppices and pollards are now largely confined to Forests where the Crown did not own the wood rights.

Early maps make it clear that the physical boundaries of most Forests were not wood-shaped or park-shaped but had concave outlines, funnelling into roads, like other large commons (Fig. 35). This can still be seen in the northern half of Epping Forest. The perimeter is not normally embanked, except in places where a private wood abuts on the (physical) Forest from outside; the woodbank here is that of the wood and not the Forest. Within the Forest, coppices may be defined by woodbanks, but otherwise there is no demarcation between areas of trees, scrubs, and treeless 'plains' or 'lawns' or heathland. Forests, like parks, had lodges, often in permanent embanked enclosures.

The division into plains and areas of trees is older than the Forests. In the New Forest, pollen evidence dates it back to the Bronze Age; the tree-land has fluctuated considerably.[16] Replacement of trees in unenclosed tree-land has been mainly by seed; the present trees tend to reflect in their ages the history of grazing on the site. In the New Forest the unenclosed trees date from 1663 to 1763, or from 1858 to 1923, or else from 1938 to 1960, periods in which records show that grazing slackened.[185] Heavy felling during the Commonwealth, and successful re-establishment of trees immediately after, are reported from a number of Forests.

Grazing is highly selective, and is doubtless responsible for the relatively poor flora, with few tree species or plants specific to woodland, of Forests compared to nearby woods. The notable rarity of hazel, ash and lime in unenclosed Forests is only partly explained by poor soils. The pollen record of the New Forest shows that it once had lime, which survived late enough to give rise to the place-name *Lynd*hurst. Lime disappeared, along with hazel, and was replaced by oak, which more gradually gave way to beech. The same sequence of changes is to be seen in the pollen record of Epping; here it was set in motion, presumably by the rise of a wood-pasture common, some centuries before Epping became a Forest.[186] In the Forêt de Fontainebleau near Paris, place-names like La Tillaie (*tilietum*, a wood of lime-trees) tell a similar story. Lime, ash, maple and hazel are more easily destroyed by browsing than oak, beech and holly. Holly tends to increase in times of slack grazing, and is now very common in Forests and parks on acid soils. It used to be encouraged because its foliage was cut as iron rations for deer and other stock in winter.[187]

We more often see fragments, or much-altered Forests, than complete examples. On paper, a large fragment of Wychwood Forest survives, but most of its historic features have gone. The distinction between Copses and Lights (wooded and grassy compartments) is

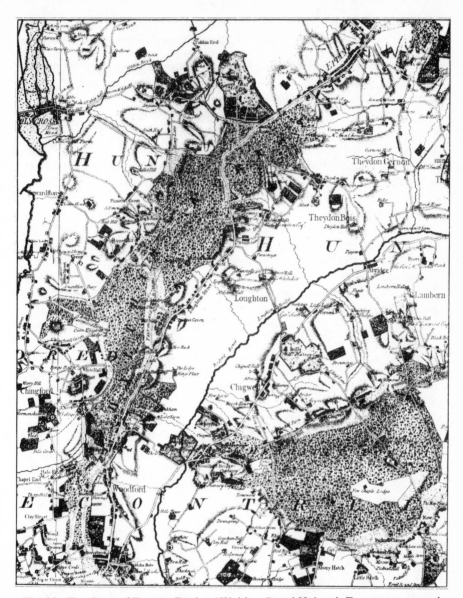

Fig. 35. The shape of Forests: Epping ('Waltham') and Hainault Forests as surveyed in 1772–4 by Chapman & André. Woodland is carefully distinguished from wood-pasture even where a wood adjoins a Forest. These Forests were not compartmented. Note the anti-highwayman trenches along some of the roads. Epping Forest, except in the south, is almost unchanged today, but only fragments of Hainault survive.

now invisible, and plantations and sycamore invasion have replaced most of the native woodland. Only the abundant maple, and the copse-banks snaking through woods and plantations, remind us of what Wychwood was. The Forest of Dean, though still at almost its full extent, has been even more thoroughly effaced by modern forestry: not by the Forestry Commission (though they did destroy the last of the greens and bogs) but by their nineteenth-century predecessors. Dean had once been famous for outsize oaks used in cathedral roofs and special bridges. The foresters of the day, thinking (as foresters do) that they could improve on this heritage, replaced the indigenous oaks, all too successfully, with 'superior' *Quercus robur* from outside, which has not prospered.

A few Forests are rich in ancient trees and in the creatures that live on them. The one remaining wood of Sherwood Forest has a wonderful landscape of timber oaks about 500 years old, all of them of bizarre shapes owing to forgotten phases of dieback long ago. (The wood is called Birkland – a Viking wood-name, 'Birchgrove'.) The oaks and beeches of the wooded corner of Windsor Forest, up to 800 years old, are preserved in Windsor Great Park. The New Forest, despite its chequered history, has an exceptional number of ancient trees, often close together; it has escaped the worst of the acid rain, and is full of deadwood. Consequently, Dr Francis Rose regards it as the nearest approximation to wildwood in Western Europe in respect of those features that the more exacting tree-inhabiting lichens require.[188]

Essex and Middlesex Forests

The six Forests of Essex, plus the royal chase of Enfield, illustrate the evolution of English wooded Forests. As an institution, the Forest of Essex was founded about 1100, and exercised a tenuous jurisdiction over most of the county until the thirteenth century. It was then reduced to Waltham Forest in the south-west, plus three smaller tracts based on the royal manors of Colchester, Writtle and Hatfield Broadoak. Perambulations of the new legal boundaries make it clear that Essex was a mainly agricultural county, with hamlets, isolated farms, hedges, greens, minor roads, groves and heathland. The Hat-field perambulation of 1298 would almost do for a description of the boundaries of that parish today.

These four *legal* Forests included six *physical* Forests (Fig. 36). All of these, together with Enfield Chase, were on poor agricultural land. Except for Kingswood, they survived almost intact into the eighteenth century. They differed in vegetation and management.

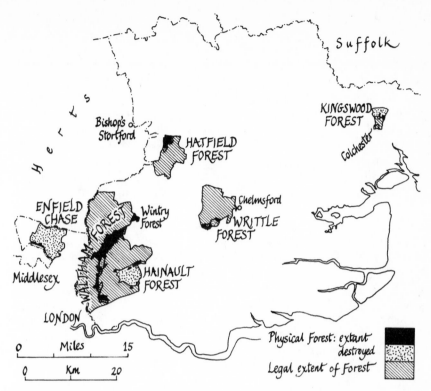

Fig. 36. Forests of Essex and Middlesex. The legal and physical Forests are distinguished.

Kingswood, the first to disappear, was partly coppice and partly heath. Henry VIII granted it in 1535 to the burgesses of Colchester, who within a hundred years disposed of it to private individuals as farmland. Some biggish woods north of the town, with lime and other ancient-woodland plants, almost certainly represent the coppices.

Enfield Chase was part of an enormous tract of wood-pasture which stretched nine miles to Hatfield (Herts). The Forestal rights belonged to the Duchy of Lancaster, and thus were technically not the Crown's (which may be why it is called a Chase), but in practice the Duchy functioned as the king's second estate agency. The medieval history was very like that of Epping Forest. Fallow deer, cattle and sheep were pastured, and appear in the records chiefly when they were stolen. Beeches, oaks and hornbeams were pollarded, both by commoners and by the Duchy (which was also landowner). The Chase was bordered by parks, which at various times encroached upon it. In the sixteenth century there were new developments: the use of the Chase for royal

177

hunts, and an attempt to increase the rights of the Duchy, particularly in timber, against the commoners. The Duchy authorities, such as Lord Burghley, were more aggressive than those of the Crown Estates as such, and did not have the Crown's traditional scruples about oppressing the tenantry. (They claimed that the common-rights had been exceeded by a growing population.) The dispute went on for two and a half centuries, sword, axe and musket being met with prison and occasionally gallows. By the 1760s the normal penalty for wood-stealing had become three months' Bridewell with a whipping in Enfield market in each month.

The outcome was to advance the timber interest at the expense of woodcutting and grazing. By 1700 pollarding had almost disappeared. Although the Chase was never compartmented, there was no difficulty – except for a short period in the sixteenth century – in securing a succession of young trees. There was a heavy felling in the 1650s, attributed to thieves in those times of unrest; but the Chase had regained at least its normal cover of trees by 1700.

The Duchy (*alias* the Crown) never got much return from the timber it had promoted at so great a cost in ill-will. In 1777 the Chase was abolished by Act of Parliament, and was later sold off to various private landowners, who had destroyed nearly all of it by 1800 and converted it to poor-quality farmland.[176]

About 2% of Enfield Chase survives on Monken Hadley Common. It is dominated by beech on the higher gravels, through hornbeam, oak and ash, to a little elm in a clayey bottom. These are timber trees, with almost no pollards or underwood; although they are of no great age, they match almost exactly a description of the Forest in 1702. A small area of plain remains.

Epping Forest, its outlier Wintry, and Hainault were pollard and grazing Forests of the uncompartmented kind. They were partly tree-land and partly heath and grassland: the earliest document describing what was to be Epping Forest, King Harold's foundation charter of Waltham Abbey in 1062, already mentions a heath. The Crown was landowner in Hainault, but in Epping and Wintry the landowning rights were divided between the Abbey and many private persons. Henry III took an average of 40 fallow and 4 red deer a year from the three Forests.

These Forests produced a little timber, and in parts of Epping a few giant beech stools indicate coppicing in the unrecorded past; but pollarding, as the main tree management, was entrenched in local custom from at least the thirteenth century. Here the commoners had undisputed rights to wood as well as grazing; but all the common wood-rights together would have amounted to less than one-third of

178

the expected growth of the trees, and there was much woodcutting by landowners as well, presumably for the London firewood market. The Forestal term 'vert' was restricted to holly, crabtree, hawthorn, blackthorn and service, which were supposed not to be cut because the deer fed on them. Tree-ring and written evidence indicate an average pollarding cycle of about thirteen years.

These Forests, unlike Enfield, had a stable history, with very little change in 700 years except for a gradual increase of trees at the expense of plains. The soils are mainly acid, with heather in the plains, and small peat-bogs. The original limewood disappeared before the memory of records. Throughout history, Epping has had mainly beech pollards on the gravelly hilltops, an intermediate zone of oak pollards, and hornbeam pollards on the clayey lower slopes, with a general scatter of the vert trees.

The fate of these Forests is a landmark in the development of the bulldozer and of the modern conservation movement. In 1851 the Crown enclosed and sold Hainault, 92% of which was quickly destroyed and was turned into poor-quality farmland. Epping and Wintry were in fragmented ownership and not so easily to be disposed of. They were saved – all but 10% – by the tenacious commoners, the infant Commons, Open Spaces, and Footpaths Preservation Society, and the intervention of the Corporation of London. By the Epping Forest Act of 1878 the Forestal rights were extinguished, and the ownerships were given to the Corporation, which was ordered to protect the 'timber and other trees, pollards, shrubs, underwood, heather, gorse, turf and herbage' which were the historic features of the Forest.

Unfortunately the Act was filed away and never read. The new Conservators undertook, as their chief duty, to 'preserve the natural aspect' of the Forest. They thought they knew what this phrase meant. They terminated the very woodcutting rights which had been the means of frustrating the destruction of the Forest. Grazing rights were continued, but no attempt was made to prevent their decline. The Conservators took a dislike to pollards, thought to be the 'maimed relics of neglect', and preferred timber trees. Not only were pollards not cut, but many thousands were destroyed in order to give room to new saplings. Plains and scrub areas were allowed to be invaded by birch and oak.

A hundred years on, much has been lost. The pollards are overgrown, and nothing grows beneath their shade. Primroses and polypody have disappeared, crab and service are rare, and even horn-beam and oak have declined; only holly and birch have prospered. Especially sad is the loss of the heather which once covered thousands of acres. We should not be too critical of the early Conservators: they would have done much worse if they had taken the advice of forestry or municipal-park interests. Nevertheless they inherited a complex and balanced system, every acre the product of centuries of peculiar land-uses, a thing of distinction and beauty unique in the world; and they set it on the way to becoming just another Chiltern-type beechwood. (Their successors now fully understand the Forest's meaning, but have come too late to reverse these changes.)

Part of Hainault Forest escaped in 1851, and now gives a rather better impression of a pollard Forest. The hornbeam, oak and thorn closely match surveys of the Forest in 1544 and 1565. Pollarding continued later and has now been revived, and the plain and heathland have been restored.

Hatfield is of supreme interest in that *all* the elements of a medieval compartmental Forest survive: deer, cattle, coppice-woods, scrub, timber trees, grassland, fen, the medieval Forest Lodge, and dozens of houses round the boundary of various dates back to the thirteenth century. As such it is unique in England and perhaps in the world. It was a small Forest of 1100 acres, which is why it survives. It supplied Henry III with about 11 fallow deer a year. The commoners had grazing rights, but the woodcutting was the landowners'. The Crown's interests ceased early, but not permanently; five of the private owners forfeited the Forest for high treason committed elsewhere. Later the Forest passed to a succession of ruffianly or litigious squires; swords and pistols were drawn, but not so often as at Enfield. In 1857 Hatfield came within an inch of sharing the fate of Hainault Forest, but most of it went as one lot to the Houblon family, who loved the Forest and preserved it as their deer-park. Only one-fifth – including, alas, most of the original Forest-shaped boundary – was lost.

Hatfield is the only place where one can step back into the Middle Ages to see, with only a small effort of the imagination, what a Forest looked like in use. In 1639, Charles I's corrupt commissioners, seeking grounds for destroying the Forest, wrote:

We find the said Forest ... to consist of Wood ground and Plains (that is to say) in Woodground usually incopsed and inclosed 646 Acres, in open Wood and Bushie ground 109 Acres, and in Playnes, Ridings and highways 240 Acres. The Forest appears irregular, full of angles and narrow Passages which wee conceive to be dangerous for the safetie of the Game of Deer there ... By reason of the ... small Quantity of Playnes, the multitude of Sheep and other Cattle that depasture there (by pretence of Commonage) ... the Deere are forced to stray abroad for their Food. ... We find little Timber in the Forest worthy valuation. The open Woods consisting of Pollard Ash and Maple of small worth ...[189]

This still holds after 350 years. The Forest (Fig. 37) consists of

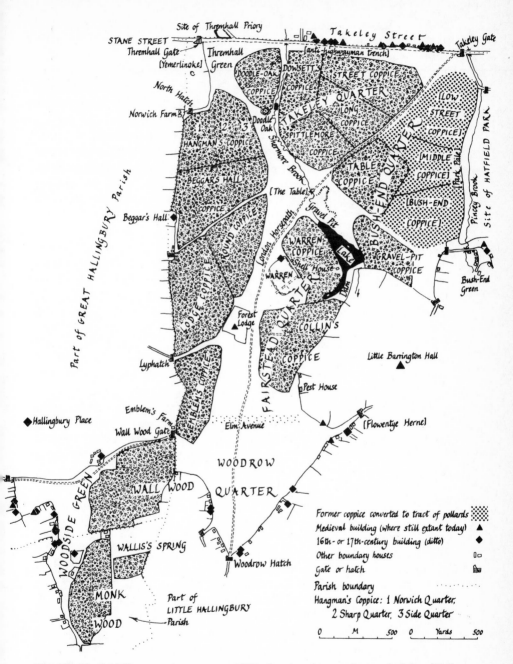

Fig. 37. Hatfield Forest as it was up to 1857, showing the coppices and plains. Wall Wood and Monk Wood were *purlieu woods*, to which some of the provisions of Forest Law applied.

181

coppices – twelve of the original seventeen survive – around a central plain. Each coppice is a separate wood with a woodbank round it. In theory, each was supposed to be cut every eighteen years, fenced against all livestock for six years, opened to deer alone for the next three, and opened to all animals for the final nine years. Outside the Forest there are two 'purlieu woods' (exclaves to which some of the Forest law applied), both of which go back to the early days of the Forest. The plains were open to deer and farm animals all the time. They contain eight kinds of pollards, including giant oaks and wonderful gnarled thorns, and tracts of 'Bushie ground'. Hatfield has the biggest maples in England, and the largest group of pollard hawthorns in the country; it is probably the chief stronghold of mistletoe in the kingdom. It has recently been shown to be a notable place for the special creatures that live on ancient trees (pp. 16,161).

Like Epping and other wooded Forests, Hatfield has a prehistoric dimension. There are Iron Age and Roman sites. The 'pillow-mounds' of a seventeenth-century rabbit warren – the commoners made it an occasion for oppressing their lord – have been adapted out of some ancient earthwork. Apart from a lake, made $c.1750$, and specimen trees of the Houblon era, Hatfield owes very little to the last 250 years.

The National Trust has owned Hatfield Forest since 1924. This period is a useful and cautionary example of the history of conservation. For many years the Trust did not know what it had, nor understand the Forest's special importance. At first the wise policy was followed of continuing what had been done before. But later the spirit of modern forestry and agriculture penetrated even here, and Hatfield suffered 'improvements' such as bulldozing tracts of coppices and replacing them with plantations. This might have been avoided had it been realized that such experiments had been tried in Georgian and Victorian times and had not succeeded. However, in recent years, Hatfield has received the sympathetic and scholarly treatment for which the Trust is famed in its treatment of historic buildings. Coppicing and pollarding have been revived, and new pollards have been started for the first time in 200 years. The special features of the Forest are now being fully catalogued and taken into account in its management.

Hatfield Forest needs all the understanding that it can get. By ill chance, a redundant wartime airfield next to the Forest became Stansted Airport in 1946, and has been growing ever since. The Trust has to deal with ever-proliferating numbers of visitors, and their cars, attracted (directly or indirectly) by the airport. Hope lies in the unfathomable mud that defends most of the Forest from incursion except in the driest weather.

And who has heard of Writtle Forest (Fig. 36)? Like Hatfield it has been in private hands for many centuries. It is not quite so well preserved – it has lost the great pollard beeches that adorned it in the Middle Ages – but most of it is still there, and in the quiet of winter is a wild and lovely place. Nearly everything one sees is of the fourteenth century or earlier: the great assart surrounded by hornbeam springs and alder slades; the heathland, pollard oaks and woodbanks; the lonely cottage, with a palfrey grazing in its pightle, on the site where King Stephen set up a solitary monk. (No Forest was really complete without a hermit.) This astonishing survival from the depths of the medieval countryside is within twenty-five miles of St Paul's Cathedral.

10

Trees on the farm:
hedges and elsewhere

The grubbing up of Hedge Rows is become general, and the Growth of Timber in them is thereby totally destroyed, owing to the great Price given for Corn since the Bounty took place for exporting of Corn and Beer, which gives every Farmer encouragement to grub Hedge Rows up, and convert them into Corn Land.

House of Commons Journal, 1792, p.318
[Grubbing of hedges was reported from 18 out of 38 counties; this entry is for Hampshire]

It should no longer be necessary to refute in detail the theory that all, or nearly all, hedges are modern, the product of the Enclosure-Act movement of the eighteenth and nineteenth centuries. It was a classic triumph of unreason that many people, from Ministers of Agriculture downwards, still believed this ten years ago – in the face of the clearest evidence to the contrary, accessible to anyone who cared to spend an hour in a county record office. This factoid was much repeated as an argument against conservation. The fact is that innumerable maps and pictures, as far back as the sixteenth century (e.g. Frontispiece), plainly depict hedges and hedgerow trees as the normal furniture of the countryside. To trace them back further calls for a little specialized knowledge; but it is no great feat of scholarship to show that they were already part of England as far back as the written record goes.

There are three ways of getting a hedge. Planting is the most familiar, the most talked-about, and the only method likely to be recorded in writing. We are therefore tempted to assume that all hedges have been planted. But hedges can also be the *ghosts* of woods that have been grubbed out leaving their edges as field boundaries. More common are hedges that have developed naturally at the edges of fields. Whenever a fence, ditch, or earthen bank is neglected for a few years, not too far from a source of tree seed, a hedge will result. Seeds are trapped in long grass or dropped by birds sitting on fence-posts; the fence protects

184

the incipient hedge. When prosperity returns, the young trees will be managed as a hedge and their origin will be forgotten. The United States has thus acquired a huge mileage of 'fence-rows', despite (in general) lacking a hedge-planting tradition. In Britain the process is uncommon in these tidy and prosperous days, but examples can be found, particularly along railways. There can be little doubt that it was common in past times of adversity.

Historians of hedges usually think in terms of 'early' or 'late enclosure', of a change (at some date or other) from an original hedgeless landscape to one with a more or less dense network of hedges. This may be unrealistic. Not all hedges form a network of enclosures. Recent work in Germany and Holland tends to back-date hedges to the Neolithic.[190] The hedgeless landscape was probably itself made by removing earlier hedges.

We now think of hedges as live fences to confine livestock, or as boundary markers, or for shelter. In earlier times they were valued also as sources of wood. A hedge might be coppiced as if it were a wood. The practice of *plashing* a hedge (which academic writers call 'laying') to make a barrier also existed; it is said to be the basis of place-names such as *Pleshey* in Essex and *Plessis* in France.

Early hedges

Ancient Rome had a long tradition of hedges, and a technique more elaborate than ours for creating them; they are described by Columella and Palladius Rutilius. Siculus Flaccus adds that some hedges can be natural, and some have hedgerow trees in them. This refers to Italy rather than Britain; but only just across the Channel, Julius Cæsar met with the practice of plashing a hedge to make it impenetrable. Hedges leave much less trace than banks or field-walls, but there is a small, but growing, body of archaeological evidence for them as antedating Roman sites. The probability is that the Romans found Britain an already hedged land.[191]

Of the Anglo-Saxon evidence there can be no doubt. Charters often include *hege*, *hegeræwe*, and various other words for hedges and hedgerows. Mentions of hazel-rows, willow-rows, etc. and compounds corresponding to our 'hawthorn' (*hagaþorn*) and 'hedge-sparrow' make it clear that it was indeed hedges, not fences, that were meant. Many charters, such as the one quoted at the head of Chapter 3, mention hedgerow and other free-standing trees. Hedges were an accepted part of the landscape; the phrase 'old hedge' occurs 24 times. They were occasionally created or destroyed: at Kington Langley

(Wilts) in 940 there was 'the hedge row that Ælfric made', and at Grimley (Worcs) in c.966 there was an 'old hedge-place'.

Hedges and non-woodland trees in the charters lend themselves to statistics. The 840 perambulations mention 14,432 objects, of which 372 were hedges and 766 were trees. Charters for what is now Ancient Countryside mention hedges 253 times; those for Planned Country-side – the medieval open-field regions – mention 119 hedges. Although Ancient Countryside has a little more charter material than Planned, it is clear that the latter had many fewer hedges. The proportion varies from N.W. Dorset, where one feature in 16 was a hedge, to the adjacent, almost hedgeless Wiltshire chalklands. Trees appear as boundary points with roughly equal frequency in the two landscapes, but the species were different. In Planned Countryside thorn was vastly predominant, followed by apple and elder; in Ancient Countryside there was a wider range of common trees (Table 6). There are a few records of pollards and other special trees.

Place-names, as we have seen, often refer to what must have been non-woodland trees. At Ashwell (Herts) a branch of the River Cam still wells out of the earth under the roots of an ash. The most frequent trees in the names of towns, villages and hamlets are thorn, ash, willow (or withy or sallow) and oak; beech, lime and service, strongly associated with woodland, are uncommon in place-names.

To summarize, over a thousand years ago there existed a peripheral England of wood and heath, hedges and hedgerow oaks, and also limes, wild pears (a tree now almost extinct) and birches. There was a central, more crowded England of few hedges, few heaths, less woodland, downland, thorns, elders and apples. In the latter the charters often mention terms relating to open-field. Since hedges and woodland tended to go together, there can be no possibility that hedges were deliberately conceived as a substitute for woodland.

The collectivization of agriculture, which created the medieval open-fields and villages of central England, was already well advanced (though still incomplete) by the time of the charters. It had destroyed many of the hedges which probably existed at an earlier period. Strip-cultivation did not spread to peripheral England until later, and then only partially. Here the landscape – the present Ancient Countryside – has always been hedged.

Medieval hedges and hedgerow trees

Hedges and trees are beneath the notice of Domesday Book, but evidence gathers from the twelfth century onward. Estate accounts

Table 6.   The Two Landscapes in Anglo-Saxon charters and Domesday Book
Figures in brackets are percentages of all features.

	Charters for Ancient Countryside		Charters for Planned Countryside	
Woods (Anglo-Saxon *wudu, graf, holt* etc.)	224	(3.0)	159	(2.4)
Hedges (*hege, ræwe, hegeræwe* etc.)	253	(3.4)	119	(1.8)
Trees: all species	389	(5.1)	368	(5.5
thorn	87	(1.15)	162	(2.43)
oak	64	(0.85)	21	(0.32)
apple (usually wild)	31	(0.40)	32	(0.48)
willow, withy, sallow	22	(0.29)	22	(0.33)
ash	29	(0.38)	13	(0.20)
elder	10	(0.15)	29	(0.44)
alder	19	(0.26)	6	(0.09)
hazel,[a] nut[a]	17	(0.23)	22	(0.33)
maple[a]	14	(0.19)	10	(0.15)
lime[a]	17	(0.23)	3	(0.05)
pear (usually wild)[a]	10	(0.15)	9	(0.14)
birch[a]	13	(0.17)	2	(0.03)
elm (*wice*)[a]	11	(0.15)	4	(0.06)
yew[a]	9	(0.12)	3	(0.05)
holly[a]	8	(0.11)	3	(0.05)
aspen[a]	6	(0.08)	4	(0.06)
blackthorn, sloethorn[a]	1	(0.01)	7	(0.11)
Heaths[a]	37	(0.48)	10	(0.15)
All features	7562	(100.0)	6664	(100.0)
Domesday Book woodland as percentage of land area	18.7		8.2	

[a] These figures include places named after the object: e.g. Apsley and Heathfield would count as 'aspen' and 'heath'.

and court rolls are the most prolific sources. Hedges were everyday objects calling for no special comment. They were managed by coppicing; the wood produced was of value and was frequently stolen. A common offence in court rolls is allowing hedges and hedgerow trees to overgrow roads, for example 'one ancient & decayed [black] poplar growing out too far over the King's highway' at Great Canfield (Essex) in 1422.[192] Timber trees and pollards often appear: for instance, at Nowton (Suffolk) in 1310 John Petye was fined 2s. for felling a poplar, and Will Gunnild felled an *abel* worth 2s. 6d.[193] At West Donyland (Essex) John Gru in 1392 was prosecuted because he had 'cut off the branches of an ancient oak amounting to 1200 billets' – like many hedgerow trees, it was a giant.[194]

Cut thorn, called *trouse*, was used for mending gaps in other hedges, and for creating temporary fences. Fitzherbert, the agricultural writer of 1523, recommends laying trouse as a protection to a newly-planted hedge or the spring of a newly-felled hedge.

In contrast to woodland, there are many records of planting both hedges and non-woodland trees. For example 18 perches [99 yards] of 'live hedge' were planted at Gamlingay (Cambs) in 1330 at a cost of 6s.[195] At Hindringham and Gateley (Norfolk) men were paid for planting ashes which had been pulled up in Hindolveston Woods.[196] There was also a nursery trade in elm, hazel, willow and poplar.[197]

Hedges increased during the Middle Ages. By the fifteenth century, they existed at least in all parts of England. In some Ancient Countryside areas they were as numerous as they have ever been: a survey of Leaden Roding (Essex) in 1439 shows every field 'enclosed by hedges and ditches'.[133] In parts of Northern England the present dry-stone walls replace medieval hedges.[198] In Planned Countryside, hedges, though less common, were present round most villages and often on parish boundaries or near woods, and there were sometimes lengths of hedge here and there in the open-fields.

Most hedges contained pollards, timber or occasionally shredded trees. There were also trees standing in fields or meadows: in 1301 an inquest was held on an Oxford schoolmaster who fell into the Cherwell from a pollard willow while cutting rods with which to beat his boys.[199] In c. 1500 Thomas Waring made a survey of trees on farms at Tanworth-in-Arden (Warwickshire). He found 1851 trees in 'heges', besides others in groves, all of them timber; two-thirds were oak and most of the rest ash. There were about three trees per acre of farmland.[200]

Oak was perhaps the commonest hedgerow tree, though not overwhelmingly predominant as it was among the timber trees of woods. Non-woodland trees could alternatively be ash, willow, elm, poplar or *abel*; elm was less common than in the twentieth century, possibly because of Elm Disease. Hedgerow trees, especially ash, were often larger and more valuable than in woodland. Many of the big timbers in medieval buildings have wide annual rings or are very crooked, suggesting that they grew outside woodland.

Tudor and Stuart hedges and trees

Numerous surveys, beginning with some of those made at the dissolution of the monasteries, list hedges or hedgerow trees. Hedges were valuable property, and are sometimes assigned acreages and coppicing rotations as if they were woods; they could be many yards in width. Wood from hedges was increasingly coveted in the terrible post-medieval centuries of the Little Ice Age and advancing poverty. Penalties for 'hedge-stealing' increased to include whipping and the stocks. Thomas Tusser in 1573 published a book called *Fiue hundred pointes of good Husbandrie, as well for the Champion or open countrie, as also for the woodland, or Seuerall.* The title emphasizes the contrast between what I have termed the Planned and Ancient Countryside. Tusser, as an Essex man, preferred the latter; he called it Woodland, not because it contained woods, but because it produced wood from hedges.

From 1580 onwards, many maps depict hedges and distinguish them from other kinds of boundary; they also differentiate between woodland and fields with many trees. The map of Earl's Colne (Frontispiece) portrays small fields, lanes and isolated farms, and a vast mileage of hedges carefully distinguished from the few fences, palings and walls. Most hedges, with a few exceptions, are shown with trees in them; here the trees are partly conventionalized, though other cartographers tried to plot them individually. This was typical of Ancient Countryside; in champion regions hedges were less common, but (despite Tusser) almost every parish in England had at least a few. Landscape paintings and engravings, such as Hoefnagel's view of Norwich in 1580, nearly always depict hedges, often astonishingly packed with hedgerow trees.

Although many of the hedges shown on early maps still exist today, there were some changes. Most maps that depict hedges also, occasionally, depict rows of trees across fields, evidently remaining from former hedges already grubbed out. In Ancient Countryside additions and subtractions probably roughly balanced. In Planned Countryside hedges increased as individual fields, and here and there a whole parish, were enclosed.

The age of the Enclosure Acts

The Great Enclosures, though not a universal transformation, were a time of more new hedging (and walling) than ever before or since. Hedges planted between 1750 and 1850, probably about 200,000 miles,

189

were at least equal to all those *planted* in the previous 500 years. Hedging, at first quite elaborate, became more commercialized and more perfunctory as the enclosure movement advanced.

The Georgians, however, saw themselves as destroyers of hedges and non-woodland trees. The protests of Clare, the poet, at the destruction of his 'ancient pulpit trees' are corroborated by the *House of Commons Journal*. Enclosures of Planned Countryside parishes incorporated some of the existing hedges but swept away others. In Ancient Countryside, fields were often enlarged: at Earl's Colne, fields averaged 5.4 acres in 1598 but 8.2 acres in 1922.

In the mid-eighteenth century there were more hedgerow trees than ever before or since. The evidence of artists is confirmed by surveys. At Roxwell (Essex) in 1734 there were 6.7 trees to the acre of farmland (Table 7), and this was far from being extreme. At Thorndon (Suffolk), *c*. 1742, a farm of 187 acres had no fewer than 6,058 pollard trees[202] – trees grew thicker on that farmland than in many wooded Forests. Numbers varied widely, but were often ten times what they are today, and could be much more.

Table 7. Trees on 603 acres of farmland in Roxwell[201]

	Maiden	Pollard
Elm	370	1848
Oak	131	715
Ash	214	376
Maple	58	309
Willow	–	30
Hornbeam	10	–
	783	3278

Farmland trees might be timber or pollards. The terms of farm leases usually reserved the timber for the landlord – apart from the tenant's housebote – but gave the pollard wood to the tenant. Pollards are usually described from the landlord's point of view and therefore disapprovingly. The Thorndon farm was 'very much incumbered' with pollards 'and if a great deal more was cut down it would be much better for the Land'. Hedges sometimes provided large or curved timber for buildings. As early as 1608–9, when over half the 'hooks', 'knees', etc. taken from Crown estates in eastern England are recorded as coming from trees in fields,[203] hedges were a principal source of special shipbuilding timbers.

From 1750 onwards, hedgerow trees generally declined. The huge numbers in Ancient Countryside were felled and not replaced, and were not balanced in numbers by new trees in Enclosure-Act hedges. The first edition Ordnance Survey 25-inch map, a miracle of cartography, tries to depict every non-woodland tree. It rarely shows much more than one tree per acre of farmland, and often less. The year 1870 probably marks a maximum number of hedges and a minimum number of hedgerow trees. It came at the end of a century of agricultural prosperity (on the whole), in which farmers had had the incentive and the means to prevent trees from growing.

Hedges and trees since 1870

Next there came long decades of stable landscape and increasing trees. Except for those destroyed by expanding cities or wartime airfields, almost every hedge that existed in 1870 was still there in 1950. In 1951 the Forestry Commission estimated that there were 56 million hedgerow and park trees in England more than 12 inches in girth – 2.3 trees per acre of farmland. I reckon that this is a slight underestimate, and compare it with the 23 million depicted by the Ordnance Survey eighty years or so earlier.[204] That there had been a big increase is confirmed by the record that nearly a third of the 1951 trees were 'saplings' of between 12 and 24 inches in girth. Most of the intervening years had been times of agricultural adversity; farmers had allowed young trees (especially elms) to grow up; and even wartime fellings had not kept pace with the growth of new trees. This marks a second maximum in the numbers of farmland trees.

After 1950 there came two sudden changes of fashion. It became the practice to grub out hedges on an unprecedented scale, and to keep the remaining hedges unprecedentedly tidy. Estimates of the rates of destruction vary widely owing to differences between regions and to the difficulty of deciding when a damaged hedge becomes a destroyed one. The richly hedged Ancient Countryside of Eastern England became cornland, in which parish after parish now has well under half the hedges shown on World War II air photographs. Much of the west and north still has a relatively complete hedge system. Huge numbers of hedgerow trees were lost to Dutch Elm Disease between 1973 and 1983. Recruitment of young trees was abruptly stopped by the invention of the mechanical hedge-trimmer, and the fashion for using it every year. Estimates of the numbers of non-woodland trees vary widely and are difficult to reconcile. Eastern England now has well under half those which it had in 1951, but other regions have lost fewer, and in Cornwall they are probably still increasing.

The meaning of hedges and non-woodland trees

In Ancient Countryside the majority of hedges are older, often much older, than 1700. There have been many piecemeal alterations, but these often cancel one another out: younger hedges tend to be more often grubbed out than older. At Lawshall (Suffolk), comparison of early maps shows that about 85% of the present hedges were already there in 1612 (Fig. 38). Even in Planned Countryside, pre-Enclosure hedges are not so very uncommon: Dr Max Hooper has shown that 62% of the hedges of Conington (Huntingdonshire) were already there in 1595.

Even ancient hedges differ from woods, especially in their herbaceous plants. Kex or cow-parsley, the most familiar of all hedgerow plants, is infrequent except in very recent woods. Hedges that are the ghosts of vanished woods are often strikingly unlike other ancient hedges. They may have strict woodland plants such as wood anemone or (in the Midlands) dog's-mercury. In lime country a ghost hedge may be a wall-like palisade of small-leaved lime stools with occasional service (both trees otherwise very rare indeed in hedges).

Most readers will know Dr Hooper's correlation between the age of a hedge and the number of tree and shrub species in it. The count of species in a 30-yard length of hedge, defined according to a standard list (Table 8), gives the approximate age in centuries. An Enclosure-Act hedge typically has one or two, for example hawthorn and ash; an older hedge will be mixed; while a hedge with ten or more trees and shrubs in 30 yards is likely to be pre-Conquest. This is an empirical relation, which holds over most of England; it is surprising how little influence management or soil have on what composes a hedge.

Why does Hooper's Rule work? Already in the Middle Ages there were mixed hedges, as illustrated by a complaint at Hatfield Broadoak (Essex) about the felling of a hedge containing 'oak, ash, maples, white thorn & black'.[207] The answer is probably through a combination of three processes. A hedge gains further species by colonization as it gets older. In earlier times it was the custom to plant hedges with more species than later on. A hedge that formed naturally would be mixed from the start; this happened more often in earlier centuries than in recent times when new hedges have usually been planted.

Hooper's Rule is not a law, and it has exceptions. A hedge may lose species through being invaded by elm, which is a strong competitor.

192

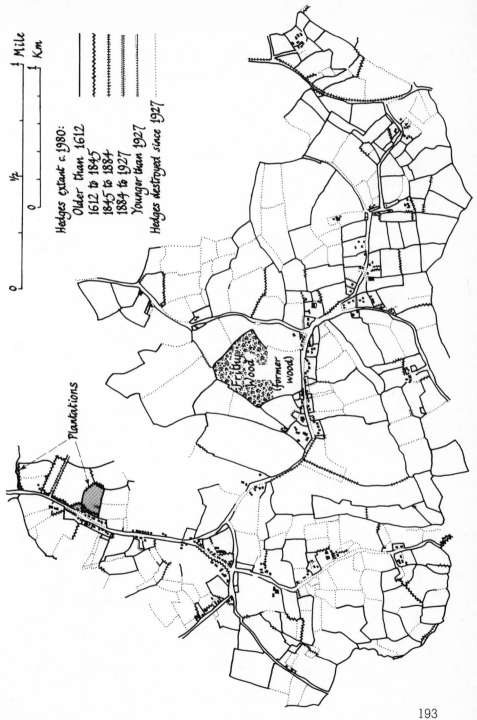

Hedges extant c. 1980:
Older than 1612
1612 to 1845
1845 to 1884
1884 to 1927
Younger than 1927
Hedges destroyed since 1927

0   ½   1 Mile
0   1 Km

Plantations

Fribuy Wood (former wood)

Fig. 38. The hedges of Lawshall (Suffolk), showing the date of each hedge now extant.[205]

Table 8. List of trees and shrubs to be counted in hedge-dating

Alder	Furze	Poplar: aspen
Apple (including crab)	Guelder-rose	black
Ash	Hawthorn: ordinary	grey
Beech	woodland[b]	white
Blackthorn	Hazel	Privet (wild)
Briar[a]	Holly	Rowan
Broom	Hornbeam	Sallow[c]
Buckthorn	Lime: ordinary	Service
Cherry	pry	Spindle
Cherry-plum	Maple	Sycamore
Dogwood	Oak: pedunculate	Wayfaring-tree
Elder	sessile	Whitebeam
Elm: wych	Pine	Willow: crack
English	Plum (including bullace)	white
East Anglian		Yew
Cornish group		
Dutch, Huntingdon etc.		

Undershrubs (e.g. bramble) and woody climbers (e.g. ivy) do not count.

[a] The three common species (*Rosa arvensis, canina, rubiginosa*) are counted separately.
[b] *Crataegus lævigata.*
[c] *Salix caprea* and *cinerea* are counted separately.

Hedges gain species more quickly where they are near a wood or an existing ancient hedge. A few hedges have arisen naturally within the last hundred years, and have far too many species for their age.

The study of hedges calls for the intelligent use of a variety of evidence, including Hooper's Rule. Victorian squires could imitate Gothic hedges, as they did Gothic churches; they also (as with churches) disguised Anglo-Saxon examples as Victorian. But the deception is seldom flawless. A perfectly straight hedge is unlikely to be ancient. A hedge will probably be old if it stands on a big bank or lynchet (p. 116) between fields, and almost certainly if it contains big coppice stools or pollards.

David Dymond and Colin Ranson examined the dispersed parish of Rougham, Suffolk, which straddles the boundary between Ancient and Planned Countryside. In the middle stands the isolated church, surrounded by 2- and 3-species hedges resulting from the enclosure of heath and open-field by Act of 1813. Farther out is a belt of hedges with 7 to 10 species – an early-medieval landscape which still contains most of the hamlets and houses. On the outer fringes of the parish, 'and sometimes between settlements, there are patches of 4- to 7-species hedges, probably later-medieval assarts into common-land or wood-pasture.[208] In the nearby parish of Felsham, Ann Hart has examined 298 hedges, with a predominance of 7 or more species (occasionally up to 14). These exceptionally rich hedges are in a highly dispersed settlement with 17 scattered homestead moats. The whole of Felsham could easily have been hedged by the early Middle Ages; it has remains of what could be a Roman or Iron Age grid of fields.

Hedgerow trees are usually of the same age as the hedge or younger. It is not known how many trees in Enclosure-Act hedges are the ones originally planted there. There are many records of trees having been planted in existing hedges, but modern experience suggests that it would have been difficult to keep them alive. Hedgerow trees, also, were promoted from the saplings, elm suckers or coppice shoots with which any mixed hedge abounds.

Hedgerow pollards and timber trees show regional variation. Oak, for instance, predominates in most of Norfolk, elm in Essex, and ash in the N.E. Midlands. This is not well correlated with either the timber trees or the underwood in local woods. In Essex, hornbeam is common in woods and among Forest pollards, but not in hedges. Oak is less often predominant as a timber tree in hedges than in woods, despite being easier to grow. Hedges (except for ghosts) are historically and ecologically different from woods.

Hedgerow pollards are now uncommon except in Eastern England. They very seldom occur in Enclosure-Act hedges, since making new pollards was in decline by that time; but it is not clear why the Welsh Border and Devon, with so many ancient hedges, should have few pollards. There are magnificent ancient wych-elm pollards in Swaledale, N.W. Yorkshire.[209]

Few remain of the innumerable, sometimes very large, trees that before 1750 used to stand on their own in fields and meadows. Pollard willows on river-banks are now the most active branch of pollarding, but individual trees seem seldom to be of any great age. On the edges of the Breckland, there are still a number of meadows with giant black poplars, and upland fields thick with pollard oaks. Pollards are also to be found in pasture-fields in S.E. Wales.

Of special interest are the ancient trees of settlements. Gnarled elm pollards are a characteristic feature of many villages and hamlets – or of places where such have been – in East Anglia and the East Midlands. At Knapwell (Cambs) vast pollard elms, of surrealist shapes, mark the deserted streets and closes of the shrunken medieval village (Plate XX). On the Lizard Peninsula (Cornwall) nearly every one of more than a hundred settlements and deserted settlements has its grove of one of the three or four local elms. There are many different kinds of settlement elms, which once introduced are almost impossible to get rid of, and maintain their distinctive characters for ever by suckering. It has been claimed that some of these elms were brought from the Continent by Bronze and Iron Age men.[115]

Any study of a deserted settlement should include ancient trees. Pollard oaks and ashes may go back to the time the settlement was inhabited, and occasionally one finds relict trees from gardens and orchards.

The best impression of pre-1750 hedgerow and field trees is to be gained from pseudo-medieval parks. The vast numbers of pollard oaks at Thorndon (Suffolk) have perished, but a small sample of their sisters survives nearby at Thornham Magna through incorporation in a Victorian park. At Ickworth (Suffolk) the great park – now National Trust – is set with some of the most imposing pollard oaks and other ancient trees in Britain. It simulates a medieval park, with later boundary woods and landscaping around the great house; but there is a church in it, which no genuine medieval park had. Ickworth parish was described field by field in 1665, and then consisted of hamlets and greens, numerous hedged fields, groves and a small open-field.[210] In 1701 the entire parish (and more) was engulfed in the park, and its trees, some already ancient, were preserved. A ring-count in elm confirms a last pollarding in *c*. 1690. Trees remain from hedgebanks and the boundaries of closes, and from former gardens. Many other pollard trees evidently stood in fields, in accordance with Breckland-edge practice.

11

Conservation
and the future

And I [the LORD] will restore to you the years that the locust hath eaten.

Joel 2, 25

For there is hope of a tree, if it be cut down, that it will sprout again, and that the tender branch thereof will not cease. Though the root thereof wax old in the earth ... *yet* through the scent of water it will bud, and bring forth boughs like a plant.

Job 14, 7–9 [c.400 BC]

The optimistic Eighties

The first edition of this book ended with a depressing prognosis. If the changes between 1950 and 1975 had continued, there would by the turn of the century be almost no ancient woodland left except in nature reserves. This will not now happen. Little ground has been lost in the last fourteen years, and much ground thought lost has been regained. The vast, intractable problems of conserving woodland have passed into history (Chapter 5), and a new set of issues has come to the fore. This is partly by historical accident – the besieging troops are no longer being paid, or have found other things to do – but partly because ancient woods are now appreciated and valued (though not always understood). Almost any threat to ancient woodland, except from forestry, is promptly challenged, often with success.

Since 1985 the expansion of farming is not a major threat. This seems to be, not a repetition of the events of 1350 and 1870, but a permanent change, which should have been foreseen. Plant breeders have enabled farmers to grow $2\frac{1}{2}$ bushels of wheat where one grew before, and sooner or later this raises the question of what happens to the land on which the $1\frac{1}{2}$ bushels used to grow. Not all the increase may be maintained, either because of crop disease or because it requires too much fertilizer, but plant breeders are capable

197

of addressing both these problems also. Far from needing yet more farmland, Europe will not be able to use all the farmland it already has. The inevitable result, unless sustained effort is put for ever into preventing it, will be a huge increase in woodland.

With forestry the story is different, and the woods themselves have played an active part. Some woods have, indeed, been successfully exterminated and replaced by conifer plantations. When the conifers are felled there is little, save woodbanks, to show that there had ever been a wood before; if not replanted, the site turns itself into a new wood just as a field does. But it has often happened that the original stools, after felling, have grown again and have competed, more or less successfully, with the planted trees. The effect has been like a rather drastic coppicing: an expensive coppicing, but expense is soon forgotten. Alternatively, both the original and the planted trees have died and the site has been taken over by self-sown ash, sallow or birch. The result is a natural wood, with much of the ground vegetation, though not the trees, of the original.

When 'restocking' ancient woods was proposed in the 1950s, it should have been realized that this had already been tried by the Victorians (if not earlier), with much the result I have described. Either this experience had been forgotten, or it was supposed that the invention of poisons like 2,4,5-T had turned the scales against the native trees. This has not been so, for three reasons. To establish a plantation in the face of existing trees calls for labour over many years in cutting back the regrowth. The task may be too expensive, the workmen may live too far away, and the work tends to be postponed and then forgotten. A felled wood, especially after machines have run over it, becomes a wetland in which transplanted trees are at an especial disadvantage. And native trees vary in their response to poisons: hornbeam is fairly susceptible, but lime recovers easily, and no venom hurts aspen, which keeps its vital parts below ground.

There are *more* ancient woods surviving in 1989 than I would have estimated that there were in 1975. Many woods, once written off as wrecked by replanting, have come back to life. This has yet to be properly measured, but my impression is that in eastern and midland England less than half the conversion attempted has resulted in a plantation, and still less in a plantation that will grow worth-while timber. In the west and north success is more likely. Replanting seldom succeeds in small woods, but has failed in large woods too. Shrawley Wood (Worcs), half of which is supposed to be a conifer plantation, is once again a magnificent lime coppice in which, in places, careful search reveals the occasional remains of a conifer. I used to mourn the loss of two-thirds of Chalkney Wood (Essex), but over the years more and more of that wood has come back.

The future of woodland is now less often presented in economic terms. It is now obvious that trees outlive industries, intended users, and money itself.* Over the time which it takes a tree to become 'mature', all economic laws are swallowed up in the Law of Unintended Consequences. The economist C. Price, asking the question 'Are there any economics of upland forestry?', persuasively argues for the agnostic answer No[211] – and yet moorland forestry avoids many of the uncertainties in woodland forestry. Even if plantations grow as expected, economic predictions about trees are, at best, a game of the mind; in the game of real life, the goal-posts will have moved by the time the trees have grown. If forestry has to be justified, there are much better grounds on which to do so. The confidence with which landowners planted trees in the 1960s has dwindled into a sad plea that 'the sale of the timber will pay for the replanting'. This bubble of fashion has burst.

The replanting threat is still not dead. The Forestry Commission, in general, has usually come to respect ancient woods, but I am disturbed by reports of what has been attempted in Herefordshire and other western counties in the name of its present broadleaved woodland grant scheme. The Commission's private imitators continue their depredations, especially in the west and north where replanting is not so conspicuous a failure. Occasionally they have the naïvety to invoke the name of conservation, or to plead Dutch Elm Disease as a pretext. I am sorry to see that the otherwise excellent Woodland Trust makes so much of planting in its propaganda, and occasionally does it even in ancient woods. The bandwagon has not come to rest, though its engine has been switched off.

There has been a big revival of traditional woodmanship. Coppicing has been continued or revived in, for example, more than a hundred woods in Essex. This is partly the work of public authorities such as Rochford District Council (Essex) and of conservation bodies – first the county wildlife trusts, recently the National Trust – who value coppicing either as an amenity or for the habitats it provides. After 1973 fossil fuels ceased to be cheap, and many woods reverted to their traditional use as sources of energy. The specialist underwood crafts

---

* Some landowners are setting out to grow high-quality oak and other timber, which commands a much higher price than timber of ordinary quality. It seems a pity to argue against this, at least as an objective for new plantations, but some words of caution are needed. This is a new enterprise: Britain has normally grown ordinary timber but imported superior timber. High-quality timber is more easily grown in France, where it is a traditional product and the special trees, environment, skills and tenacity of purpose already exist. And, alas, who can tell what will count as high-quality timber in a hundred years' time?

have shown unexpected resilience and a modest revival.

Ancient woodland is now valued in its own right, not as vacant land which ought to be growing something. For example, in 1988 there were public inquiries into proposals for new roads which would partially destroy Oxleas Wood in Greenwich and Birkham Wood near Knaresborough. At the time of writing one case had apparently been lost, and the other was unresolved. But it is a change in public appreciation that the destruction even of part of an ancient wood should be grounds for an objection to a main road, with at least a fair chance of winning. There are occasional losses of woods to quarries and development, but this (since 1950 only the third most important cause of loss) shows no sign of increasing.

There is apprehension that trees in Britain are threatened by the blight, popularly attributed to acid rain, that has killed great areas of conifers in Central Europe. Symptoms, supposedly of a similar nature, have been widely reported in spruce, beech, oak and various exotic trees in Britain. The symptoms, such as defoliation, are vague and mild and have seldom been claimed to have killed the tree. On present evidence I am sceptical. The Forestry Commission has surveyed the symptoms and finds no clear link with the geography of pollution.[212] The argument depends on an assumption that the normal state of all trees is vigorous health, and that any departure from the norm is 'damage' and has an ascertainable cause. In fact, trees can have thin foliage by reason of genetics, weather, age, soil, or through having flowered well the previous year. If the symptoms are pathological, pollution is one among many possible causes, biological and non-biological. Trees have had their ups and downs for centuries – the 1920s were a bad period for oak – and will continue to do so. Most of the symptoms are from *planted* trees, which cannot be expected always to flourish, because many of them have been put in unsuitable situations.

The effects of acid rain on lichens are very well known. Lichens are much more sensitive to sulphur dioxide than trees; many species of tree grow perfectly well in an atmosphere acid enough to kill even the most resistant lichens. Acid rain has been with us as long as men have burnt coal. Jacobean London was alarmed about 'the corroding quality of the Coale smoake, especially in moist weather' dissolving Old St Paul's Cathedral.[79] We now burn vastly less heavy oil (the worst producer of brimstone) than we used to, and rather less coal: the lichenological literature has many reports of the atmosphere getting better, not worse. The matter is not quite settled, but those who claim that trees in Britain are now threatened by pollution must explain how it is that there are any trees more than 60 years old in, for example, east London or the Welsh mining valleys.

Destruction of hedges and hedgerow trees has much diminished since 1975. I now see about one destroyed hedge a year, although I am told that this is less rare in parts of the west and north. The Dutch Elm Disease epidemic has largely run its course, leaving a good many elms alive outside English Elm territory. Suckering elms (including English) are returning. Even wych-elm, though it does not sucker, grows easily from seed and produces more seed when quite young. In some areas I find more wych-elms now than there were in 1960.

Hedges and non-woodland trees have fared best in times of past neglect. They fare badly in this age of tidiness and machinery. In the past, a hedge was plashed or coppiced every so many years; the work was done carefully, with due regard to the succession of trees. The work is now done hastily and grudgingly every year. No chance is given for damaged hedges to recover, or for new trees to arise within the hedge. One man with a machine cuts off ten thousand young trees in an hour, without noticing that they are there. Instead, ten young trees may be planted and left to die. Tree-planting has come to usurp the place of conservation.

Tidy-mindedness can perhaps be overcome with education. By 1987 there were signs of progress even on this front, and the prospects for conservation looked better than ever since 1945, when a remarkable event let Unreason loose once again.

The 'Great Storm'

On 16 October 1987 there was one of the great storms of history, affecting south-east and east England as far as a line from Southampton to Newmarket and Cromer. As measured by instruments, or by damage to buildings (other than by trees falling on them), the wind speed was not specially remarkable; there was little shipwreck and not much loss of life. But the effects on trees were spectacular; the storm was exceptional in coming when the trees were in leaf and when the ground had been weakened by previous heavy rain. The ecological effects are outside the scope of this book. Here I am concerned with the anthropological effects.

Four days after the storm, my telephone rang, and this conversation took place:

Dr Rackham, this is the Editor of [a famous national newspaper]. We hear you are knowledgeable about trees. We would like you to write us an article about the effects of the Great Storm.
I don't know much about the effects yet, but I will do what I can. The day after tomorrow

I am going to London on business, and I was intending to spend the afternoon finding out what the effects are.
Oh no, Dr Rackham. We can't wait for you to find out. We need that article now.

The article duly appeared – but I did not write it – and many others within a week of the storm. The storm was universally treated as a disaster and a tragedy; it was bad for conservation; it had 'destroyed ancient woodland'; it was unprecedented, but the pundits took only two days to make up their minds what to do about it. The destruction had come about because there had not been enough planting in recent decades and the country was full of old, 'geriatric' trees. Like all tragedies, it could be put right by Money. Within five days the Government knew what was wanted: on October 22 a grant of £3 million was announced for 'restoring the nation's ravaged woods and parks'. (This did not mean putting uprooted trees back in their holes.) Within ten days the storm had a complete pseudo-history: a newly-built Temple of Unreason, with an angel with a fiery sword posted at the door to keep out fresh information. The public had come to believe that this was the greatest storm for 300 years, and that 15 million trees had been 'lost'; and still believes these figures, unshaken by later investigation.

There was an immediate sense of urgency, stoked up by the press. 'Action was a substitute for thought.' All through that very wet winter, machines galumphed through the woods, getting out timber which was sold at bottom prices. Men were found to clear 'dangerous' trees, sometimes losing their own lives in that ill-advised task. Young trees were hastily bought from somewhere and stuck in the ground. Ecological damage done by clearing-up and replanting exceeded that done by the storm itself.

The storm was an insult to people's ideas of a tidy world, and to preconceptions of what a tree is and how it behaves. The sense of haste, to do something rather than wait and see, was understandable. Conservation bodies should have realized that the storm was a rare and wonderful event, good for wildlife and to be made the most of; but many of them joined the panic with the same squeals as everyone else. A few kept their heads. The organization Common Ground instantly commissioned and published a set of postcards on the theme 'Don't Chop Them Down; Don't Chop Them Up'. Rochford District Council (responsible for many of the woods described in my *South-East Essex* book) decided to do the minimum necessary to reopen the footpaths, and was not to be deflected from its coppicing programme, and published a leaflet to explain why.

What had really happened was gradually found out. Most affected were young trees which had recently reached full size; they had developed maximum windage but not the massive stems and roots

202

which might have resisted the gale. A famous example were the Seven Oaks of Sevenoaks, planted in 1902. Conifer plantations, set too close together and seldom properly thinned, were often flattened. Least affected were ancient trees. Staverton Park stands relatively intact, surrounded in all directions by vast pine plantations in which nearly every tree was snapped or uprooted. I know a place in Kent where ancient pollard hornbeams withstood not only the storm but also having a poplar plantation collapse on them.

Next summer it emerged that most of the trees 'lost' in the storm had not actually been killed. Broadleaved trees, if broken, resumed growth as they would have done if pollarded. Most uprooted trees, apart from beeches on thin soils, were in at least normal health, and some were flourishing horizontally. They had kept enough roots in the ground to sustain them through the wet summer of 1988. Even conifers, which are set in their ways, lived more often than not. This outcome, correctly predicted by Common Ground, is so wildly outside most people's expectations that even when taken out and confronted with the evidence they refuse to believe it.

These observations belong to the real world, and were kept out of the Temple of Unreason. On the anniversary of the storm more articles appeared, regretting that so much clearing and replanting had still to be done, reproaching landowners who had not begun, and calling for yet more money. Conservation bodies, even outside the main area of the storm, were embarrassed by (but seldom refused) grants to be spent on tree-planting by the end of the financial year.

Spectacular damage was mostly in formal plantings. Ancient woodland was let off lightly, with boughs broken and the occasional uprooting. Overgrown coppice stools, especially of chestnut, were overturned; these survived, and will either go back into their holes at the next coppicing, or will be objects of wonder and legend for centuries to come. A horizontal tree – alive or dead – is at least as good a habitat as an upright one. Patches of uprooted trees have sometimes revived the coppicing flora of a long-neglected wood.

The myth of the Tree as Artefact

The Great Storm was a setback to woodland conservation, not directly, but because it drew public attention to trees and woods without adding to public understanding. It gave opportunities for circulating further the myth that a tree is an artefact, a kind of gatepost with leaves, that comes out of a nursery and dies when cut down or blown down. The ravages of the storm could be 'restored', or so we were told, by spending money on planting trees in replacement of those 'lost'.

Where the trees blown down were themselves known to have been planted, replanting was, maybe, the right course of action; although even here there should have been a pause for thought. Planted trees almost certainly fared disproportionately worse in the storm than wild ones. Part of this was due to factors such as poor root development, which should be studied before replacement is attempted.[213] To replant risks setting up the same circumstances – a landscape of big, young, poorly-rooted trees – in which the effects will be repeated when there is next a high wind in, say, seventy years' time.

Planting is all very well for replacing trees definitely known to have been planted, in plantations, gardens and arboreta. In the landscape at large, there are good reasons why it should not be a normal conservation practice. It has a poor record of success. A transplanted tree is, inevitably, a damaged tree, like a man shot in the stomach. Even in the intensive care of a garden (or of Essex County Council, who know what they are doing), it does not always survive. Planted and forgotten in a hedge or a wood, a planted tree has a hard, often a losing, struggle against competition from the plants already there. A campaign of tree-planting propaganda has been going on for twenty years. What is there to show for all the trees planted in the 'Plant a Tree in '73' enthusiasm?

Where they do succeed, planted trees too often dilute the values that conservation should stand for. They destroy existing vegetation patterns and meanings, such as giant coppice stools, and replace them with an arbitrary selection of fashionable trees. It is counter-productive to plant rare trees, whose value lies in their being rare and meaningful: every small-leaved lime or service planted arbitrarily into a hedge or wood diminishes the wonder and meaning of pry and service.* There is a more subtle reason why conservationists should be cautious about planting native trees. Much of the value of wild trees depends on their variation (pp. 124–5). For over 150 years, foresters have sought to eliminate this variation, and instead to grow 'supertrees', all of the same genetic stock, having qualities thought desirable at the time of planting. There is now a fashion, thoughtlessly written into Common Market legislation, for planting only trees of officially approved strains. Even on its own terms, this is not as clever as it might seem. Super-oaks failed to live up to their reputation in the Forest of Dean (p. 176); the English Elm, a genetically uniform

---

* Black poplar is probably an exception, for it seems not to have had an adequate means of propagating itself in recent centuries.

super-elm widely propagated in the more distant past, proved disastrously susceptible to the new form of Dutch Elm Disease; superpoplars, planted for match-making on meadows in the 1950s, outlived the industry that they were grown for. Conservationists should resist the tendency: a world in which all oaks and ashes are genetically selected will have lost much of the meaning and beauty of oak and ash. Trees for planting should not be accepted from commercial suppliers unless they are known to be of local provenance. If in doubt, don't plant.

Problems of the 1990s

With diminished pressure on land, the survival of ancient woods is no longer in question. They will continue to be nibbled at by the forestry interest, though much of this damage is self-reversing; they will occasionally be taken for roads and perhaps development. But a sign of the times is the change in emphasis within the Nature Conservancy Council – the State conservation service – from Sites of Special Scientific Interest to the Inventory of Ancient Woodland. In the desperate 1960s, it seemed possible, at best, to try to schedule and protect about one-tenth of the ancient woods. In the 1980s, although the SSSI system is still in use, the listing of *all* ancient woods is by no means an impossible goal. It is also more objective: most woods either are or are not ancient, but who can say whether a wood has just enough scientific interest to qualify it as an SSSI? A first Inventory is almost complete, although it will doubtless continue to be revised over many years as the list of historic buildings has been.

Coppicing brings to life the traditional working of a wood and all its plants and animals. The practice continues to grow, and to benefit from new inventions in handling and using 'small roundwood'. Complaints have begun that too many woods are now coppiced, but as yet are hardly justified. Now, and into the next century, a majority of ancient woods are likely to remain uncoppiced. What is to happen to them? In the 1960s, any land not doing something was classed, reproachfully, as 'derelict'. Conservationists, including myself, claimed that derelict coppices would lose their meaning and value as a habitat; some expected them to vanish altogether. Twenty years later, these evils have not happened. The effects of too much shade are at their worst soon after coppicing is abandoned, and thereafter tend to diminish. Doing nothing may not be the best option in conservation terms, but is a good second-best. Landowners who are content with inaction should not be reproached nor prodded into action. There is no such thing as a derelict wood.*

The chief threat to woodland is grazing. Most ancient woods in Wales, Scotland and Highland England have been ravaged for decades by sheep, which get in through breaches in the boundaries. Sheep devour woodland herbs and young trees, and leave just trees plus grass. Although woods can long survive in this state, a comparison with Cornwall – where similar woods are protected – shows how much has been lost. The simplest and most effective conservation measure is three strands of barbed wire.

In Lowland England there are now more deer than there have been for a thousand years. Within twenty miles of where I sit in Cambridge (the worst deer terrain in England) there are established herds of two native and three naturalized species. Deer eat shrubs, young trees such as ash, and rare plants such as oxlip. Parts of Hayley Wood now begin to look like a Welsh wood; even the birds are affected. Coppicing becomes impossible outside an expensive deer-fence. Learning to live with deer is the chief problem for the 1990s. I do not know the answer. Shooting deer is difficult in a wood, and the survivors can easily spend more time in the wood and do the same damage.

A main issue in the 1990s will be De-Coniferization. Landowners often disapprove of their fathers' replanting of the family woods, and seek advice on how to reverse it. Worcestershire Nature Conservation Trust has acquired Tyddesley Wood, and Suffolk Wildlife Trust has Reydon Wood near Southwold; in both of these the original wood is recoverable. How far is it worth-while to undertake more difficult cases, where less of the ancient wood survives?

A related question is what to do with Woods with Too Many Oaks. Many big woods are now full of oaks, planted or encouraged in the 1820s. These outlived the industries for which they were destined, escaped felling in the World Wars, and are now big trees. They are liable to be felled whenever the price of oak-trees picks up again. What then happens to the site? Not enough of the underwood survives to continue the wood. These woods are very wet and full of deer. Replanting, if attempted, will cause great disturbance and public protest (as happened recently in Salcey Forest, Northants), and stands a poor chance of success.

There is some sign of progress in the conservation of pollards and ancient trees. Their virtue lies in their age and meaning, and they are not conserved by establishing young trees as successors. There will always be middle-aged trees; it is old trees, and big dead ones, that

---

* It is, however, important to prevent woodland grassland – rides and glades – from being shaded.

are rare and precious. This is now better appreciated, and ancient trees are less at risk from being tidied away. Ancient trees are not 'senile' or 'geriatric'; it is a false analogy to suppose that a 500-year-old oak has a life expectancy comparable with that of a 90-year-old man. The Great Storm (which invites an analogy with the battlefield, not the almshouse) should have put paid to the myth that these trees are, in general, dying or unstable or 'dangerous'. Pollarding has been resumed in several places, and occasionally new pollards have been started, for example by the National Trust at Hatfield Forest. When pollards have not been cut for over a century, re-pollarding is unpredictable, and should first be experimented with.

How do we transmit our ideas about trees or woods to the next generation? Few people managing woods for any purpose, including conservation, set down their objective in writing. They expect it to be obvious to their successors; but experience in, for example, Epping or Hatfield Forests shows that it is not. What may have seemed inevitable in the 1950s is a mystery in the 1980s. In practice a site passes through a sequence of conservationist fashions, losing something of its character with each. Now that conservation has become a profession with a career structure, the human generation time is shortened from thirty to less than five years. A management plan should solve this problem, but in my experience management plans are seldom read – especially if they are in the form required under the Wildlife & Countryside Act, which makes them unreadable.

A management plan for a wood should not be a bald list of biological features and prescriptions, but should set out all that is now valued – especially what is rare and wonderful and has meaning. A test is that it should be possible to delete the name of the wood and still recognize it as, say, Hayley Wood. Readability is all-important, and all else depends on it. A plan written to a prescribed form, or platitudinous, or full of economics or officialese or conservationists' claptrap, will not be read, and might as well not exist. A plan should be thought of as a guide for the next thirty years, to be revised only in response to advances in knowledge or method or to genuine changes of circumstance. For a public wood the management plan should be published.

If I have to make a new prognosis, it is that woodland conservation is in danger of drowning in money. In the 1960s and 1970s benefactors subscribed what seemed enormous sums to purchase threatened woods, or to subsidize a revival of coppicing. This was real generosity, and without it this book could not have been written. But money is not God, and does not solve all problems. The original need for it has diminished, as threats of destruction have receded, land values have fallen, and coppicing has become re-established; but money continues to pour in, especially after the Great Storm. Not much of the extra money seems to be spent on real and important problems such as the control of grazing. Some of it goes counter-productively to tree-planting and tidiness. Much of it pays for professional staff in the conservation movement who do the work formerly done by amateurs. In this way some excellent ecologists have been been recruited as professionals into woodland conservation. But there are also others who bring with them preconceptions from their professional training, and who fail to discover what woodland is about; or who leave in a few years to pursue careers elsewhere. The good which pro-fessionalization has brought to woodland conservation is balanced by many examples of harm. The last thing that ancient woodland deserves is too much money.

For native trees the 1980s have been a time of prosperity and recovery. The prospects are good, but education still has far to go. Planting is not conservation, but an admission that conservation has failed. One can be a lifelong woodland conservationist but never plant a single tree. The conservation of woods is not the same as that of buildings: troubles (apart from that of deer) have a habit of getting better, not worse, if neglected. We need to know each kind of tree and how to work with, not against, its natural properties. Conservation is about letting trees be trees, not gateposts with leaves.

Bibliography

HSF   Anderson ML 1967 *A history of Scottish forestry* Nelson, London

Fitzrandolph HE and Hay MD 1926 *The rural industries of England and Wales. I. Timber and underwood industries and some village workshops* Oxford

Godwin H 1981 *The archives of the peat bogs* Cambridge

Harding PT and Rose F 1986 *Pasture-woodlands in lowland Britain* Monks Wood

FD   Hart CE 1966 *Royal forest: a history of Dean's woods as producers of timber* Clarendon, Oxford

Linnard W 1982 *Welsh woods and forests: history and utilization* Cardiff

WCM   Peterken GF 1981 *Woodland conservation and management* Chapman & Hall, London

Peterken GF and Harding PT 1975 'Woodland conservation in Eastern England: comparing the effects of changes in three study areas since 1946' *BC* **8** 279–98

Pollard E, Hooper MD and Moore NW 1974 *Hedges* Collins, London

HW   Rackham O 1975 *Hayley Wood: its history and ecology* Cambs & Isle of Ely Naturalists' Trust, Cambridge

AW   Rackham O 1980 *Ancient woodland: its history, vegetation and uses in England* Edward Arnold, London

EF   Rackham O 1978 'Archaeology and land-use history' *Epping Forest: the natural aspect?* ed. D Corke *Essex Naturalist* **NS 2** 16–75

Rackham O 1985 'Ancient woodland and hedges in England' *The English landscape: past, present and future* ed. SRJ Woodell Oxford 68–105

HC   Rackham O 1986 *The history of the countryside* Dent, London

SEE   Rackham O 1986 *The ancient woodland of England: the woods of South-East Essex* Rochford District Council

Rackham O 1987 'The countryside: history & pseudo-history' *The Historian* **14** 13–7

Rackham O 1988 'Wildwood' *Archaeology and the flora of the British Isles*, ed. M Jones *Oxford Committee for Archaeology Monograph* **14** 3–6

HF   Rackham O 1989 *The last Forest: the story of Hatfield Forest* Dent, London

Roden D 1968 'Woodland and its management in the medieval Chilterns' *Forestry* **41** 59–71

Tubbs CR 1986 *The New Forest* Collins, London

References

BAR   British Archaeological Reports
BC   *Biological Conservation*
CRO   Cambridgeshire Record Office
EHR   *Economic History Review*
ERO   Essex Record Office
ESRO   Suffolk Record Office (Ipswich)
FS   *Field Studies*
JE   *Journal of Ecology*
MCOR Merton College, Oxford, Records
NC   *Nature in Cambridgeshire*
NNRO   Norfolk & Norwich Record Office
NP   *New Phytologist*
PRO   Public Record Office
QJF   *Quarterly Journal of Forestry*
SF   *Scottish Forestry*
TNNS   *Transactions of Norfolk & Norwich Naturalists' Society*
VA   *Vernacular Architecture*
WSRO   Suffolk Record Office (Bury St Edmund's)

1 Peterken GF 1974 'Developmental factors in the management of British woodlands' *QJF* **68** 141–9
Peterken GF 1974 'A method for assessing woodland flora for conservation using indicator species' *BC* **6** 239–45
Tittensor RM 1970 'History of the Loch Lomond oakwoods' *Scottish Forestry* **24** 100–18
Tubbs CR 1968 *The New Forest: an ecological history* David & Charles [see also Tubbs 1986, in Bibliography]
2 Barfield T and others 1984 *A Herefordshire woodland survey* Herefordshire & Radnorshire Nature Trust
Best JA 1983 *King's Wood Corby* 3 vols Nene College, Northampton
Edwards ME 1986 'Disturbance histories of four Snowdonian woodlands and their relation to Atlantic bryophyte distributions' *Biological Conservation* **37** 301–20
Kingsbury JG 1984 'Nunnery and Perry Woods, Worcester: historical ecology

and land-use changes' *Transactions of Worcs Archaeological Society* **3rd ser.** **9** 67–85

3 Colebourne P and others 1983 *Hampshire's countryside heritage. 2. Ancient woodland* Hampshire County Council
Jones M 1986 'Coppice wood management in the eighteenth century: an example from County Wicklow' *Irish Forestry* **43** 15–31
Watts WA 1984 'Contemporary accounts of the Killarney woods 1580–1870' *Irish Geography* **17** 1–13

3a Redmonds G 1983 'Spring woods 1500–1800' *Old West Riding* **3** 4–9

4 *HC* p.54–7

5 Cross JR 1975 'Biological Flora of the British Isles: *Rhododendron ponticum* L.' *JE* **63** 345–64

6 Shigo AL 1983 *Tree defects: a photo guide* United States Government Printing Office, Washington, no. 001–001–00586–0

7 Mitchell AF 1966 'Dating the 'ancient' oaks' *QJF* **60** 271–6

8 Menzies W 1864 *The history of Windsor Great Park and Windsor Forest* Longmans, London

9 *HW* p.92

10 Tansley A 1939 *The British Islands and their vegetation* Cambridge

11 Milne-Redhead E 1983 'The black poplar survey' *Botanical Society of the British Isles News* **33** 6

12 E.g. WSRO: E2/9/1

13 Meikle RD 1975 '*Populus* L.' *Hybridization and the flora of the British Isles*, ed. CA Stace, Academic Press, London, p.303

14 Translated by M. Robson; by permission of Danmarks Geologiske Undersøgelse

15 West RG 1977 *Pleistocene geology and biology with especial reference to the British Isles* 2nd ed. Longmans, London
Godwin (see bibliography)

16 Dimbleby GW 1985 *The palynology of archaeological sites* Academic Press, London

17 Bennett KD 1983 'Devensian Late-glacial and Flandrian vegetational history at Hockham Mere, Norfolk, England' *NP* **85** 457–87

18 Huntley B and Birks HJB 1983 *An atlas of past and present pollen maps for Europe: 0–13000 years ago* Cambridge

19 Birks HJB, Deacon J and Peglar S 1975 'Pollen maps for the British Isles 5,000 years ago' *Proceedings of the Royal Society, London* **B189** 87–105

20 Birks HJB 1988 'Long-term ecological change in the British uplands' *Ecological change in the uplands* ed. MB Usher and DBA Thompson, Blackwell, Oxford 37–56

21 Birks HH 1972 'A radiocarbon-dated pollen diagram from Loch Maree, Ross and Cromarty' *NP* **71** 731–54

22 Turner J and Hodgson J 1981 'Studies in the vegetational history of the northern Pennines. II. An atypical pollen diagram from Pow Hill, Co. Durham' *JE* **69** 171–88

23 Rackham O 1986 'The ancient woods of Norfolk' *TNNS* **27** 161–77

24 E.g. Sims RE 1972 'The anthropogenic factor in East Anglian vegetational history ...' *Quaternary plant ecology*, ed. HJB Birks and RG West, Blackwell, Oxford 223–36

25 E.g. Cronon W. 1983 *Changes in the land: Indians, colonists, and the ecology of New England* Hill & Wang, New York

26 Dimbleby GW 1962 *The development of British heathlands and their soils* Clarendon, Oxford

27 Bush MB and Ellis S 1987 'The sedimentological and vegetational history of Willow Garth' *East Yorkshire – field guide*, ed. S Ellis, Quaternary Research Association, Cambridge

28 *AW* p.259–66; *HC* p.240–6

29 Girling MA 1988 'The bark beetle *Scolytus scolytus* ... and the possible role of elm disease in the early Neolithic' *Archaeology and the flora* ... (see Rackham 1988 in Bibliography) 34–8

30 Scaife RG 1988 'The Elm Decline in the pollen record of south east England and its relationship to early agriculture' *ibid.* 21–33

31 Turner J 1962 'The *Tilia* decline: an anthropogenic interpretation' *NP* **61** 328–41

32 *HC* chapter 14

33 Coles J 1973 *Archaeology by experiment* Hutchinson, London

34 *HF* chapter 10

35 McGrail S (ed.) 1982 *Woodworking techniques before A.D. 1500* BAR International Series **129**

36 *Somerset Levels Papers* passim

37 Pryor F, French C and Taylor M 1986 'Flag Fen, Fengate, Peterborough. I: discovery, reconnaissance and initial excavation (1982–85)' *Proceedings of the Prehistoric Society* **52** 1–24

38 Millett M and McGrail S 1987 'The Hasholme Logboat' *Archaeological Journal* **144** 69–155

39 Rackham O 1977 'Neolithic woodland management in the Somerset Levels: Garvin's, Walton Heath, and Rowland's Tracks' *Somerset Levels Papers* **3** 65–71
Rackham O 1979 'Neolithic woodland management in the Somerset Levels: Sweet Track I' *Somerset Levels Papers* **5** 59–61

40 The key to charters is: Sawyer PH 1968 *Anglo-Saxon charters: an annotated list and bibliography* Royal Historical Society, London. Most of the texts are published in: Kemble JM 1839–48 *Codex diplomaticus* 6 vols London; or: Birch W de G 1885–93 *Cartularium saxonicum* 3 vols London. Commentaries are provided by: Hart CR 1966 *The early charters of Eastern England* Leicester (companion volumes for other regions)

41 Peglar SM, Fritz SC and Birks HJB 1989 'Vegetation and land-use history at Diss, Norfolk, England' *JE* **77** 203–22

42 Cleere H 1976 'Some operating parameters for Roman ironworks' *Bulletin of the Institute of Archaeology* **13** 233–46
AW p.108–9

43 Liversidge JEA 1968 *Britain in the Roman Empire* Routledge, London

44 *SEE passim*

45 Brooks H 1987 *Relics and runways*, and other preliminary reports on the Stansted investigations

46 Brodribb ACC, Hands AR and Walker DR 1968–73 *Excavations at Shakenoak* [privately published]

47 Rodwell W and Rodwell K 1977 *Historic churches: a wasting asset* Council for British Archaeology Research Report **19**

48 Turner J 1970 'Post-Neolithic disturbance of British vegetation' *Studies in the vegetational history of the British Isles*, ed. D Walker and RG West, Cambridge 81–96

48a Losco-Bradley PM and Salisbury CR 1988 'A Saxon and a Norman fish weir at Colwick, Nottinghamshire' *Medieval fish, fisheries and fishponds in England* ed. M Aston BAR British Series **182** 329–52

49 For details see *AW* pp 111–27

50 Witney KP 1976 *The Jutish forest* Athlone Press, London
Everitt A 1986 *Continuity and colonization: the evolution of Kentish settlement* Leicester

51 Ford WJ 1976 'Some settlement patterns in the central region of the Warwickshire Avon' *Medieval settlement: continuity and change*, ed. PH Sawyer, Edward Arnold 274–94
Schumer B 1984 *The evolution of Wychwood to 1400: pioneers, frontiers and forests* Leicester

52 *FD* chapter 1

53 Rackham O, Blair WJ and Munby JT 1978 'The thirteenth-century roofs and floor of the Blackfriars Monastery at Gloucester' *Medieval Archaeology* **22** 105–22

54 Lennard R 1945 'The destruction of woodland in the eastern counties under William the Conqueror' *EHR* **15** 36–43

55 Hatcher J 1977 *Plague, population and the English economy* Macmillan, London

56 Moore SA (ed.) 1897 *Cartularium monasterii Sancti Johannis Baptiste de Colecestria* Chiswick, London

57 Room A 1986 *A dictionary of Irish place-names* Belfast

58 PRO: E143/9/2

59 British Library: Cott. Claud. C xi **or** Gonville & Caius College Cambridge MS 485–9

60 ESRO: HA1/BA/3/10 and HA1/BC/1/2

61 Rackham O 1968 'Medieval woodland areas' *NC* **11** 22–5

62 Hockey SF 1975 *The account-book of Beaulieu Abbey* Royal Historical Society, London
AW p.140–2

63 NNRO: Dean & Chapter Rolls 4739–93

64 Rackham O 1969 'Knapwell Wood' *NC* **12** 25–31

65 Pembroke College, Cambridge: MS I 1–3

66 Harris R 1974 'Poplar crucks in Worcestershire and Herefordshire' *VA* **5** 25

67 Rackham O 1972 'Grundle House: on the quantities of timber in certain East Anglian buildings in relation to local supplies' *VA* **3** 3–8
SEE chapter 6
HF pp 185–6

68 MCOR: 5342–99

69 Beevor HE 1924 'Norfolk woodlands, from the evidence of contemporary chronicles' *TNNS* **11** 488–508

70 ERO: D/DB L1/9/1

71 Troup RS 1952 *Silvicultural systems*, 2nd ed. Oxford

72 I am indebted for this analysis to HJB Birks, P Adam and H Prentice

73 E.g. *Calendar of Inquisitions Miscellaneous* **5** 56 (1388)

74 PRO: E134 (21 Chas II Mich. 7) (with acknowledgement to DP Dymond)

75 WSRO: microfilm of Chicago University Library, Bacon Collection, Brandon Compotus Rolls 653–63; Iveagh Suffolk MS 148 (with acknowledgement to the late JT Munday)

76 *Calendar of Liberate Rolls*

77 Davis EM 1984 in *The Three Blackbirds: a medieval house in Ely, Cambridgeshire*, ed. APB Holton-Krayenbuhl, Ely Preservation Trust

78 Rackham O 1982 'The growing and transport of timber and underwood' *Wood-*

   working techniques (ref. 35) 199–218
79 Dugdale WD 1658 *The history of St Paul's Cathedral* ... Warren, London
80 Dent J 1970 *The quest for Nonsuch* London Borough of Sutton
81 Hewett CA 1980 *English historic carpentry* Phillimore, London
82 *Statutes of the Realm* 34–5 Hen. VIII c.3
83 *HW* pp25–8
84 ESRO: HA1/BD3/1
   PRO: E178/4564
85 ERO: D/DQ 16/1
86 Lord Tollemache's muniments at Helmingham Hall
87 *AW* chapter 11
   Brown EH and Hopkins SV 1956 'Seven centuries of the prices of consumables, compared with builders' wage-rates' *Economica* **23** 296–313
88 Smith TP 1985 *The medieval brickmaking industry in England 1400–1450* BAR British Series **138**
89 Flinn MW 1959 'Timber and the advance of technology: a reconsideration' *Annals of Science* **15** 109–20
   Hammersley G 1973 'The charcoal iron industry and its fuel' *Economic History Review* **2nd ser. 26** 593–613
90 Schubert HR 1957 *History of the British iron and steel industry* London
91 Rackham O (forthcoming) *Ancient woodland of England: the woods of the Helford River, Cornwall*
92 [Defoe D] 1724 *A Tour thro' the whole Island of Great Britain* London
93 Yarranton A 1677 *England's improvement by sea and land*
94 Rees W 1933 *The historical map of South Wales and the Border in the fourteenth century* Cardiff
95 Gilbert JM 1979 *Hunting and hunting preserves in medieval Scotland* John Donald, Edinburgh p. 237
96 Tittensor (ref. 1)
   Rymer L 1977 'The exploitation of woodlands in the parish of North Knapdale, Argyllshire' *SF* **31** 244–50
97 Loudon JC 1838 *Arboretum et fruticetum britannicum* London
98 *HSF*
99 *The Civil Survey AD 1654–1656* ed. RC Simington 10 vols Stationery Office, Dublin
   HC pp 112–5
100 Kelly DL 1981 'The native forest vegetation of Killarney, south-west Ireland: an ecological account' *JE* **81** 437–72
   Watts WA 1984 'Contemporary accounts of the Killarney woods 1580–1870' *Irish Geography* **17** 1–13
101 Wallace PF 1982 'Carpentry in Ireland: the Wood Quay evidence' *Woodworking techniques* (ref. 35) 263–300
102 McCracken E 1971 *The Irish woods since Tudor times* Newton Abbot
103 Sparke J 1723 *Historiae Anglicanae scriptores* vol.2
104 *AW* pp 290–1
105 Anderson (see bibliography)
106 Ketton-Cremer RW 1962 *Felbrigg* Hart-Davis, London
107 Pitt-Rivers AH 1890 *King John's House*
108 Information derived chiefly from *House of Commons Journals, Navy Lists*, and from:
   O'Connor TV 1929 'Shipping' *Encyclopædia Britannica* 14th ed.

Davis R 1962 *The rise of the English shipping industry in the seventeenth and eighteenth centuries* Newton Abbot

109 Albion RG 1926 *Forests and sea power* Massachusetts
Holland AJ 1971 *Ships of British oak* Newton Abbot

110 Merriman RD 1961 *Queen Anne's navy* Navy Records Society

111 Tittensor (ref. 1)

112 Hart and Tubbs (see bibliography)

113 Clarkson LA 1974 'The English bark trade 1660–1830' *Agricultural History Review* **22** 136–52
AW p. 154

114 *AW* chapter 11

115 Richens RH 1983 *Elm* Cambridge

116 *AW* p.229–30

117 James W and Malcolm J 1794 *General view of the agriculture of the county of Buckingham* London
Roden (see bibliography)

118 Fitzrandolph and Hay (see bibliography)

119 Sinclair J 1845 [published 1936] *The new statistical account of Scotland* Edinburgh

120 NNRO: 30D5 12554

121 *HF* chapter 6

122 Rubner K 1960 *Die pflanzengeographische Grundlage des Waldbaues* Radebeul

123 *AW* pp296–7

124 Peterken and Harding (see bibliography)

125 Southgate GJ 1969 'Helicopter spraying to kill overhead cover at Lavenham Forest, Suffolk' *Journal of the Forestry Commission* **36**

126 Smith AH 1956 *English place-name elements* Cambridge

127 ERO: survey of Earl's Colne by Israel Amyce (1598)

128 CRO: map of Kingston Wood Manor

129 Ryan GH and Redstone LJ 1931 *Timperley of Hintlesham* Methuen, London

130 MCOR: 6/17

131 ERO: D/DAb E5

132 ERO: D/DB T16/6

133 ERO: D/DHf M19

134 United States National Archives, Cartographic Division, Washington, DC, 20408: Group No. 373

135 *Statutes of the Realm* i 97

136 Clarke JW 1907 *Liber memorandorum ecclesiae de Bernewelle* Cambridge

137 Linnard (see bibliography) chapter 2

138 Tollemache (ref. 86) B1/11

138a Gulliver R 1989 'Reconstructing a historic landscape' *Landscape Design* June 1989, 38–41

139 CRO: Q/R Dc19
Cambridge University Library: Ely Diocesan Registry H1/1–9

140 *SEE* chapter 5

141 *HC* chapter 16

142 *HC* chapter 8

143 Hawksworth DL (ed.) 1974 *The changing flora and fauna of Britain* Academic Press
HF chapter 11
Harding & Rose (see bibliography)
Paul CRC in *HW* chapter IV.9

144 Rodwell J *National vegetation classification* Nature Conservancy Council [unpublished at the time of writing; I have seen draft of 1986]

145 *AW* p. 250

146 Peterken GF and Jones EW 1987 'Forty years of change in Lady Park Wood: the old-growth stands' *JE* **75** 477–512

147 Woodruffe-Peacock EA 1918 'A fox-covert study' *JE* **6** 110–25

148 *HW* chapters III.5, III.6

149 Peterken GF 1974 'A method for assessing woodland flora for conservation using indicator species' *BC* **6** 239–45

150 Pigott CD and Taylor K 1964 'The distribution of some woodland herbs in relation to the supply of nitrogen and phosphorus in the soil' *JE* **52 suppl.** 175–85

151 Based in part on a map by GF Peterken

152 May S 1988 ['Overhall Grove'] *The Conduit* **17** 43–6

153 Downing College, Cambridge, archives *re* E Hatley

154 Winthrop Papers 1929 vol.1 Massachusetts Historical Society

155 I regret that I have not the name of the gentleman who drew my attention to these oaks

156 Birch (ref. 40) no. 898
Tittensor A and Tittensor R 1977 *Natural history of The Mens, Sussex* Horsham Natural History Society

157 Ault WO 1972 *Open-field farming in medieval England* Allen & Unwin, London

158 Anderson MD 1964 *A saint at stake* Faber, London
Supple WR 1917 *A history of Thorpe-next-Norwich* Norwich

159 Watson CE 1932 'The Minchinhampton custumal and its place in the story of the manor' *Transactions of the Bristol & Gloucs Archaeological Society* **54** 203–385

160 PRO: E134/5 Jas I Hil/26

161 Le Sueur ADC 1955 *Burnham Beeches* Corporation of London

162 WSRO: 1066

163 *HC* chapter 6

164 For England after Cantor LM 1983 *The medieval parks of England: a gazetteer* Loughborough
For Wales after Rees (ref. 94) and Linnard (bibliography)
For Scotland after Gilbert (ref. 95)

165 Original in Long Melford Hall; another translation is in Parker W 1873 *The history of Long Melford* London

166 *Rotuli Hundredorum* HMSO, London (1810) **1** 155

167 Rackham O 1974 'The oak tree in historic times' *The British Oak*, ed. MG Morris and FH Perring, Classey 62–79

168 Peterken GF 1969 'Development of vegetation in Staverton Park, Suffolk' *FS* **3** 1–39

169 Rackham O forthcoming ('The king's deer') *Nonsuch Celebrations* ed. M Exwood

170 Shirley EP 1867 *Some account of English deer parks* Murray, London

171 Harding and Rose (see bibliography)

172 Addison W and Hewett CA [1975] *Queen Elizabeth's Hunting Lodge and Epping Forest Museum* City of London Corporation

173 Phibbs JL 1980 *Wimpole Park Cambridgeshire* National Trust

174 *Calendars of Close and Liberate Rolls*

175 Putman RJ 1986 *Grazing in temperate ecosystems: large herbivores and the ecology of the New Forest* Croom Helm, London

Grant R 1959 'Royal Forests' *Victoria County History: Wiltshire* **4** 384–457 Oxford

Gilbert: see ref. 95

176 Pam D 1984 *The story of Enfield Chase* Enfield Preservation Society

177 Young CR 1979 *The royal Forests of medieval England* Leicester

178 *AW* chapter 12

179 Cummins J 1988 *The hound and the hawk: the art of medieval hunting* London, Weidenfeld & Nicholson

180 *EF; HF* chapter 4

181 PRO: LRRO/5/39

182 Hammersley G 1957 'The Crown woods and their exploitation in the sixteenth and seventeenth centuries' *Bulletin of the Institute of Historical Research* **30** 136–61

183 Thompson EP 1975 *Whigs and hunters: the origin of the Black Act* Allen Lane, London

184 Hart: see bibliography

185 Tubbs CR 1968 *The New Forest: an ecological history* Newton Abbot

186 Baker CA, Moxey P and Oxford PM 1978 'Woodland continuity and change in Epping Forest' *FS* **4** 645–69

187 Peterken GF and Lloyd PS 1967 'Biological Flora of the British Isles: Ilex aquifolium L.' *JE* **55** 841–58

188 Rose F and James PW 1974 'The corticolous and lignicolous [lichen] species of the New Forest, Hampshire' *Lichenologist* **6** 1–72

189 PRO: E178/5297

190 Kreuz A 1988 'Holzkohle-Funde der ältestbandkeramischen Siedlung Friedberg-Bruchenbrücken: Anzeiger für Brennholz-Auswahl und lebende Hecken?' *Der prähistorische Mensch und seine Umwelt*, Festschrift für Udelgard Körber-Grohne, Stuttgart, 139–53

191 *HC* chapter 9

192 Eland G 1949 *At the courts of Great Canfield, Essex* Oxford

193 WSRO: E2/9/1

194 ERO: D/DHt M145

195 MCOR 5382

196 NNRO: Dean & Chapter Rolls 4755, 4899

197 Rogers JE Thorold 1866–1902 *A history of agriculture and prices in England* Clarendon, Oxford

198 Moorhouse SA 1979 'Documentary evidence for the manor of Wakefield during the middle ages' *Landscape History* **1** 44–58

I am indebted to Dr Andrew Fleming for further evidence

199 Coulton GG 1967 *Life in the Middle Ages* Cambridge p.74

200 Smith LDW 1981 'A survey of building timber and other trees in the hedgerows of a Warwickshire estate, *c.* 1500' *Transactions of the Birmingham & Warwickshire Archaeological Society* **90** 65–73

201 ERO: D/Dc E15/2

202 ESRO: T1/1/16

203 PRO: E178/3785, 4564, 4988

204 *HC* chapter 10

205 ESRO: HA93

WSRO: Lawshall tithe map

206 Pollard and others (see bibliography)

207 ERO: D/DK M1

208 *HC* Fig. 9.5

209 Shown me by Andrew Fleming

210 Hervey J (ed.) *Ickworth Survey Boocke Ano 1665* Ipswich. The park has been fully studied by J. Phibbs and C. Gallagher

211 Price C 1988 'Are there any economics of upland forestry?' *Ecological change in the uplands* (ref. 20) 295–309

212 Innes JL and Boswell RC *Forest health surveys 1987* Forestry Commission Bulletin **74, 79**

213 cf Geddes H, letter to *The Times*, 17 Oct. 1987

Index and Glossary

Words here given a definition are printed in **_bold italic_**. Further definitions or explanations are to be found on pages numbered in **_bold italic_**. Page-numbers in **bold** are main references.

Bu	Buckinghamshire	Mx	Middlesex
Ca	Cambridgeshire	Nf	Norfolk
Co	Cornwall	Nh	Northamptonshire
Do	Dorset	Nt	Nottinghamshire
Ex	Essex	Ox	Oxfordshire
Gl	Gloucestershire	Sf	Suffolk
Gm	Glamorgan	So	Somerset
Ha	Hampshire	Sx	Sussex
He	Herefordshire	Wa	Warwickshire
Ht	Hertfordshire	Wi	Wiltshire
Hu	Huntingdonshire	Wo	Worcestershire
Kt	Kent	YN	Yorkshire (North Riding)
Li	Lincolnshire	YW	Yorkshire (West Riding)

gardens 91, 138, 160, 196, 204
Gateley Nf 188
gazelles 152
gean see *cherry*
Germany 101, 185
Gernon Bushes (S.W. Ex) 147
Geum see *avens*
ghost: destroyed wood (or other feature) whose outline remains as a hedge (or soil-mark or parish boundary). See *hedges*
Gilbert J. M. 165
glaciations 26, 119
glades 33, 46, 71
glass 40, 43
Glemsford Sf Fig. 22d
Glen Lyon (Perthshire) 88
Glenmore (Inverness) 88
Gloucester 55
goats 36
goosegrass *Galium aparine* 135
gorges 131, 132, 150
graffiti 14, Fig. 4
Grant R. 165
grassland 34, 40, 133, 180
  woodland 33, 132, 206
grazing 70, 171, 180 and see *browsing*
Great Canfield Ex 188
Great Horwood Bu 144
Great Ridge (wood in S. Wi) 123
Greece 16, 94
green: a small *common* 149, Fig. 32, 176, 196
Greening R. 162
Greensted Ex 43
gregarious trees 20–1, 130
Groton Wood Sf Fig. 23, 140–3, Fig. 29, Plate I
ground-elder *Ægopodium podagraria* 138
grove: a small wood 45, *46,* 61, 145
Grovely Forest (S. Wi) 41, 171
grubbing see *destruction* under *Forest: hedges; woodland*
Gulliver R. 114

Hadstock Ex 43
hag 108
Hainault Forest Ex 164, 173, Figs 35 and 36, 178–80
Hallingbury Ex 144
Hammersley G. 84, 86

Hampton Court Mx 158
Harding P. 104
Hardwick Wood Ca 64–6, 68–9, 75, 134
hare 152, 169–70
Hart A. xviii, 195
Hart C. E. 165
Harvey J. 91
Hatfield Broadoak Ex 161, 192
  Forest 25, 68, 94, 163, 172, 176, **180–2, Fig. 37**
    National Trust 207
    perambulation 109
    trees 14, 101, 123, 125, 128, 207, Plate XV
    wood-pasture operation 36, 70, 171
Hatfield Chase YW 166
hawthorn *Cratægus monogyna* 19, Fig. 16, 127, 134, 179
  ancient and pollard 14, 160, 182
  hedges of 2, 115, 185, 192
  woodland species (*C. lævigata*) 123, 132, 138
  and see *thorn*
Hayley Wood Ca 94
  deer 206, Plate XXII
  medieval history 59, 61, 64, Fig. 16, 75, 107
  plants 132–4, Plate VIII
  post-medieval 82, 103
  trees 16–17, 127, 138, Plate XI
  woodbank Fig. 23, 118
hazel *Corylus avellana* 4, 123–4, 136, 140
  behaviour 6, 10, 28, 103
  early history 44, 46, 174
  medieval 71–2, Fig. 16, 87, 187
  nuts 34, 70
  prehistory 27–32, 34, 37
  woods of 18, 30, 93, 126–31, 138
Hearse Wood Sf 108
heath 56–7, 102, 112, 176
  Anglo-Saxon 44, 186–7
  becoming wood 19, 122–3, 130, 145
  creation 34, 144–5, Fig. 30
  and wood-pasture 153, 157, 166, 169, 177–80
  and see *moorland*
heather *Calluna vulgaris* 27, 34, 179
Hedera see *ivy*
hedges Frontispiece, xiv, 2, 10, 138, 150
  destruction 184–5, 189–92, Fig. 38, 201
  difference from woods 132–3, 192, 195